INTERNATIONAL FEMINIST PERSPECTIVES IN CRIMINOLOGY

INTERNATIONAL FEMINIST PERSPECTIVES IN CRIMINOLOGY

ENGENDERING A DISCIPLINE

Edited by
**NICOLE HAHN RAFTER AND
FRANCES HEIDENSOHN**

OPEN UNIVERSITY PRESS
Buckingham · Philadelphia

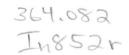

Open University Press
Celtic Court
22 Ballmoor
Buckingham
MK18 1XW

and
1900 Frost Road, Suite 101
Bristol, PA 19007, USA

First Published 1995

A catalogue record of this book is available from the British Library

ISBN 0 335 19389 7 (hb)   0 335 19388 9 (pb)

Library of Congress Cataloging-in-Publication Data

International feminist perspectives in criminology : engendering a
    discipline / Nicole Hahn Rafter and Frances Heidensohn, editors.
        p.   cm.
    Includes bibliographical references and index.
    ISBN 0–335–19389–7 (hb).   ISBN 0–335–19388–9 (pb)
    1. Feminist criminology.   I. Rafter. Nicole Hahn, 1939– .
II. Heidensohn. Frances.
HV6030.I495   1995
364′.082—dc20   95–10580
                                                          CIP

Typeset by Graphicraft Typesetters Ltd, Hong Kong
Printed in Great Britain by Biddles Ltd, Guildford and King's Lynn

For everyone at Mont Gabriel, July 1991

Contents

List of contributors

The editors

FRANCES HEIDENSOHN is Professor of Social Policy and Head of the Department of Social Policy and Politics, Goldsmiths' College, University of London. She has written and researched widely on the subjects of feminism and criminology. Her publications include *Women and Crime* (second edition, Macmillan, 1995) and *Women in Control? The Role of Women in Law Enforcement* (Oxford, 1992).

NICOLE HAHN RAFTER, Professor of Criminal Justice at Northeastern University, Boston, coedited one of the first books on gender and crime. Her other books include *Partial Justice: Women, Prisons, and Social Control*, the first full-scale history of the US women's prison system.

The contributors

CHRISTINE ALDER is an Associate Professor in the Criminology Department at the University of Melbourne. Juvenile justice issues have been a focus of her research and she has recently co-edited *The Police and Young People in Australia* (Cambridge University Press, 1994) and *Family Group Conferencing: the Way Forward or Misplaced Optimism?* (Australian Institute of Criminology, 1994). Christine has also published articles on gender and violence and is currently researching the issue of child homicide.

MARIE-ANDRÉE BERTRAND is full Professor of Criminology at the School of Criminology, University of Montreal, Canada. She is a research associate with the International Centre for Comparative Criminology at the University of Montreal. She received her doctorate in criminology from the University of California at Berkeley in 1967. Her first major work on women and criminology was *La femme et le crime* (l'Aurore, 1979). Some of her recent feminist works are detailed in the references to Chapter 6.

DOROTHY E. CHUNN is Associate Professor at the School of Criminology, Simon Fraser University, Canada, and Co-Director of the Feminist Sociolegal Network (FEMNET). Her publications include *From Punishment to Doing Good* (University of Toronto Press, 1992), *Investigating Gender Bias* (co-edited, Thompson Educational, 1993) and *The Law of Homicide* (co-authored, Carswell, 1994). She is currently working on feminist histories of intra-familial violence against women and of the welfare state in British Columbia.

KATHLEEN DALY is a Visiting Associate Professor of Sociology at the University of Michigan. She has written on how gender and race structure patterns of law-breaking and criminal court process, formal and informal responses to violence against women, and the relationship of feminist theory to criminology, law and justice. Her book *Gender, Crime, and Punishment* (Yale University Press, 1994) analyses men's and women's pathways to felony court, the social organization of their law-breaking and the theories of punishment judges use in justifying their sentences.

DESIRÉE HANSSON has been actively involved in both the feminist and anti-apartheid movements in South Africa since the early 1980s. She is the former Director of the Institute of Criminology at the University of Cape Town and also practises as a registered clinical psychologist. Desirée is currently spending her sabbatical leave as a visiting scholar at the Cambridge Institute of Criminology in England.

DORIE KLEIN is a senior researcher at the Western Consortium for Public Health, Berkeley, California, where she is conducting policy research on issues related to women and substance use, and public responses to driving under the influence. She directed court services for the judiciary in Alameda County, California, for five years, and has taught at the University of California, National Judicial College and California State University, among other institutions. Dr Klein co-organized the International Conference on Women, Law and Social Control in 1991, consulted to the UN Crime Prevention Branch on violence against women and served on the founding board of directors of one of the early community-based perinatal women's drug treatment programmes. She works with a local task force on the needs of women inmates. Her doctorate in criminology is from the University of California at Berkeley.

ROBERT MENZIES is Professor and Associate Director at the School of Criminology, Simon Fraser University, Vancouver, Canada. He has written a variety of works on the sociology of criminology, on the role of experts in judicial and carceral contexts, and on the relationship between psychiatric and penal control systems. His books include *Transcarceration: Essays in the Sociology of Social Control* (Gower, 1987, co-edited with John Lowman and Ted Palys) and *Survival of the Sanest* (University of Toronto Press, 1989). He is currently working on a historical study of medico-legal regulatory practices in the province of British Columbia.

JAMES W. MESSERSCHMIDT is Professor of Sociology at the University of Southern Maine. His research interests focus on the interrelation of class, gender, race and crime, and he has authored *The Trial of Leonard Peltier* (South End Press, 1983), *Capitalism, Patriarchy and Crime: toward a Socialist Feminist Criminology* (Rowman and Littlefield, 1986), *Criminology* (second edition, with Piers Beirne, Harcourt Brace Jovanovich, 1995) and *Masculinities and Crime: Critique and Reconceptualization of Theory* (Rowman and Littlefield, 1993).

TAMAR PITCH is Associate Professor of the Sociology of Law, University of Camerino. She has made major contributions to the study of women, law and social control and has published on a range of related topics in both Italian and English. Her main publications include *Donne in Carcere* (Women in Prison, Milan, 1992) and *Responsabilità Limitate* (Milan, 1989).

MONIKA PLATEK teaches law, criminal justice, criminology and comparative criminology courses at the Law Faculty, Warsaw University, Poland. She has recently introduced a new interdisciplinary subject, feminist jurisprudence, which she teaches with two other female professors. The course is popular among both female and male students.

DEBORAH J. STEPHENS is a doctoral candidate in the Department of Sociology at the University of Michigan. Her research interests are black women and crime, black feminist theory, criminal behaviour and programmes for black youth, drugs and crime, and violent crime. She plans to conduct her dissertation research on the correlates of recidivism for adolescent lawbreakers.

Preface

Criminology has long suffered from what Jessie Bernard has called the 'stag effect'. It has attracted male scholars who wanted to study and understand outlaw men, hoping perhaps that some of the romance and fascination of this role will rub off. Among the disciplines, it is almost quintessentially male. That is why, when I was asked to write the preface to a volume on the possibility of an international feminist criminology, I jumped at the chance. This edited collection, like the conversations and conferences (notably the Mont Gabriel Conference on Women, Law and Social Control) that gave it birth, is making intellectual history. Suddenly, women are daring to speak about crime and social control in ways that place women at the centre rather than the periphery of the inquiry.

No surprise, given the field's history and character, then, that the issue that haunts the essays in this volume is the question first posed by Betsy Stanko: 'Is Feminist Criminology an Oxymoron?' Can macho criminology be re-invented or as the volume's title suggests, 'engendered'. Many of these authors address this dilemma from the perspective of feminist scholars with a deep interest in the issues of social control, the law, and the place of women. Because of the variety of countries represented by the authors in this volume, it is no surprise that they come down on different sides of the debate. What will fascinate the reader more than their specific answers is the richness of their arguments. Most of the authors in this book first consider the state of criminology in their particular setting and then the place of feminist scholarship in that particular framework. Their accounts establish both the diversity of what constitutes criminology in different countries and the consistent resistance in this field, however diverse, to women scholars and their work.

Even in countries such as the United Kingdom, arguably the birthplace of feminist criminology, one of the book's co-editors, Frances Heidensohn, describes the particular isolation and hostility that feminist scholarship has experienced. She dubs this the 'Falklands factor' and explains how feminist scholarship is generally treated as this British dependency was: 'remote, unvisited and ignored'. As her metaphor suggests, though, there may be only one thing worse than being neglected and that is receiving attention and exploration from the dominant power. That, she argues may well prove 'unwelcome and lead to conflict'. I would go on to suggest that, in the United States, this unwelcome scrutiny has occurred in the areas where feminist scholars and activists have made the most headway: sexual assault and sexual harassment. The backlash in these areas has begun with a vengeance. Adding a touch of humour, Tamar Pitch notes that criminology in Italy has largely ignored the work of feminist scholars and activists. This, it turns out, is not necessarily a problem since Italian criminology, unlike feminism, is completely ineffective in the public policy arena.

Again and again, though, these accounts document Bernard's powerful point about the hard work facing feminist scholars. We not only pull a double shift as workers and wives and mothers (as all women do); we must also pull a double shift intellectually. We must establish our legitimacy and ability in traditional criminology, and we must undertake the daunting task of creating a feminist perspective on crime and social control. Added to this, we must do this work in universities and other settings that are, at best, tough places for women to work. Each of these essays deals with this marginality, but Chunn and Menzies' essay documents the barriers with the most painful detail. Generally speaking, graduate school is harder for women to manage financially (especially if they have children); they face sexual harassment in the classroom and office; and once out they confront an uncertain future. All the while, they watch their male counter-parts get funded, mentored, and published. Certainly, though, our experiences as women and as scholars prepare us well to engage in the hard work of building a new field. As the old adage has it: whatever a woman does, she must do twice as well as a man to be considered half as good.

What would criminology look like if women's experience was at the centre rather than the periphery of the inquiry? Suddenly, as Messerschimdt's work documents, men have a gender. Male violence, in particular, takes on a very different meaning if women's relative non-violence were the normal response to life, and men's aggression the aberration. The violence, fear and victimization that are so much a part of many women's lives (that is, the other side of male violence) are suddenly important areas of study and research. One can immediately see why feminist perspectives have so invigorated criminology in the countries where they are the most established, and why they will be an irresistible force in those that are just being exposed to them. Even in countries of the first wave though, the progress has been uneven.

In the US, for example, the construction of woman as victim has made great headway, since the recognition of women's victimization both created 'new' crimes to study, and new men to jail, but it did not fundamentally challenge androcentric criminology. It appeals, in part, because the victimized woman does not challenge core notions of patriarchal ideology; she – the plundered waif – after all, needs male protection and assistance. These comments should not be taken to mean that women's victimization is not horrific, but rather that the study of women's victimization (long considered, in some circles, to be co-extensive with feminist criminology) caused the least resistance in the field itself.

The study of women in conflict with the law and out of control, by contrast, languished. Perhaps, the existence of these women suggests that male domination is not as complete as it might be? These women were certainly trouble for theories of male criminality which were long described as theories of crime. So the 'offending' women were ignored, and those who studied them did so from the very edges of the field. This meant of course that the lives of women of colour in the US and Australia, as the work of Daly and Stephens as well as that of Alder document – who were the overwhelming victims of this control – were left undocumented and unexplained. Their race and their class simply placed them outside a slightly modified criminology where men (assumed to be poor and non-white) are criminals and women (assumed to be docile, good and white) are victims. That reality is more complex than this explains why there is still so much work to do in our field.

Should we attempt to do this work? Is engendering criminology a worthy undertaking? Some might contend (as one Norwegian did) that the effort, like this book, would focus too extensively on the 'inside hierarchy of the university' and too little on the content and impact of the discipline outside the university. Yet this is a tension that threads its way through these varied discussions. Feminist scholars shoulder many burdens, but perhaps the most daunting is the one articulated by Liz Kelly and re-visited in Frances Heidensohn's essay 'Feminist research investigates aspects of women's oppression while seeking at the same time to be a part of the struggle against it'.

Certainly, as Klein argues, it is not clear that the academic criminologists, including feminist criminologists, are prepared to take on the virulent backlash against women and minorities in the US. Yet, this is precisely what we must do, since crime has become a code word for race in the US, and imprisonment rates are soaring. The clearest victims of the current imprisonment binge are African-American males (one out of four of whom are under correctional supervision), but women's prison populations are also swelling with non-white, petty offenders as well. In 1980, there were roughly 12,000 women in prison; today, there are over 60,000 – more than a five-fold increase in a little over a decade. Moreover, as the US slides into a sort of unapologetic, carceral apartheid, we beggar our children to fund the US love affair with racism.

Americans are not alone in facing daunting problems. As this volume clearly documents, sexism comes in a wide variety of forms and offers feminist scholars a staggering array of mind numbing challenges – different in form from those in the US – but no less challenging. Take, for example, the situation of Polish women. In this country, as Monika Platek so powerfully documents, women criminologists are suddenly given leave to think freely about crime and justice after decades of Soviet repression, only to discover this same licence is being used to justify embracing some of the worst features of Western sexism with unapologetic enthusiasm. These patterns produce a sort of intellectual and political whiplash.

From Hansson's work in the new South Africa comes a more hopeful story. Since the overthrow of apartheid, there is a receptivity to critical criminology (a possibility that seems unthinkable to US scholars), and vigorous debates as to which sort of version of the equal rights amendment should be incorporated into the new constitution. Models of working collaboratively with feminist women in government bureaucracies comes from Alder's review of the accomplishments of Australian feminists, as does the notion of a pragmatic and politically informed feminist criminology.

In short, this volume provides us all with a rich set of readings that ably document the enormous achievements of women scholars worldwide – accomplishments that are all the more remarkable when placed in their disciplinary contexts. It is no mystery that women are everywhere oppressed; what is endlessly discouraging and fascinating are the variations of the challenges that women in different cultures must face while attempting, at the same time, to go on with their lives and their work. The debate will continue about whether a feminist criminology is possible, but what comes across clearly in this reading is the value of seeking to understand what Nicole Hahn Rafter and Frances Heidensohn call the 'collision' between gender consciousness and issues of crime and social control.

Meda Chesney-Lind

Acknowledgements

As we indicate in our introductory chapter, this book records and reflects the impact of feminism on the study of crime and criminal justice. It does so in an international context. That this is possible is very much a result of the First International Conference on Women, Law and Social Control, held at Mont Gabriel, in the province of Quebec, in July 1991. This conference brought together a group of scholars and activists from across the world, including both of us. Since then many of the participants have continued to meet, correspond and, as this volume shows, work together on scholarly endeavours. We are therefore immensely grateful to Marie-Andrée Bertrand, Kathy Daly and Dorie Klein, who organized the Mont Gabriel congress so well.

Some of the chapters in this collection are based on papers originally given at the British Criminology Conference at Cardiff in July 1993, where Nicky Rafter organized and chaired a panel. We acknowledge the support of Becky Dobash and her colleagues who organized the BCC, as well as the encouragement and response from the audience there. In November 1994, Nicky Rafter chaired and ran a panel at the American Society of Criminology Meetings at Miami, Florida, at which papers based on several chapters from this book, as well as an important contribution from Chinita Heard, were given. Once again we appreciated the support of conference organizers.

The ideas and histories presented in this book have thus been explored and developed in large gatherings across the English-speaking world. In addition, we have received vast amounts of advice, support and helpful criticism from friends and colleagues around the world. Jacinta Evans responded promptly and with enthusiasm to our proposal to publish this work. She and Joan Malherbe have continued to support and advise on the project with tact and grace. Many others deserve our special thanks; in particular, we should like to mention Kathy Daly, Jim Messerschmidt and Betsy Stanko for their comments on an earlier draft of the Introduction and Dorie Klein for her incisive summary at Miami. Frances Heidensohn would like to thank Marisa Silvestri and Martin Heidensohn for their help with research, Shirley Angel for much kindness and Klaus Heidensohn for practical assistance. She also records with thanks financial support for conference attendances from the British Council of Canada, the Centre for Comparative Criminology, Montreal, and the Ginsberg Fellowship. Nicky Rafter owes her strongest thanks, as always, to Robert S. Hahn, without whom she couldn't get through a day, much less a book. In addition, she too thanks Klaus Heidensohn, who didn't blink when she came for dinner and stayed a week, but rather became chef, chauffeur and companion. She owes an enormous debt, as well, to the relatives, friends, former students and colleagues who have provided such strong support and good cheer in a difficult time of her life.

As editors, we have appreciated the patience and good humour of all our contributors, who have responded to our requests and requirements so well. Last, but no means least, we should like to salute each other. Authors sometimes claim that their efforts are a chore; we, on the contrary, should like to record how much we have enjoyed working with each other on this book. It has been very much a transatlantic initiative and would have been impossible without our fax machines. We trust that some of the stimulus and excitement, the challenges and friendship which this project has meant to us, will come through to the readers of *International Feminist Perspectives in Criminology*.

Nicole Hahn Rafter and Frances Heidensohn

1

Introduction: the development of feminist perspectives on crime

**NICOLE HAHN RAFTER AND
FRANCES HEIDENSOHN**

This book is concerned with the results of an encounter – what some would call a collision – between gender consciousness on the one hand and crime and social control issues on the other. A few years ago we would have described our topic as the impact of 'feminism' on 'criminology', and those terms, although no longer entirely satisfactory, still serve to describe key aspects of our project. This collection is one of the first book-length attempts to assess the influence of feminism on the academic discipline of criminology.[1] It is also (to our knowledge) the first international and multicultural survey of feminism's effects on criminology.[2] Finally, this book is an act of documentation, an effort to show where, after twenty-five years, feminism has carried the criminological enterprise.

However, the work this collection analyses has burst the boundaries of 'feminism' and 'criminology' as they are usually conceived. In some cases this work has been conducted by activists or bureaucrats who, though focused on women's issues, would not call themselves feminists. In other cases the work has been carried out by men and women who might call themselves 'feminists' but are primarily concerned with crime–masculinity relationships. In aim, scope and influence, moreover, these activities have frequently by-passed the academic discipline of criminology. Another goal of this collection, then, is to show how feminist analyses are in some places redefining and in others replacing 'criminology' as the site where crime is addressed.

Our goals are both retrospective and prospective. Retrospectively this collection records significant chapters in the history of feminism and criminology. Whereas feminists' entry into and impact on other academic fields has been well documented, until now this story has remained by and large untold for the field of criminology. In this volume, leading scholars take steps towards a collective history by recording how they and others recognized the limitations of traditional criminology and developed alternative analyses. They begin by chronicling criminology's evolution as a formal field of study in their countries – a second retrospective aspect of this collection and one that, by demonstrating tremendous variation, suggests that we might better speak of 'criminologies'. Prospectively, this volume forecasts directions that feminist analyses of crime and social control will take in the years ahead. It proposes agendas and furthers the current globalization of efforts to recognize how criminological writings, criminal behaviours and the administration of justice are gendered.

In this introduction we trace the trajectories of twentieth-century feminism and Western academic criminology and then turn to the much-discussed issue of the results of their encounter, a debate we attempt to reframe and broaden. Next we identify factors that have fostered the recent globalization of feminist criminological analyses. We conclude by specifying key issues that those concerned with gender, crime and social control – however far-flung geographically or diverse in their immediate concerns – are likely to grapple with during the next twenty-five years.

Feminism in the late twentieth century

We begin with Western academic feminism, partly because it has been the international leader in feminist analyses of crime and criminology, partly because it is the territory with which we, as American and British academics, are most familiar. This volume covers a broader terrain, however, just as feminism ranges freely beyond the academy and Western world.

The immediate roots of twentieth-century Western feminism lie in the liberation movements of the 1960s: the European and American student movements and, in the United States, the civil rights movement as well. Idealistic young women were shocked to realize that male colleagues in these egalitarian movements regarded them as no more than secretaries or sexual playmates. Shock gave birth to indignation, indignation to a resolve to promote the liberation not only of others but of women themselves.

For guidance, newborn feminists turned to *The Second Sex*, Simone de Beauvoir's (1952) analysis of women's ubiquitous treatment as Other. Beauvoir made it painfully clear that this was a world in which the chief interpreters of women were men. Soon the new feminists were producing analyses and manifestos of their own (Friedan 1963; Millet 1970). And so began a new 'women's movement' (actually a group of interlocking movements) focused, initially, on issues that were political (reproductive rights), economic (equal wages), social (equal household responsibilities) and relational (equal status). Throughout the Western world, especially in countries with strong democratic traditions, women challenged discrimination (for example, the assumption that the best jobs would go to men), exclusion (for example, the assumption of masculinity as normative) and representation (for example, the lack of women's history). Simultaneously, they began campaigning around issues such as abortion rights and childcare. The personal (as one of their most effective slogans put it) became political.

The new feminists gave a name to what they saw as the underlying problem: *sexism*. As they grasped the consequences of marginalization and negation, silences became matters to fight against. Through the collective efforts that were such a striking characteristic of the early phase of the women's liberation movement, a crucial distinction was made between *sex* (often defined biologically, in terms of female and male) and *gender* (often defined socially, in terms of feminine and masculine). It became clear that gender subordination was neither inborn nor inevitable. Once made, the sex–gender distinction enabled feminists to break free of crippling roles and eventually to imagine cultures in which sexual and gender identities might be mixed, matched and even multiplied.[3]

In the United States and to a lesser extent other countries, the movement carried women on to campuses, where they demanded more opportunities for female scholars and students, together with courses in women's studies. Female students increased in number; in some North American departments, women scholars became regular faculty members, eligible (at last) for tenure and promotion; and the colleges and universities began to approve subjects such as women's history. But the victories were costly, and they remain contested to this day.

Crucial though the contribution of academics was to the development of feminist criminological analyses, other activists contributed with equal force. In fact, much of the original impetus for Western scholars to focus on crime issues came from *outside* university settings, from grassroots movements to help battered women, rape victims and prisoners (Rafter 1990). Participants in these movements would not necessarily have called themselves 'feminists'. Similarly, today the feminist label might seem inappropriate to the Sicilian and Calabrian women whose anti-Mafia work Tamar Pitch describes in Chapter 5 and to the academic women of colour whose criminological dilemmas Kathleen Daly and Deborah Stephens review in Chapter 10. As part of the movement to challenge the gender structures of criminology and social control we might even include people whose primary agendas have little to do with feminism – producers of television shows about female cops, for example, and women who have sued to work in men's prisons.[4] Moreover, although we know that on various continents women are campaigning against domestic violence, forced prostitution, political terrorism and other human rights violations, we don't know the degree to which these campaigns are fuelled by feminist concerns (Papanek 1993). Thus 'feminist' may not be a particularly good way to describe efforts by women and their allies to improve the quality of justice. Arguably, 'feminist' trivializes such movements by conceptually reducing them to the concerns of Westerners who identify as feminists.

Moreover, the meaning of 'feminist' is changing. What began as an egalitarian 'women's liberation' movement expanded to include the recognition of gender as a basic element in social structures throughout the world. The goal of feminism broadened to embrace an understanding of how gender shapes verbal interactions, education, identities, organizations and other aspects of culture, such as crime rates, definitions of crime and social control traditions. What began with concern about 'sexism' grew to include the social construction of femininity and enlarged again to include masculinity (Messerschmidt 1993; Newburn and Stanko 1994). Moreover, as Daly and Stephens (Chapter 10) and other studies in this volume show, feminists now investigate how multiple dimensions of power – age, geographical location, race, sexuality, social class and so on – combine with gender to affect human lives. These investigations have fractured the notion of gender, turning it into one of multiple 'femininities' and 'masculinities' (see, for example, Jim Messerschmidt's analysis of girl gang violence in Chapter 9). Feminism has rendered problematic concepts whose meanings not long ago seemed self-evident: gangs, Mafia, rape, victims, violence (even 'feminism' itself). It has also challenged the epistemological status of theories of crime.

Late twentieth-century criminology

'Criminology' too is by no means the straightforward term it may first appear. In Italy, Tamar Pitch tells us (Chapter 5), criminology has long been a 'clinical' speciality. In Eastern Europe, Monika Platek explains (Chapter 7), criminology was until recently a tool for extolling socialism's 'crime-free' societies. Australian criminology, Christine Alder observes (Chapter 2), continues to be heavily influenced by law and lawyers; the same is true of criminology in some European nations (Bertrand, Chapter 6). In South Africa (Hansson, Chapter 3), Great Britain (Heidensohn, Chapter 4), and the United States (Klein, Chapter 11), the 1970s brought critiques of traditional criminology, variously called 'critical', 'neo-realist', 'progressive realist' or the 'new' criminology. Our authors build on – and against – these diverse criminologies.

These diversities notwithstanding, it is still possible to generalize about mainstream Western criminology. This academic discipline was ripe for intervention and change at the time of its first encounters with feminism. Having flourished in the late nineteenth and early twentieth centuries, by the 1970s the field had become stagnant. Mainstream or official criminology remained insistently positivist in its methods, intent on mapping a straightforward world 'out there', dedicated to measuring crime and criminals. Because the vast majority of crimes were committed by men and men constituted over 90 per cent of all prisoners, criminologists felt justified in ignoring women. On the rare occasions on which they mentioned female offenders, they treated women's low crime rates as the phenomenon to be explained. 'It was women's lack of criminality that was seen as the intellectual problem', Robert Connell (1993: x) quips. Men were taken as the norm and women as departures from it: 'deviants from the deviance, so to speak'. Moreover, as Messerschmidt (1993: 15) observes, 'While criminological theory and research have concentrated on men and boys as the normal subjects, the *gendered* man and boy, like women, has been notoriously hidden from criminological history' (emphasis in original). In addition, criminologists slighted the offences most likely to victimize women: domestic violence, incest and rape. Even labelling theorists and critical criminologists, the self-appointed progressives of the 1960s and 1970s, ignored women.

In fact, late twentieth-century mainstream criminology was the most masculine of all the social sciences, a speciality that wore six-shooters on its hips and strutted its machismo. Political science had to acknowledge women because they could vote. The history profession might not welcome women's history, but it could not deny that women had existed in the past. Even law – another highly gendered field – paid more attention to women, perhaps because they constituted more than a tiny fraction of potential cases. But the gatekeepers of criminology and criminal justice apparently assumed that sexism was inherent in their field.

Unpersuaded, three fledgling feminists began questioning criminology's androcentrism (Bertrand 1967; Heidensohn 1968; Klein 1973). Working separately, in three different countries, they none the less raised related issues. What motivated Bertrand, Heidensohn and Klein to produce these foundational texts? Marie-Andrée Bertrand (1994) reports an evolution through the 1960s, from an initial awareness of the sexual double standard in delinquency proceedings, through her Berkeley dissertation critiquing 'the biases of statistics and the sexism of the criminal law', to her more explicitly feminist work of the late 1960s. Dorie Klein (1994) recalls that she was inspired by the student and other liberation movements of the 1960s. Frances Heidensohn began her researches into women and crime in 1965, before she was influenced by American feminism. Initially she was interested in the criminological questions of why female crime rates are lower than male rates; given this, why conventional criminology had not been interested in this topic; and finally, why this lack of interest was so widespread. But all three pioneers were involved as academics in the study of criminology – Klein as a student at Berkeley, Bertrand as a staff member of the University of Montreal while doing her PhD research at Berkeley, Heidensohn as a lecturer at the London School of Economics – and their work reflected growing feminist interests.

By the mid-1970s, several book-length studies of women and crime had been published (Adler 1975; Simon 1975; Smart 1977). It was becoming possible to talk of a feminist criminological agenda. The agenda's authors, moreover, had passed through their pioneering stage and were now entering a second phase, 'consolidating and expressing key ideas more confidently' (Heidensohn 1994: 1013). Developments occurred most swiftly in the United States, where feminists with degrees in criminology or related topics were joining the academy, doing research on women and crime, and developing the first courses in this area. Courses called for texts; collections of articles on women and crime began appearing (Price and Sokaloff 1982; Rafter and Stanko 1982). Publishers, recognizing a new market, added studies of women and crime to their lists. Simultaneously, more women were entering the traditionally male domains of policing, guarding male prisoners and court work, thus providing new data for researchers (e.g. Martin 1980; Zimmer 1986). And a powerful new branch of feminist work, victimological studies, was starting to flourish (e.g. Dobash and Dobash 1979; Russell 1982; Stanko 1985, 1990).

As yet we know next to nothing about the social organization of criminology on an international scale, but research in this area might help us understand the diffusion of feminist ideas in academic criminology as well as variations in their acceptance. How does criminology's location in the academies of various nations encourage or block the acceptance of feminist analyses of crime and social control? In countries where criminology is an adjunct of law or another entrenched discipline, as Marie-Andrée Bertrand shows (Chapter 6), criminological studies may be relatively weak and feminist criminological studies more marginal still (but see Alder, Chapter 2). Where criminology is part of a sociology department (as is often the case in the United States), there is apparently more room for it and, within it, for courses in women and/or gender and crime. In sociology departments where there is great demand for crime-related courses (and again this is often true in the United States) gender-related studies may be particularly likely to thrive. We can hypothesize that departments in which students can take a wide range of crime-related courses without restriction are those in which feminist work is most likely to flourish. These matters call for investigation, but it may be that diffusion and receptivity are even more strongly affected by other factors, such as the general strength of feminist movements within a geographical area or linguistic traditions (English being the dominant language of academic feminist criminology).[5]

The long-term health of Western criminology as both an academic speciality and a tool for social improvement may well lie in its willingness to open its boundaries to feminist analyses, postmodernist ideas and interdisciplinary endeavours (Rafter 1990). Academic specialities are always in a state of flux, but today many are experiencing particularly rapid change: new cross-disciplinary fields are emerging and less flexible specializations are becoming backwaters. For some time the most interesting theoretical developments in the understanding of crime and social control have been occurring in other areas: epistemology, gender studies, history, legal theory. In some countries criminology may be able to assimilate (at least partially) the new currents flowing around it; elsewhere it is likely to remain a rock in the stream, impervious to change. In either case, feminist work on crime and social control will probably continue unabated, for its primary aim has always been to improve not criminology but people's lives.

Analysing the impact

Feminist criminological studies have multiplied remarkably over the past two decades, becoming more sophisticated, extending their range and depth, developing new methods and recognizing diverse standpoints. How has this work affected mainstream criminology?

Feminists divide in their answers to this question. A discouraged response has been given by Americans Kathleen Daly and Meda Chesney-Lind (1988: 498), who argue that 'With the exception of feminist treatments of rape and intimate violence,' criminology 'remains essentially untouched' by feminist thought. It is true that whereas feminists began their criminological critique with the neglect of women as *offenders*, their greatest achievement has been in developing new theories about and policies for women (and children) as *victims*. But other evidence contradicts Daly and Chesney-Lind's pessimistic conclusion. As they themselves show, by the early 1980s feminists working in Australia, Canada, Great Britain and the United States had raised two central criminological issues. One was the *generalizability problem*: can supposedly gender-neutral explanations of offending apply to women as well as to men, and if not, why not? Today, the burden of explaining why a theory cannot be generalized to both sexes falls on the theorist; to ignore the female case is usually no longer acceptable. The second key issue, which Daly and Chesney-Lind call the *gender ratio problem*, asks why females are less involved than males in nearly every type of criminal behaviour. Feminist work has moved this issue, too, to centre stage in criminological inquiries.

A second and more positive assessment, this one by British sociologist Pat Carlen (1990), holds that feminists' achievements include: putting women on the criminological map; critiquing traditional criminology's essentialist and sexualized view of women; promoting justice campaigns for women and other victims; exploring the possibilities of founding a feminist criminology; challenging the preoccupation with women as offenders; and investigating the potential of feminist jurisprudence. Like Daly and Chesney-Lind (1988), Carlen describes an international endeavour which, while conducted mainly from the English-speaking world, includes Scandinavia and other parts of Europe. Carlen does go on to explore arguments against feminists studying women and crime, but these, as Heidensohn suggests in Chapter 4, may be a particularly British concern.

To answer the impact question we might compare feminism's influence with that of some other body of thought that has affected criminology. The most obvious candidate is the critical or 'new' criminology of the 1970s. Both reform efforts have objected to official criminology's claims to neutrality and objectivity; both have presented a new vision of equality and social justice; and both are overtly political. But as the comparison reveals, feminism's impact has been more profound. Feminists have produced a greater volume and range of work; this work has demonstrated greater staying power; and whereas so-called critical criminologists made no mark outside the academy, feminism has transformed criminal justice practices.

Throughout the world, as the following chapters illustrate, feminists have challenged others' pronouncements about the nature and causes of crime. They have questioned some basic concepts of the discipline and revitalized others (see, for example, Chapter 5, in which Tamar Pitch shows how feminism has reinvigorated the notions of *social control* and *moral entrepreneurship*). Although much of their work is empirical, feminists have replaced a threadbare positivism – the scientistic belief in objectivity,[6] reliance on unproblematized concepts such as 'race' and 'crime' – with new methodologies. These emphasize the importance of the researcher's standpoint, stress epistemological issues and sometimes merge victimology with criminology (see also Gelsthorpe 1990; Klein, Chapter 11 in this volume).

Moreover, feminists have developed a new criminological agenda that includes child abuse, domestic violence, sex and gender offences, fear of crime and the causal role that prior victimization may play in offending. They are researching the involvement of women in social control through studies of policing (Heidensohn 1992), judging (Rush 1993) and prison management (Zimmer 1986; Hawkes 1994). Some feminists are now reconceptualizing the meanings of criminal justice itself: taking a leaf from feminist legal theorists (Minow 1990; Guinier 1994), they are looking for ways to move beyond simplistic either/ors in which one party wins and the other loses, searching instead for third-type solutions that maximize benefits for all and minimize social costs. For example, the emerging battered women's defence (Browne 1987) would give women the right (one men have had for centuries) to choose self-protection as an alternative to tolerating severe physical abuse or facing homicide charges. The interest in developing new conceptions of justice is evident as well in studies of sentencing leniency for 'familied' defendants (Daly 1987) and arguments for differential sentencing of defendants with dependent children (Rafter 1989).

Our authors show varying degrees of interest in the question of feminism's impact on traditional criminology. Dorothy Chunn and Robert Menzies (Chapter 8) subject the question to sustained analysis by surveying former and current graduate students at three anglophone Canadian universities. Other authors assess feminism's impact on other aspects of the study of crime. Both are useful reactions. As these chapters demonstrate, we can monitor the effects of feminist criminological discourses within and outside academe simultaneously. This volume is organized around a question – how feminist movements in various parts of the world have affected crime and crime control – that enables us to look inward to scholarship and outward to activism at the same time.

International developments

Domestic violence, sexual abuse, rape – these issues cut across national boundaries. Sharing fears of male violence, women around the globe are already bound by strong ties. But recent years have witnessed an internationalization of women's concerns about crime and justice. More than a recognition and acknowledgement of mutual interests, this phenomenon is self-consciously feminist. And it aims explicitly at creating transnational and transcultural alliances that will respect diversity.

One factor encouraging globalization is the collapse of old political orders in Eastern Europe (Platek, Chapter 7), the Balkans and South Africa (Hansson, Chapter 3). In country after country, patriarchal regimes that silenced dissent have been overthrown. Out of the rubble are emerging a host of new minorities – ethnic, feminist, nationalist – contending for participation in the new regimes. Internationalization has also been fostered by the trend toward postmodernism – the fragmentation of old explanatory structures and acceptance of multiple perspectives. Interest in discourses, identities, representations: these facets of postmodernist thought have all contributed to a renewed interest in the origins and effects of cultural difference. Globalization has been further promoted by the simple fact that, throughout the world, feminists and their allies have entered work in criminology and criminal justice, creating a critical mass capable of giving voice to women's concerns. Throughout the world we now find crusades against domestic violence and other forms of victimization of women. Participants in these movements now constitute an international audience for information on gender, crime and social control.

Much as international conferences solidified the global women's movement during the 1980s, a conference on Women, Law and Social Control drew feminists together in the early 1990s, internationalizing concerns about crime and justice. Held at Mont Gabriel, Quebec, in 1991 and organized by an international team,[7] the meeting brought together over sixty delegates from eighteen countries (Bertrand et al. 1992). Follow-up meetings were held at the 1993 British Criminology Conference in Wales and the 1994 American Society of Criminology meeting in Miami. Facilitating the exchange of feminist concerns and agendas across national lines, the conferences also challenged assumptions of an uncomplicated, uniform 'sisterhood'.

Common themes and future directions

Some of the following chapters forecast future directions for feminist criminological work in general; others set new agendas for particular countries. Several look mainly to next steps within academic criminology; all are ultimately concerned with transforming conditions under which people lead their lives. Most future-directed and transformative in thrust is the essay by Dorie Klein (Chapter 11), who calls for nothing less than a complete 're-envisioning' of the field she helped to create, a reorientation so radical that 'feminist thinking on crime and justice' would 'make an intellectual and political difference'. That has always been the central goal of feminist criminological work, and by definition it will continue to be so.

Within academic criminology, what can we expect in the years ahead? According to these chapters, three issues will be particularly important. First, *is a 'feminist criminology' possible or rather a contradiction in terms*? This question is raised in part by feminists' mistrust of positivism and of state crime control programmes, which all too often have been thinly disguised women control programmes.[8] The question stems as well from current feminist efforts to keep gender on a par with other aspects of social location and experience, such as race and sexuality. If we aim at 'feminist criminology', are we not giving preference to gender over other dimensions of power? Why not instead label our goal 'anti-racist' or even 'multicultural' criminology? In fact, few feminists would be surprised or distressed if their project lost its current identity by spilling over into others. Inclusiveness has long been a feminist goal, one actively advanced by insistence on the embrace of multiple standpoints and the value of crossing boundaries.

The perception of a fundamental incompatibility between feminism and criminology surfaced first and most forcibly in England (Cain 1986, 1990a,b; Smart 1990; and see Heidensohn, Chapter 4 in this volume). But as this collection indicates, doubts about whether feminism and criminology can coexist have become widespread. Alder (Chapter 2) shares these doubts but sees no cause for alarm; in Australia, multiple disciplines and even the state have contributed to feminist work on criminal justice issues and are likely to continue doing so. Similarly, writing from Italy, Pitch (Chapter 5) expects feminist work on crime to persist despite official criminology's indifference. Klein (Chapter 11) suggests that if feminism is to fulfil its promise and retain vitality, it will keep a wary distance from the criminological establishment. And, as Daly and Stephens (Chapter 10) point out, women of colour may find neither feminism nor traditional criminology congruent with their concerns. Over and over in these chapters we observe a search for what Pitch calls a new 'site', a berth within the academy that will nurture investigations of gender, crime and social control. In all likelihood, we will have to continue creating that site for ourselves.

Second, *in the years ahead how will feminists deal with the anglo- and ethnocentrism of current work on crime and justice*? For historical and economic reasons, feminism and criminology are both strongest in Western nations, particularly English-speaking countries (Margolis 1993). As a result, problems have tended to be stated in anglocentric and ethnocentric terms. In other parts of the world women often face more serious crime and justice problems, including genital mutilation and widespread sexual slavery. In some places conditions for women are deteriorating (Platek, Chapter 7), owing to cutbacks in welfare services and the growth of inequality and violence. In theory at least, white Westerners seek a more heterogeneous feminism and would welcome a decentring of their own traditions. But the alternatives are not yet clear, especially as sex-equality movements elsewhere are often weaker and more fragmented (Margolis

1993). What directions will or should feminist efforts in criminology take in future?

Third, in the years ahead feminists will have to confront the question: *to what degree are criminology and crime control policies implicated in the construction of hierarchies based on gender, race, class and sexuality?* Traditional criminology has mainly asked how to achieve crime control. Feminists have asked how crime control achieves gender – how control systems contribute to the maintenance of 'female' as inferiority. And feminists have tended to view criminology itself as a tool for reinforcing inequality. (This tendency is reflected in the many chapters of this volume that analyse criminological discourses.) Continuing to turn positivism on its head, feminists will doubtless continue to explore how criminology and crime control policies contribute to and reinforce structures of power and hegemony.

These are difficult questions – harder than many posed by mainstream criminologists. They demonstrate the conflicts and contradictions, the differences and divergences that characterize contemporary feminisms. But they also illustrate the magnitude of the feminist criminological enterprise. Ultimately, this is a project of self-obsolescence, for if the discipline were engendered and crime control policy transformed as feminists recommend, they could retire from the field. But then, the field itself as we now know it would no longer exist.

Organization of this volume

Work on this collection repeatedly reminded us of how difficult it is actually to break the fetters of anglocentrism. We solicited chapters on Asian nations, central and northern African countries, and Central America and the Caribbean, but without success. Thus although this book covers a broader cultural range than other criminological texts, that range is narrower than we had hoped.

Part I, on the South, deals with Australia and South Africa, countries that share a colonial past but today differ markedly in racial composition, political stability and crime control problems. These differences have pushed feminist criminological concerns in divergent directions.

Part II, on Europe, also embraces diverse cultures. Starting with a chapter on England, it then turns to feminist criminological work in other relatively stable nations: Germany, Denmark and Finland. Italy, the focus of the next chapter, is currently experiencing political upheaval, an upheaval precipitated in part by past governments' inability to control the Mafia and bureaucratic corruption. This turmoil is reflected in the criminological and legal theorizing of Italian feminists. As the last chapter in this section shows, feminists in Poland and other Eastern European countries are confronting yet another set of difficulties brought on by the collapse of communism.

Part III, on North America, opens with a chapter analysing feminism's impact on criminological communities in anglophone Canada. It is followed by three chapters that grow out of the experiences of US feminists but carry far broader implications. One demonstrates how recent theory about the social construction of gender can help us understand the gender content of law-breaking behaviour, including female violence, a category that most criminologists have studiously avoided. The following chapter sets a theoretical and research agenda for black and multi-ethnic feminist perspectives in criminology. The final chapter seeks nothing short of a total revitalization of feminist thinking about crime and justice. Sending jolting reminders of the transformative aims of our criminological enterprise, it proposes goals for the next twenty-five years of feminist work in criminology.

Acknowledgements

Thanks are due to Kathleen Daly, Jim Messerschmidt and Elizabeth Stanko for their helpful comments on earlier versions of this introduction.

Notes

1 We are using the term 'discipline' loosely, to indicate a field or area of academic inquiry. As far as we know, the only earlier book-length assessment of feminism's influence on criminology is Gelsthorpe and Morris (1990), a work that concentrates on Great Britain. For article-length assessments of the impact, see Daly and Chesney-Lind (1988), Gelsthorpe and Morris (1988), Simpson (1989) and Heidensohn (1994).

2 *The Incidence of Female Criminality in the Contemporary World*, Adler's 1984 collection, was also international in scope, but its purpose was criminological rather than feminist.

3 For more on the criminological history and significance of the sex–gender distinction, see Heidensohn (1994: 997–8) and Messerschmidt (Chapter 10) in this volume. However, the sex-gender distinction is being challenged.

4 Zimmer (1986) discovered that US women who sued and otherwise struggled to be hired as guards in men's prisons did so primarily because the jobs offered convenience and/or good pay, not out of a sense of feminist mission.

5 Piers Beirne and Jim Messerschmidt contributed ideas to this discussion of diffusion and receptivity.

6 For a critique of the myth of objectivity, see Daly and Chesney-Lind (1988). Feminists are certainly not monolithic in their attitudes towards objectivity, however. For a more positive view, see Platek (Chapter 7 in this volume).

7 The Mont Gabriel conference on Women, Law and Social Control was organized by French-Canadian Marie-Andrée Bertrand and two Americans, Kathleen Daly and Dorie Klein.

8 Alder's chapter (Chapter 2) contains the fascinating suggestion that feminists' mistrust of the state is to some extent ill-conceived. In Australia, Alder indicates, the legacy of colonialism includes a strong state bureaucracy or 'femocracy' that today actively furthers feminist goals. Platek's chapter suggests that the mistrust of positivism may also need rethinking.

References

Adler, F. (1975). *Sisters in Crime*. New York: McGraw-Hill.

Adler, F. (ed.) (1984). *The Incidence of Female Criminality in the Contemporary World*. New York: New York University Press.

Beauvoir, S. de (1952). *The Second Sex*. New York: Knopf.

Bertrand, M. (1967). The myth of sexual equality before the law. In *Proceedings of the Fifth Research Conference on Delinquency and Criminality*. Montreal: Quebec Society of Criminology.

Bertrand, M. (1994). Information about my own history. Memorandum to Nicole Hahn Rafter of 11 April.

Bertrand, M., Daly, K. and Klein, D. (eds) (1992). *Proceedings of the International Feminist Conference on Women, Law, and Social Control*. Mont Gabriel, Quebec, 18–21 July 1991.

Browne, A. (1987). *When Battered Women Kill*. New York: Free Press.

Cain, M. (1986). Realism, feminism, methodology, and law. *International Journal of the Sociology of Law*, 14, 255–67.

Cain, M. (1990a). Realist philosophy and standpoint epistemologies, or feminist criminology as a successor science. In L. Gelsthorpe and A. Morris (eds) *Feminist Perspectives in Criminology*. Milton Keynes: Open University Press.

Cain, M. (1990b). Towards transgression: new directions in feminist criminology. *International Journal of the Sociology of Law*, 18, 1–18.

Carlen, P. (1990). Women, crime, feminism and realism. *Social Justice*, 17(4), 100–23.

Connell, R.W. (1993). Foreword to J.W. Messerschmidt. *Masculinities and Crime*. Lanham, MD: Rowman and Littlefield.

Daly, K. (1987). Discrimination in the criminal courts: family, gender, and the problem of equal treatment. *Social Forces*, 66(1), 152–75.

Daly, K. and Chesney-Lind, M. (1988). Feminism and criminology, *Justice Quarterly*, 5(4), 497–535.

Dobash, R.E. and Dobash, R.P. (1979). *Violence against Wives: a Case against Patriarchy*. New York: Free Press.

Freidan, B. (1963). *The Feminine Mystique*. New York: Norton.

Gelsthorpe, L. (1990). Feminist methodologies in criminology: a new approach or old wine in new bottles? In L. Gelsthorpe and A. Morris (eds) *Feminist Perspectives in Criminology*. Milton Keynes: Open University Press.

Gelsthorpe, L. and Morris, A. (1988). Feminism and criminology in Britain. *British Journal of Criminology*, 28(2), 221–40.

Gelsthorpe, L. and Morris, A. (eds) (1990). *Feminist Perspectives in Criminology*. Milton Keynes: Open University Press.

Guinier, L. (1994). *Fundamental Fairness in Representative Democracy*. New York: Free Press.

Hawkes, M.Q. (1994). *Excellent Effect: the Edna Mahan Story*. Laurel Lakes, MD: American Correctional Association.

Heidensohn, F.M. (1968). The deviance of women: a critique and an enquiry. *British Journal of Sociology*, 19(2), 160–75.

Heidensohn, F.M. (1992). *Women in Control? The Role of Women in Law Enforcement*. Oxford: Oxford University Press.

Heidensohn, F.M. (1994). Gender and crime. In M. Maguire, R. Morgan and R. Reiner (eds) *The Oxford Handbook of Criminology*. Oxford: Clarendon Press.

Klein, D. (1973). The etiology of female crime: a review of the literature. *Issues in Criminology*, 8(2), 3–30.

Klein, D. (1994). Twenty years ago . . . today. In B. Price and N. Sokaloff (eds) *The Criminal Justice System and Women*, 2nd edn. New York: McGraw-Hill.

Margolis, D.R. (1993). Women's movements around the world: cross-cultural comparisons. *Gender and Society*, 7(3), 379–99.

Martin, S.E. (1980). *Breaking and Entering: Policewomen on Patrol*. Berkeley: University of California Press.

Messerschmidt, J.W. (1993). *Masculinities and Crime*. Lanham, MD: Rowman and Littlefield.

Millet, K. (1970). *Sexual Politics*. New York: Doubleday.

Minow, M. (1990). *Making All the Difference: Inclusion, Exclusion, and American Law*. Ithaca, NY: Cornell University Press.

Newburn, T. and Stanko, E. (1994). *Just Boys Doing Business?* London: Routledge.

Papanek, H. (1993). Theorizing about women's movements globally: comment on Diane Margolis. *Gender and Society*, 7(4), 594–604.

Price, B.R. and Sokoloff, N.J. (eds) (1982). *The Criminal Justice System and Women*. New York: Clark Boardman Company.

Rafter, N. (1989). Gender and justice: the equal protection issue. In L. Goodstein and D.L. MacKenzie (eds) *The American Prison: Issues in Research and Policy*. New York: Plenum.

Rafter, N. (1990). The social construction of crime and crime control. *Journal of Research in Crime and Delinquency*, 27(4), 376–89.

Rafter, N. and Stanko, E.A. (1982). *Judge, Lawyer, Victim, Thief: Women, Gender Roles, and Criminal Justice*. Boston: Northeastern University Press.

Rush, S.E. (1993). Feminist judging: an introductory essay. *Southern California Review of Law and Women's Studies*, 2(2), 609–32.

Russell, D.E.H. (1982). *Rape in Marriage*. New York: Macmillan.

Simon, R.J. (1975). *The Contemporary Woman and Crime*. Rockville, MD: National Institute on Mental Health.

Simpson, S.S. (1989). Feminist theory, crime, and justice. *Criminology*, 27(4), 605–31.

Smart, C. (1977). *Women, Crime and Criminology*. London: Routledge & Kegan Paul.

Smart, C. (1990). Feminist approaches to criminology or postmodern woman meets atavistic man. In L. Gelsthorpe and A. Morris (eds) *Feminist Perspectives in Criminology*. Milton Keynes: Open University Press.

Stanko, E. (1985). *Intimate Instrusions: Women's Experience of Male Violence*. London: Routledge & Kegan Paul.

Stanko, E. (1990). *Everyday Violence*. London: Pandora.

Zimmer, L. (1986). *Women Guarding Men*. Chicago: University of Chicago Press.

Part I
The South

2

Feminist criminology in Australia

CHRISTINE ALDER

Introduction

Feminist criminology is relatively new to Australia. While from the mid-1970s in the United States there was a marked increase in feminist criminology, in Australia it was the early 1980s before more than a couple of lone voices were speaking out. However, in the 1994 Annual Conference of the Australian and New Zealand Society of Criminology, ninety of 196 appearances on the programme were by women, and feminist (broadly defined) sessions constituted 23 per cent of the programme. Feminist voices are being raised in Australian criminology.

As activists, feminist criminologists in Australia are engaged with local matters, but their research and writing is frequently published in international forums. The work of some feminist Australian criminologists would be known more widely outside of their country than within. While this is indicative of the resonance of Australian material with other nations, there are also some distinctive features of the development and context of feminist criminology in Australia to which I hope to introduce the reader in this chapter.[1]

Background: Criminology in Australia

The form of feminist criminology in Australia is in some ways founded in the historical development of Australian criminology. Law and lawyers dominated the formation of criminology and continue to have significant input even though a greater social science component developed in the

1980s. Of the eighteen feminists whose curricula vitae I reviewed for this chapter, half had law degrees. The institutional basis of criminology in law in part accounts for the significant legal and criminal justice policy reform framework of Australian criminology (O'Malley and Carson 1989). If criminology can be crudely divided into two bodies of concern, one with theories of causation, the other with punishment and control (Cohen 1988: 1–7), it is the latter that has dominated Australian criminology.

In the USA and Britain, the empiricism and positivism of criminology were challenged in the 1960s and early 1970s by sociologists. However, this did not occur in Australia, where it is only relatively recently that sociology has developed as an autonomous discipline; it is still not as extensive nor does it have the same standing in the social sciences as in the USA (O'Malley and Carson 1989). The relative underdevelopment of sociology as a discipline in part explains two features of Australian criminology in general: the relatively small number of explicitly theoretically focused debates and theoretically driven research; and the limited development of social science research methods.

Nevertheless, social scientists in particular played a significant role in challenging the traditional subject matter of criminology through a strong body of research which critically analysed areas such as corporate and white collar crime and its regulation (see Braithwaite 1984; Grabosky 1989; Grabosky and Sutton 1989). Radical criminologies also emerged in Australia in the 1970s and have continued to play an active and influential role in the development of Australian criminology. Most of the academics who contributed to this development were located in law schools. David Brown and Russell Hogg argue that the legal location 'gave an interventionist impetus to the emerging radical criminology, aligning it to concrete criminal justice struggles and, in particular, prison movement and community legal centre organisations' (Brown and Hogg 1992: 207). Thus radical criminology as it developed in Australia could not be dismissed for not 'taking crime seriously' and could not be characterized as the 'left idealism' in opposition to which 'left realism' defined itself in Britain. While there is some affinity between British left realism and the recent theoretical, programmatic and policy work of radical criminologists in Australia, the Australian work has not 'been sponsored under a left realist banner' (Brown and Hogg 1992: 218). In exploring the reasons for this, David Brown and Russell Hogg (1992) raise a number of reservations they have about British left realism, while at the same time indicating some of the differences in the theoretical, historical and political contexts of Britain and Australia.

Overall, pragmatic or policy-directed research remains a significant component of criminological research in Australia. However, contemporary criminology, including some feminist research, while often emerging from policy-related concerns rather than explicitly stated theoretical concerns, has a critical edge that was less often found in the past. The March 1994 issue of the *Australian and New Zealand Journal of Criminology*, edited by a feminist, Kathy Laster, is evidence of a more self-reflective stance regarding the pragmatism of criminology and the 'lure of relevance'.

Feminism and criminology in the universities

Academic criminology in Australia, as elsewhere and in other disciplines, has been and still is dominated by men (Naffine 1987). Overall, the number of feminist criminologists in Australia is small, they are dispersed across the country and across disciplines, and in general they feel somewhat isolated from other academic feminists with similar areas of interests.

In a by now familiar story, men have dominated not only the corridors of the universities but also the pages of the academic journals. An analysis of the *Australian and New Zealand Journal of Criminology* from 1974 to 1993, and *Current Issues in Criminal Justice* from 1989 to 1994, revealed that of a total of 497 articles, 14 per cent were written by women, and 10 per cent had women as joint authors. The proportion of articles by women has not altered significantly in recent years. Further, only 7 per cent of articles either included gender or sex as a key component of the analysis or dealt with issues specifically related to women.[2]

The publication of feminist work in local journals may be minimal, but the work of academic feminist criminologists is frequently informed by, and places itself within the context of, debates in the international forum, and therefore their work is published more extensively in overseas journals. Further, it is not uncommon for feminist criminologists to have educational and research experiences overseas and to participate in international conferences. Perhaps this in part accounts for the openness to feminist ideas from a variety of Euro-American sources that Curthoy (1994: 2) notes as a distinctive feature of Australian feminist discourse. Given our geographical isolation, feminist discourse might be anticipated to be parochial; on the contrary, more so perhaps than feminists in either the UK or the USA, in general academic feminist criminologists in Australia draw upon and engage in the debates of feminist criminology from across both of these locations.

A feature of the work of Australian feminist criminologists is its breadth. It is not uncommon for Australian feminist criminologists to publish on topics that are not overtly identifiable as 'feminist', that is, the focus of their work is not always gender or issues that are specific to women.[3] For example, Ngaire Naffine (1992), Christine Alder and Joy Wundersitz (1994), Faye Gale, Ngaire Naffine and Joy Wundersitz (1993), Jenny Bargen (1990), and Julie Stubbs (1991a) have written on juvenile justice issues; Ann Aungles (1994) on the interdependence of prison and family life; and Kathy Laster and Veronica Taylor (1994) on 'Interpreters and the Legal system'. Sharon Anleu (1991) considers the literature on *Deviance, Conformity and Control* and, Anne Edwards Hiller (1988) in her book *Regulation and Repression* explores the complexity of social control across law and criminal justice, medicine and social welfare.

Particularly for those who do not have a law background, it is not uncommon for Australian feminist criminologists to research and write in areas that are not directly related to crime as traditionally defined. Health and medical related issues have been the subject for several academic feminist criminologists; for example, Linda Hancock's work on informed consent and defensive medicine (Hancock 1993), Jocelynne Scutt's work on reproductive technologies (Scutt 1988) and Suzanne Hatty's (1994) work on 'medicalizing discipline'.

It is not always their feminism that leads women to these other topics. Feminist criminologists with whom I spoke in preparing this chapter spoke of 'social justice', 'justice', 'rights', concerns or other standpoints that arise from their ethnic or class background. Thus the work of Australian feminist criminologists is not necessarily bounded by 'crime'; their concerns range across the breadth of women's lives and across institutions other than those of the legal and criminal justice systems. Nor is feminism necessarily the only standpoint from which feminist criminologists pursue their work. This diversity of approach and subject matter adds a breadth to feminist criminology which has the potential to facilitate further challenges to the boundaries of traditional criminology.

Feminism and criminology in the community and the bureaucracy

'A distinctive feature of Australian research on women and crime has been the dual commitment of many of the researchers not only to academic investigation, but also to concrete action on behalf of women who are unjustly treated by police and courts' (Broom and Richmond 1982: 65). Many academic feminists work in a range of ways with government departments and community groups outside the universities. These include federal government departments such as the Australian Law Reform Commission, the Human Rights and Equal Opportunity Commission and The National Committee on Violence Against Women. State government agencies include the Community Council against Violence (Victoria), the Criminal Justice Commission (Queensland), the Women's Advisory Offices and the State Law Reform Commission. Other work is with community-based groups such as The Children of Prisoners Support Groups, Academics for Justice and the Women and Girls in Custody Group. Many more research reports and analyses of issues related to women and crime have been produced from these sites than from universities. These reports and studies are far too numerous for me even to begin to give an overview or analysis of them in a chapter of this length, but they address issues such as rape law reform (e.g. The Law Reform Commission of Victoria 1991), domestic violence (e.g. Family Violence Professional Education Taskforce 1991), violence against women (National Committee on Violence against Women 1993) and domestic homicide (NSW Bureau of Crime Statistics and Research 1992; Women's Coalition against Family Violence 1994). In recent years there has been a significant increase in the proportion of publications on women and crime produced by the Australian Institute of Criminology in Canberra (see, for example, the work of Patricia Easteal 1992 a,b,c, 1994).

The work on women and crime produced at these sites is not necessarily always feminist. However, there is a good deal of research, particularly that produced by women's collectives (e.g. Women's Coalition against Family Violence 1994), that could be described as 'standpoint feminism', and is the work of feminists engaged in struggle at both the intellectual and the political levels (Smart 1990: 80). The extent of this material, and perhaps its greater impact in Australia, is in part a consequence of the extent and power of what has been described as the 'femocracy', feminists in senior positions in state and federal bureaucracies. The power of femocracy may be a distinctive feature of Australian feminism. In contrasting the political strategies of feminists in Australia with those in the USA, Anne Summers (1994) comments on the flexible and pragmatic ways in which Australian feminists have learned to work successfully in the political mainstream. In Europe, Gisela Kaplan (1994) argues, the concept of femocrat is strange to feminists since bureaucracies have a more limited administrative character than in Australia, where the post-colonial legacy means they are a site of power. The working together of femocrats, activists outside the bureaucracies and academics has not been without some tensions (Stubbs 1994: 5). Nevertheless, in Australia the extent of feminist research and policy development, particularly in the areas of violence against women, has in no small way, directly and indirectly, been facilitated by feminists holding key positions inside government bureaucracies (McGregor and Hopkins 1991).

The early days

Feminist criminology, or any research on women and crime, developed later in Australia than it did in either the UK or the USA. In the early 1980s in Australia, Anne Edwards Hiller could comment that 'the sociology of female crime in Australia and New Zealand is at an elementary stage' (Edwards Hiller 1982: 82). The first book which was explicitly about 'women and crime' was published in 1981 (Mukherjee and Scutt 1981). The works collected together in this book indicate that the concerns of feminist criminologists in Australia were similar to those of their feminist colleagues elsewhere. They were keen to point out the relative absence of women from criminological theory and the invisibility of women as victims of men's violence. They were critical of the assumptions and 'myths' about women that underpinned the law, criminal and juvenile justice processing and theories of female crime. Authors called for the placing of women's crime in its social and economic context. Questions were raised about the adequacy of official statistics for understanding female crime and victimization, and the processing of women in the criminal and juvenile justice systems was critiqued.

In her review of feminist criminology to that point, Anne Edwards Hiller (1982) noted that while some work had been done which criticized police and court handling of domestic violence and rape cases, the whole question of sexism received 'scant attention' in Australia relative to the work being carried out overseas. Nevertheless, she observed that the 'chivalry' of the legal and criminal justice systems was being questioned in some more extensive work on the handling of young women in the juvenile justice system. Some features of early feminist criminology noted by Edwards Hiller were to continue, in particular the absence of 'theoretical, sociological work' on female crime and a focus on women as victims of men, both outside and within the criminal justice system.

Later reviews tend to oversimplify this earlier work; for example, analyses of 'sexism' in the juvenile and criminal justice systems were not always as naive as is sometimes presented. For example, in the frequently quoted works on sexism in juvenile justice in Australia, Linda Hancock and her co-authors explicity addressed the relevance of class and family relations in decisions regarding young women. Their arguments were not solely based on comparisons between the experiences of boys and girls: key components of the analysis were the welfare and rehabilitation concepts, which were central to the dominant discourse and philosophy of juvenile justice; the sufficiency of legal change was challenged; a recognition of the broader social and political factors involved in this area was called for; and the recommendations for change were never simply in terms of treating girls and boys equally (e.g. Hancock 1980; Edwards Hiller and Hancock 1981; Hancock and Chesney-Lind 1982).

Certainly as the research on sexism accumulated, it became apparent that the issue was more complex than initially anticipated (Edwards 1989). However, it is crucial that we consider this earlier work in its historical context. This feminist work was groundbreaking: early feminist criminologists were struggling for, and needed to struggle for, the recognition of women; for women and their definition by and treatment within the legal and criminal justice systems to be made visible and challenged. It may now be argued that the call for the inclusion of women was not sufficiently penetrating, but it would be hard to claim that at that time it was not necessary. Further, there is a complexity and diversity to this work that is sometimes obscured in order to create an 'other' which can be devalued and dismissed in order to establish the value of more recent work. That is, reviews of past feminist work to some extent engage in the process of conflating diversity in order to advance broad propositions. This is an age-old academic enterprise, and perhaps as feminists we need to think of alternative processes.

Contemporary work

Throughout the 1980s and into the early 1990s the major issues addressed by feminists in most Australian states have included: prostitution law reform;

rape law reform; policing and legislation regarding domestic violence; and women's imprisonment. Thus the focus has been on legal and criminal justice reform. The substance of the struggles in these areas would be familiar to feminists worldwide. However, this does not capture the entirety of feminist criminology in Australia and the following is an introduction to some of the other areas of interest being pursued by predominantly academic feminist criminologists.

A dominant concern of feminist criminologists over the past decade has been violence against women. Within this broader topic homicide has more recently been the subject of feminist analysis. A recent book by a feminist collective documents the stories of women victims of male violence (Women's Coalition against Family Violence 1994). Other works have examined homicide cases with gender as a central component of the analyses (Wallace 1986; Easteal 1992c). The use of the battered women's syndrome in cases where women are accused of murdering their husbands has been the subject of some debate: Patricia Easteal (1992a) advocated its use, and Julie Stubbs has been a critic (1991b; Stubbs and Tolmie 1994).

The Lindy Chamberlain case[4] in Australia, which involved the conviction and subsequent acquittal of a mother for the murder of one of her children, was the subject of intense public debate and raised a number of issues, including the effects of 'trial by media' and the representation and construction of the female offender in legal discourse and the media. These issues have subsequently been taken up by feminists, in terms of that particular case (Howe 1989; Johnson 1984) and other individual cases (Carrington 1994), and in more general terms with regard to women who kill (Naylor 1990; Wilczynski 1991).

Representations of women in crime fiction have also captured the attention of Australian feminist criminologists. Suzanne Hatty suggests that it might be 'fruitful to deconstruct the cultural division of the crime text into "factual" or "fictitious" literature' (Hatty 1993a: 13). Hatty notes that in the USA and Australia, feminist creative writers, including criminologist Jocelynne Scutt using a pseudonym, 'have been reworking the convention of the crime narrative, and problematizing the received ideas about gender, criminality and representation' (Hatty 1993a: 13).

The study of crime in Australia, including feminist research, infrequently arises from the explicit posing of a theoretical question. However, theoretical discussion has not been absent: for example, Anleu (1991) reviews primarily sociological theories of 'deviance, conformity and control'; Laster (1989) considers feminist theories of female crime in the light of historical material on infanticide; Hatty (1993b) examines the concept of dependence in definitions of and responses to female crime; and Howe argues for women's 'gender specific injuries . . . to be taken into account in any valid jurisprudence of social justice' (Howe 1987: 435).

Particularly distinguished in the body of theoretical work by Australian feminists is Naffine's (1987) book, *Female Crime: the Construction of Women in Criminology*. Through an analysis of existing theories of female crime, Naffine endeavours to 'lay bare the gendered theories and methods of criminologists' (Naffine 1987: 127). She draws particular attention to the portrayal of women as weak, passive and dependent, in contrast to the daring, aggressive and sometimes heroic portrayal of men. Naffine sees her project as contributing to the 'larger feminist project of reconstructing knowledge so that it no longer reflects exclusively a male social reality' (Naffine 1987: 127).

Another feminist book which explicitly addresses theoretical issues is Judith Allen's historical study of crimes involving Australian women. Rejecting reliance on official statistics and overall official trends, Allen claims that in her study 'the monolith "crime" has been deconstructed, and crimes relevant to relations between the sexes detached and relocated within the social history of the options and experiences of men and women' (Allen 1990a: 244). Central to her work is analysis of 'the oppression of the sex women by the sex men' (Allen 1990a: 255).

Judith Allen's book is one of a very few feminist historical studies of women and crime. Another example is Helen Daniels's (1984) collection of works on 'Women and prostitution in Australian history'. While there have been many social historical studies of crime-related matters (Brown and Hogg 1992: 211), unfortunately history and criminology have rarely come together in Australia (Phillips 1991). In fact, Judith Allen and Adrian Howe (1990), both feminist historians working on criminological issues, have distanced themselves from criminology as a discipline as they define it. Nevertheless, recently there have been calls for greater interaction between the two disciplines and an expansion of feminist historical work in Australian criminology. For example, in 1991 Kathy Laster was the editor of a special issue of the *Australian and New Zealand Journal of Criminology* on 'History and Crime', which included an article by Debra Oxley, 'Women transported: gendered images and realities' (Oxley 1991). Laster's own work has included historical studies of infanticide (1989) and the death penalty (1994).

In the introduction to her edited book on feminist criminology internationally, Ngaire Naffine comments on the difficult task of attempting to categorize the work of feminist criminologists: 'none of the divisions between the different styles stands firmly . . . they are . . . misleading because of the refusal of most of these writers to observe strictly the canons of any one tradition of thought' (Naffine 1994b). Naffine's words ring true for me as I have tried in this very brief overview to provide some indication of the breadth of the work being dealt with by a relatively small number of Australian feminist criminologists. The diversity of the work applies not only to subject matter, of which I have tried to give some indication, but also to methodology and related epistemological positions, which I have not attempted to deal with in this chapter. Further, the range applies not only across the work of different feminists, but also within the work of most individual women. It is a breadth that for me defied collapsing into meaningful categories.

Aboriginal women: not seen and not heard

In the 1991 census 1.2 per cent of all Australian women identified themselves as Aboriginal or Torres Strait Islander (Australian Bureau of Statistics
1993: 10). In 1989, Aboriginal women represented 16 per cent of the
female prison population (Payne 1993: 66) and in 1990–1, 16 per cent of
all female victims of homicide in Australia were Aboriginal (Strang 1992:
25). Such figures make clear that in terms of both criminalization and victimization, Aboriginal women in Australia are significantly over-represented
in the few statistics available which address these issues. While this fact
has been noted by Australian feminists from time to time (Hartz-Karp 1981;
Howe 1988; Scutt 1990a), the situation of Aboriginal women has rarely
been considered at any length. A recent exception is Kerry Carrington's
observations regarding Aboriginal young women in the juvenile justice
system, from which she argues that the extraordinary level of Aboriginal
criminalization is 'more complex, more subtle and more deeply imbedded'
(Carrington 1993a: 49) than allowed for by traditional explanations in
terms of either over-policing or over-offending.

In recent years Aboriginal women have spoken out against white women's
omission and oppression of their voices. In particular, some Aboriginal
women have rejected the privileging of gender over race in white women's
analyses of male violence against women. For example, in Australia the
dominant feminist approach to violence against women in the home has
not supported strategies involving working directly with violent men. In
contrast, some Aboriginal women have argued that in their communities,
acknowledging and responding to male violence against women 'must
involve Aboriginal men and indeed cannot work without the support of
Aboriginal men, who . . . are also victims of society' (Sam 1992). An Aboriginal historian and writer, Jackie Huggins, has commented that 'In asking
Aboriginal women to stand apart from Aboriginal men, the white women's
movement was, perhaps unconsciously, repeating the attempts made over
decades by welfare administrations to separate Aboriginal women and use
them against their communities.' (Huggins 1994: 70).

At the same time, Aboriginal women have noted the difficulty of discussing male violence against women in some Aboriginal communities where
talking of such matters is considered to be damaging to the community
and 'giving further ammunition to an already racist situation' (Greer 1994:
68). Nevertheless, Pam Greer describes the progress that has been made in
the development of domestic violence-related services and programming
for women in Aboriginal communities. In so doing, Greer cautions against
assuming that the problems and needs of specific communities are shared
across the 'extremely diverse and pluralistic Aboriginal cultures' (Greer
1994: 66).

Aboriginal women point out that their stories have been denied not only
when white feminists ignore race but also when they fail to acknowledge
their own sins: white feminists have been 'silent about relationships between

white women and Black women' (Huggins 1994: 72). Jackie Huggins reminds us that white women oppressed black women both in the domestic sphere, where brutal treatment was not unknown, and in the fields of welfare and education, where 'White women were and are still a major force in the implementation of government policies of assimilation and cultural genocide.' (Huggins 1994: 73).

White feminists' failure either to acknowledge the situation of Aboriginal women or to listen to them has led to the construction of 'culturally insensitive, alienating and inadequate feminist theories and policies' (Huggins 1994: 78). We can no longer ignore Huggins's (1994: 73) observation that the continued imposition of white feminist politics on Aboriginal women is 'most certainly an attempt at intellectual colonisation.'

Matters of debate

Pragmatism and theory

While the work of Australian feminist criminologists is diverse, at the same time, if one looks to the issues which have been the subject of more extensive discussion, there is apparent a continuing concern with legal and criminal justice reform. In some ways, this emphasis is consistent with the legal foundations and pragmatic traditions of Australian criminology. However, the pragmatism of feminist research does not necessarily involve collusion in the sense invoked by traditional criminology. Rather it is consistent with feminist calls for activist research strategies, and Kerry Carrington has observed that 'feminist discourses have been strident in their critique of the treatment of female offenders by the criminal and juvenile justice systems' (Carrington 1993a: 5).

At one level, feminists have achieved some hard-fought-for changes; for example, rape laws in most Australian states have undergone significant change; most states have introduced some form of restraining order provisions which can be invoked by women in situations of domestic violence; evidence of gender bias in judicial sentencing drew national attention, which resulted in the development of a judicial education programme; and the Australian Law Reform Commission has completed a report on women's access to the legal system (Australian Law Reform Commission 1994). In general, Sandra Egger concludes, 'Feminist critiques of law and society have informed and shaped Australian debate on law reform in areas of domestic violence, homicide, sexual assault and child sexual assault' (Egger 1994: 96; see also Scutt 1990b).

Nevertheless, Australian feminists are also questioning 'whether law reform in general should be so central to feminist campaigns' (Egger 1994: 98; see also Laster and Naylor 1991). For example, Ngaire Naffine comments on the intractability of ineffective rape law reform, as 'constantly the feminist struggle meets with resistance and assimilation' (Naffine 1994a:

103), and the theme of Julie Stubbs's recent edited volume is an assessment of the 'possibilities and limits of law(s) in the context of domestic violence' (Stubbs 1994: 1). Concerns about the sufficiency of law reform include the doctrine of equality which underpins some law reform agendas, the masculinity of legal discourse and the specificity of legal reform (e.g. Hatty 1993a; Naffine 1994a).

Concerned about a focus on legal and criminal justice reform, Egger (1994: 98) suggests that it may be worth taking the time to explore other options in the pursuit of social change. Certainly in the policy area, recent documents on violence against women have advocated strategies across a range of areas including education, health and industrial relations, as well as law (National Committee on Violence against Women 1993; Ollis and Tomaszewski 1993). Such documents are the consequence of a feminist analysis of crime which situates it in the broadest structural and cultural terms. However, there remains a question of the extent to which feminist criminological research should be directed by debates in the policy arena.

Some Australian feminist criminologists have expressed concern about the potential for unintended consequences of a pragmatic reform agenda. Laster and Naylor (1991) contemplate the linkages between the concerns of some feminist reform work and conservative law and order movements. Drawing upon some of the overseas evidence, Hatty (1993b: 25) warns that 'the promotion of the criminal justice system as the primary solution to male violence against women has the potential to increase state control over families, particularly female members of those families.'

Thus feminists engaged with policy reform face dilemmas not unfamiliar to other critical/radical movements concerned with social change; these include the priority given to immediate over long-term objectives; the cooptation of reform agendas for conservative projects and the subversion of apparent achievements. In addition, feminist activism is now challenged by readings of postmodernism that question the possibility of change and the engagement in direct action based on belief in social progress. However, other feminists question the depoliticizing tendencies of this theoretical position.

As feminists, by definition trying to find new ways to work in new areas, it is essential that we engage in an ongoing self-reflective process. As part of this process some Australian feminist criminologists are questioning the pragmatism of their research and writing. But in reviewing this research I wonder if we ought not to begin by questioning the categories as they are sometimes established. For example, does pragmatic research necessarily preclude theory, and vice versa? Is the division between theory and practice an example of a binary logic which establishes difference to be understood as a deficit (Kirkby 1994)? For some feminists knowledge is not divided from values and politics, but rather arises from engagement (Smart 1990: 80). For feminists ultimately concerned with transformation, the challenge is discovering the processes through which this is obtained.

Universality and difference: men

As noted earlier in this chapter, feminists in government bureaucracies in Australia have attained considerable power and have been influential in the direction of research and policy in the area of women and crime. Male violence against women has dominated discussions, research and policy initiatives generated by these sources in recent years. The analysis of violence against women in much of this material calls for violence to be understood and addressed as a problem founded in structural power differences between men and women, and cultural understandings of masculinity and violence.

This material eschews analysing male violence in terms of the circumstances of individual men or groups/classes of men (e.g. Ollis and Tomaszewski 1993; National Committee on Violence against Women 1993; Women's Coalition against Family Violence 1994). For example, some feminists publicly rejected a study of domestic homicides which found that low status areas have higher rates of domestic homicide (New South Wales Bureau of Crime Statistics and Research 1992). One of their concerns was basically political; that is, they feared that such findings would be used to establish 'excuses' for male violence and would detract from the recognition of the fundamental structural and cultural issues (related to gendered power differences and masculinity) that need to be addressed.

The rejection of findings regarding the variability of male violence has provoked the retort that 'where the theoretical construct of universal gender oppression does not fit the facts, it seems the facts tend to be sacrificed' (Carrington 1993b: 15). Further, theoretical concerns have been raised regarding the essentialism of an argument which attributes a unitary masculinity to all men that 'can be isolated and described independently of race, class, sexual orientation, and the other realities of experience' (Carrington 1993b: 6; see also Alder 1992).

Taking a somewhat different stance, Judith Allen begins by questioning the sex/gender distinction inherent in other works, arguing that the subsequent focus on masculinity removes from men, as *men*, any responsibility for women's oppression (e.g. Allen 1988, 1990a,b). Allen goes on to argue that it is to men-as-a-group that we should turn our attention and ask 'What it is about men, not as working class, not as migrant, not as underprivileged, but as *men* that induces them to commit crime?' (Allen 1990b: 39).

In the Australian context, then, there are two positions that are posed by feminist discussions of male violence towards women: to one, hegemonic masculinity and the universal maleness of violence is central; the other speaks of masculinities and male diversity. These are positioned as oppositional, but need that necessarily be the case? In his pioneering work on gender, the Australian sociologist R.W. Connell (1987: 183) argued that 'Ethnic differences and generational differences as well as class patterns come into play' in the construction of differing versions of masculinity, or masculinities. Further, he noted that hegemonic masculinity is 'always constructed in relation to various subordinated masculinities as well as in relation to women.' That is, recognition of male diversity need not undermine acknowledgement of the importance of broader cultural definitions of masculinity and structured gender differences in power relations.

These discussions mark a new point in criminology in Australia. In the late 1980s, Judith Allen could legitimately observe that 'masculinity' was rarely considered as 'a variable, an analytic dimension, a causal factor, a discursive condition' (Allen 1988: 16) by non-feminists and feminists alike. In Australia, analysis of the maleness of criminal men was made even more unlikely by the romantic identification of the Australian national identity, needless to say 'male', with a certain disrespect for authority. There is likely to be a warm smile on a person's face as they refer to a young man as a 'bit of a lair/larrikin/hoon': to be 'bad' is not totally unacceptable if you are an Aussie bloke. Nevertheless, by the mid 1990s, Sandra Egger was able to observe that 'masculinity is recognised as central to most forms of violence in Australian society' (Egger 1994: 96). At the same time, Egger noted that 'At conferences the most politicised, passionate and, at times, angry debate occurs in those sessions dealing with gender issues' (Egger 1994: 96). While it is a contentious issue, the question is no longer whether we talk of masculinity, but how.

Universality and difference: women

An important theme in Kerry Carrington's (1993a) book *Offending Girls* is a rejection of the gender essentialism that she perceives to have characterized earlier work in this area. Carrington argues that:

> girls are not a homogenous lot subject to a seamless web of male oppression. They are noticeably differentiated in their vulnerability to the repressive forms of regulation that operate through juvenile justice. Any unity imposed upon 'girls as a group' and their treatment by the justice authorities is a fictive one.
>
> (Carrington 1993a: 4)

Carrington is drawn to this conclusion by her observations of the experiences of young women from public housing estates and aboriginal young women in the juvenile justice and associated systems. Carrington correctly notes that the differential treatment of these young women has not generally been the focus of feminist research on female crime and delinquency in Australia.

Contemporary Australia identifies itself as 'multicultural'. In August 1992, 16 per cent of Australian women had been born in non-English speaking countries: in the state of Victoria the proportion is 21 per cent (Australian Bureau of Statistics 1993: 9). It is sometimes held that multiculturalism has made us more aware of diversity than is the case in the more homogeneous European states (Kaplan 1994). However, Patricia Easteal's (1992b) book *The Forgotten Few: Migrant Women in Australian Prisons* is a rare example of a study which focuses on the criminal justice experiences of women from non-English speaking backgrounds. Both Easteal and Blanche Hampton (1993) comment on the particular difficulties these women face as minority groups inside women's prisons.

With regard to domestic violence, Julie Stubbs (1994: 4) points out that while considerable gains have been made in terms of legal protections for women, 'Aboriginal women, women in rural areas, and those from non-English speaking backgrounds remain the least protected'. Stubbs argues that in theory and policy development in this area we need to be responsive to the 'difference in experience, difference in perspective and difference in need' of these women. 'In Australia this task is particularly pressing' (Stubbs 1994: 4).

Such examples of the increasing awareness of the diversity of women's lives challenge our tendency to speak of universal womanhood, and consequently there have been calls for analysis in terms of the specific contexts of women's lives. But are these two positions mutually exclusive? If we look to our own experiences of everyday life, we are constantly reminded of our membership of the group, women. At the same time we are aware of our uniqueness, our self, our difference to other women. Women-as-a-group are paid less than men; but some women are more vulnerable to the realities of this than others, and there are differences in the meaning of this in the everyday lives of women. When we look to judicial decision-making with regard to women and media representations of them, we observe them to be founded in 'dominant cultural scripts of womanhood, sexuality and mothering' (Maher 1992: 154). These generalized cultural assumptions and expectations, which at the same time draw upon others with regard to class and race, are a part of, and impact upon, the everyday reality of the lives of a diversity of women.

As feminists we are facing the dilemma of how to understand and talk about both the diversity and the convergence of women's lives: posing these as oppositional may obscure our understanding of women's lives as they experience them. Vicki Kirby (1994: 130) has argued that 'to attempt to replace the pretensions to universal truth with the specificity of our situated knowledges' is simply to reverse the binary logic of our argumentation to this point. In interpreting difference 'as something which is defined by its isolation, or distance from a universal . . . we confuse the notion of specificity with autonomy, and completely erase the constituitive nature of binary relationships'. The challenge which confronts us is to be able to recognize the 'value of a shared political stance as women . . . in a manner which acknowledges the differences amongst women' (Stubbs 1994: 4).

One way in which we hope to learn of women's experiences of the world as members of the group, women, and the diversity of their experiences is by listening to individual women's accounts of their lives. In Australian feminist criminology, as elsewhere, there is interest in facilitating this process. For example, Patricia Easteal's (1994) book *Voices of the Survivors* documents women's stories of sexual assault, and Lisa Maher is completing her study of the day-to-day lives of women who use crack cocaine in Brooklyn, New York (e.g. Maher 1992) (see also Alder 1986; Women's Coalition against Family Violence 1994).

Criminal women

In Australia as elsewhere, one of the major achievements of feminist criminology has been the contribution to the increasing awareness of the extent of male violence against women, and the significance of this for the production and maintenance of male power and authority over women in patriachial societies. Not only have feminists made male violence in the home visible, they have also contributed significantly to it being named as criminal behaviour. However, recently the preponderance of this work has led to some questions being raised about the consequences of focusing on women as victims (Laster and Naylor 1991; Carrington 1993b).

Barely visible in feminist criminology in Australia are women who break the law, but there are exceptions. For example, Jocelynne Scutt in 1980 noted women's engagement in some forms of violence and argued that 'The "criminal woman" must be seen in the context of the real social and political structure of the society in which she operates; until then she remains a cardboard character whose purpose is to reinforce principles of sexism underlying an unjust social system' (Scutt 1980: 551). Two other Australian feminists have also questioned the construction of 'woman' in theories of female offending (Naffine 1987; Laster 1989).

However, in general in Australian feminist research, 'There are profound silences about the actual girls and women whose lives are affected by the operation of the criminal justice system' (Carrington 1993b: 19). This is particularly true of the women who are in the system as offenders. When criminal women do enter the literature, it is primarily as the subjects of judicial decision-making or imprisonment, and so the debates revolve around matters of law and penal policies, and their gendered assumptions.

As neccessary and important as these discussions may be, without some counterbalancing studies of the lives of the women themselves, they may contribute to a narrow representation of criminal women. Kerry Carrington has commented that 'The female offender has emerged in this feminist discourse as a unitary subject. She is the hapless victim of a patriarchal legal system' (Carrington 1993b: 5). Drawing upon her own experiences, Blanche Hampton writes of women's imprisonment and laments that many ' "well meaning" people portray women inmates as victims, which is not how the women see themselves' (Hampton 1993: xvii).

As feminists have struggled to obtain social and judicial recognition of the violent victimization of women by men, they have been somewhat reluctant to research the lives of women law-breakers. In Australia, this is in part a consequence of the institutional basis of criminology in law and a legal discourse which entails a clear distinction being drawn between victims and offenders. However, when we look to the everyday lives of women the rigidity of this distinction is challenged. In her ethnographic study of women crack cocaine users, Lisa Maher illustrates how this form of research can 'challenge the nature of legal ideology' (Maher 1992: 152) including the rigid distinction drawn between victims and offenders. In Maher's research the resistance, struggle and agency evident in their everyday lives makes apparent the appropriateness and at the same time, the insufficiency of the construction 'victim' for describing criminal women.

In calling for more attention to be paid to 'the specificity of the margins and less devotion to the unexamined claims about universal female oppression' Carrington (1993b: 19) suggests that women who come into contact with the criminal justice system have very little in common with the vast majority of women who do not. On the other hand, I have argued elsewhere that through examination of the totality of individual women's everyday lives, of which for some women criminal activity makes up only a part, traditional stereotypes of offending women will be undermined and the elements of convergence between the lives of offending women and others will become apparent (Alder 1991). If we were to listen to women's accounts of the complexity and diversity of their lives, both of these observations would in all probability be supported.

Conclusion

The study of crime in Australia has not been dominated by 'criminologists'; there are very few Australians whose academic training, or current disciplinary affiliation, is in 'criminology'. The study of crime has had a strong legal basis, and it is only more recently it has become a multidisciplinary subject area. Nevertheless many of the problems, not infrequently loosely identified with positivism and/or empiricism, that some feminists have identified with 'criminology', have also been a feature of the study of crime in Australia. The Australian situation challenges the assumption that these problems can be understood as the vagaries of a single subject discipline named 'criminology'.

In any case academic feminists have never felt particularly constrained by traditional disciplinary boundaries. While there remains a significant law component to feminist criminology in Australia, there are increasing numbers of feminist criminologists from various social science backgrounds who teach in an array of different university departments. Australian feminist criminologists do not limit their work to studies of crime in the traditional sense: health, education and youth issues are other subjects to which they have turned their attentions. Nor is their feminism always the dominant standpoint from which they work. There is thus a breadth of interests and perspectives among Australian feminist criminologists that works towards opening up criminology by placing 'crime' and 'control' issues in domains other than law and criminal justice.

The influence of the legal tradition in studies of crime in Australia is probably most evident in the continued emphasis on legal and criminal justice reform. Research or discussion of the 'causes' of crime is negligible in both feminist and non-feminist criminology in Australia. Significant in this regard is the high level of criminological research that is conducted outside the universities. For feminist criminology the power of feminists in government bureaucracies in Australia has been influential in setting both research and reform agendas around violence against women. Much has been achieved by feminists working both in and outside of universities in terms of legal reform and policy changes in the criminal justice system and related areas of health and education. To this point, activism and academic work are not necessarily distinct for feminist criminologists in Australia. Nevertheless, the inevitable frustrations have led feminist criminologists in Australia to examine the relationships between pragmatism, reform, the process of change and theory.

Australian feminist criminologists are often involved in, and are writing and researching about local law and policy matters, yet the broader issues that emerge from this work resonate with those being considered by feminists in other countries. Thus academic Australian feminists are able to place their work in the international arena. Perhaps more so than feminists in either the UK or the USA, feminist criminologists in Australia draw upon and engage with the work of feminists from both of these sites. While it is feasible that this convergence of concerns and issues may be a product of an international sharing of ideas by a particular group of feminist academics, it is also possible that some issues transcend specific sites.

By the very act of writing and researching on 'crime' as feminists, we are doing criminology in some ways differently from how it has been done before. There are of course as many differences in the way feminists study crime as there are differences among feminists. So how do we examine the affect of this? Do we look to see if the old boys are changing their ways? With few exceptions, in Australia the answer to the latter is an unequivocal no. But in reviewing the work of my feminist colleagues, I am left wondering whether that is what really matters.

Notes

1 In preparing for this chapter I reviewed the curricula vitae of eighteen self-identified feminists who presented papers at criminology conferences and/or published in criminology journals on issues specifically concerning women or which entailed a gender analysis. I also specifically discussed the subject matter of this chapter with eleven feminists. I therefore wish to express my gratitude to the following women: Sharon Anleu, Anne Aungles, Jenny Bargen, Kerry Carrington, Patricia Easteal, Linda Hancock, Suzanne Hatty, Kathy Laster, Jeanette Lawrence, Lisa Maher, Gwen Murray, Ngaire Naffine, Bronwyn Naylor, Jocelynne Scutt, Julie Stubbs, Ania Wilczynski, Joy Wundersitz.

2 I am also grateful to Ms Krista Breckweg, who assisted me in the preparation of this document by analysing the following publications: the *Australian and New Zealand Journal of Criminology* from 1974 to 1993; *Current Issues in*

Criminal Justice from 1989 to 1994; and the publications of the Australian Institute of Criminology from 1974 to 1993. Ms Breckweg also collated information regarding the staff profiles of six university departments and research institutes.

3 In light of this observation, I initially intended to consider the impact on criminology of women who self-identified themselves as feminists in other aspects of their lives but whose research and written work in criminology was not explicitly feminist, and did not focus on gender or issues specifically related to women. Time and space did not allow for the development of this line of thought in this chapter, but it might be worth placing on future agendas.

4 This case formed the basis of a movie starring Meryl Streep which has two different titles: *Cry in the Dark* and *Evil Angels*.

References

Alder, C.M. (1986). 'Unemployed women have got it heaps worse': exploring the implications of female youth unemployment. *Australian and New Zealand Journal of Criminology*, 19, 210–24.

Alder, C.M. (1991). Economic conditions, gender and family: a response. In M-A. Bertrand, K. Daly and D. Klein (eds) *Proceedings of the International Feminist Conference on Women, Law and Social Control*. Montreal: University of Montreal.

Alder, C.M. (1992). Violence, gender and social change. *International Social Science Journal*, 132, 267–76.

Alder, C.M. and Wundersitz, J. (eds) (1994). *Family Conferencing and Juvenile Justice: The Way Forward or Misplaced Optimism*. Canberra: Australian Institute of Criminology.

Allen, J. (1988). The 'masculinity' of criminality and criminology: interrogating some impasses. In M. Findlay and R. Hogg (eds) *Understanding Crime and Criminal Justice*, pp. 1–24. North Ryde, NSW: Law Book Company.

Allen, J. (1990a). *Sex and Secrets*. Melbourne: Oxford University Press.

Allen, J. (1990b). 'The Wild Ones': the disavowal of *men* in criminology. In R. Graycar (ed.) *Dissenting Opinions: Feminist Explorations in Law and Society*, pp. 21–40. Sydney: Allen and Unwin.

Anleu, S.R. (1991). *Deviance, Conformity and Control*. Melbourne: Longman Cheshire.

Aungles, A. (1994). *The Prison and the Home*. Sydney: The Institute of Criminology Monograph Series.

Australian Bureau of Statistics (1993). *Women in Australia*. Canberra: Australian Bureau of Statistics, Catalogue No. 4113.0.

Australian Law Reform Commission (1994). *Equality before the Law: Women's Access to the Legal System*. Sydney: The Law Reform Commission.

Bargen, J. (1990). Families in the juvenile justice system. In *Kids in Justice: A Blueprint for the 90's*, pp. 149–73. Sydney: Youth Justice Coalition/Law Foundation.

Braithwaite, J. (1984). *Corporate Crime and the Pharmaceutical Industry*. London: Routledge.

Broom, D.H. and Richmond, K. (1982). Women and crime. *Australian and New Zealand Journal of Criminology*, 2, 65–8.

Brown, D. and Hogg, R. (1992). Essentialism, radical criminology and left realism. *Australian and New Zealand Journal of Criminology*, 25, 195–230.

Carrington, K. (1993a). *Offending Girls: Sex, Youth and Justice*. St Leonards, NSW: Allen and Unwin.

Carrington, K. (1993b). Essentialism and feminist criminologies: relevant to all – specific to none! *Critical Criminology*, 5, 5–20.

Carrington, K. (1994). Representations of guilt, crime and sexuality in the Leigh Leigh case. *Australian Feminist Law Journal*, 3, 3–29.

Cohen, S. (1988). *Against Criminology*. London: Transaction.

Connell, R.W. (1987). *Gender and Power. Society, the Person and Sexual Politics*. Sydney: Allen and Unwin.

Curthoy, A. (1994). Australian feminism since 1970. In N. Grieve and A. Burns (eds) *Australian Women: Contemporary Feminist Thought*, pp. 14–29. Melbourne: Oxford University Press.

Daniels, H. (1984). *So Much Hard Work: Women and Prostitution in Australian History*. Sydney: Fontana.

Easteal, P.W. (1992a) Battered women syndrome: misunderstood? *Current Issues in Criminal Justice*, 3, 356–9.

Easteal, P.W. (1992b). *The Forgotten Few: Migrant Women in Australian Prisons*. Canberra: Bureau of Immigration Research, Australian Government Printing Service.

Easteal, P.W. (1992c). *Killing the Beloved: Homicide between Adult Sexual Intimates*. Canberra: Australian Institute of Criminology.

Easteal, P.W. (1994). *Voices of the Survivors*. Melbourne: Spinifex Press.

Edwards, A. (1988). *Regulation and Repression*. Sydney: Allen and Unwin.

Edwards, A. (1989). Sex/gender, sexism and criminal justice: some theoretical considerations. *International Journal of the Sociology of Law*, 17, 165–84.

Edwards Hiller, A. (1982). Women, crime and criminal justice: the state of current theory and research in Australia and New Zealand. *Australian and New Zealand Journal of Criminology*, 15, 69–90.

Edwards Hiller, A. and Hancock, L. (1981). The processing of juveniles in Victoria. In S.K. Mukherjee and J. Scutt (eds) *Women and Crime*, pp. 92–127. Sydney: George Allen and Unwin in association with the Australian Institute of Criminology, Canberra.

Egger, S. (1994). An examination of feminist contributions to law reform. *Australian and New Zealand Journal of Criminology*, 27, 95–100.

Family Violence Professional Education Taskforce (1991). *Family Violence: Everybody's Business, Somebody's Life*. Melbourne: Education Press.

Gale, F., Naffine, N. and Wundersitz, J. (1993). *Juvenile Justice: Debating the Issues*. St. Leonards, NSW: Allen and Unwin.

Grabosky, P. (1989). *Wayward Governance: Illegality and Its Control in the Public Sector*. Canberra: Australian Institute of Criminology.

Grabosky, P. and Sutton, A. (eds) (1989). *Stains on a White Collar*. Sydney: Federation Press.

Greer, P. (1994). Aboriginal women and domestic violence in New South Wales. In J. Stubbs (ed.) *Women, Male Violence and the Law*, pp. 64–79. Sydney: The Institute of Criminology Monograph Series No. 6.

Hampton, B. (1993). *Prisons and Women*. Kensington, NSW: New South Wales University Press.

Hancock, L. (1980). The myth that females are treated more leniently than males in the juvenile justice system. *Australian and New Zealand Journal of Sociology*, 63, 4–13.

Hancock, L. (1993). *Professional Indemnity Review*. Canberra: Australian Government Publishing Service.

Hancock, L. and Chesney-Lind, M. (1982). Female status offenders and justice reforms: an international perspective. *Australian and New Zealand Journal of Criminology*, 15, 109–23.

Hartz-Karp, J. (1981). Women in constraints. In S.K. Mukherjee and J. Scutt (eds) *Women and Crime*, pp. 167–96. Sydney: George Allen and Unwin.

Hatty, S.E. (1993a). Narratives on crime. *Critical Criminologist*, 5, 3–4, 13.

Hatty, S.E. (1993b). Invisible lives: women, dependence and the law. In P. Easteal and S. McKillop (eds) *Women and the Law*, pp. 21–35. Canberra: Australian Institute of Criminology.

Hatty, S.E. (1994). Medicalizing discipline in the Age of the Epidemic: Australian and US perspectives. *Humanity and Society*, 18, 53–73.

Hatty, S.E. and Davis, N.J. (1995). *Youth, Justice and Social Changes: Toward the Twenty-First Century*. Westport, CT: Westview Press.

Howe, A. (1987). 'Social injury' revisited: towards a feminist theory of social justice. *International Journal of the Sociology of Law*, 15, 423.

Howe, A. (1988). Aboriginal women in custody: a footnote to the Royal Commission. *Aboriginal Law Bulletin*, 30, 5–7.

Howe, A. (1989). Chamberlain revisited: the case against the media. *Refractory Girl*, 31–32, 2–8.

Howe, A. (1990). Prologue to a history of women's imprisonment: in search of a feminist perspective. *Social Justice*, 17, 5–22.

Huggins, J. (1994). A contemporary view of Aboriginal women's relationship to the white women's movement. In N. Grieve and A. Burns (eds) *Australian Women: Contemporary Feminist Thought*, pp. 70–80. Melbourne: Oxford University Press.

Johnson, D. (1984). From fairy to witch; imagery and myth in the Chamberlain case. *Australian Journal of Cultural Studies*, 2, 90–107.

Kaplan, G. (1994). Women in Europe and Australia: feminisms in parallel? In N. Grieve and A. Burns (eds) *Australian Women: Contemporary Feminist Thought*, pp. 40–53. Melbourne: Oxford University Press.

Kirkby, V. (1994). Viral identities: feminisms and postmodernisms. In N. Grieve and A. Burns (eds) *Australian Women: Contemporary Feminist Thought*, pp. 120–33. Melbourne: Oxford University Press.

Laster, K. (1989). Infanticide: a litmus test for feminist criminological theory. *Australian and New Zealand Journal of Criminology*, 22, 151–66.

Laster, K. (1994). Arbitary chivalry: women and the death penalty in Victoria, Australia 1842–1967. *Women and Criminal Justice*, 6, 67–97.

Laster, K. and Naylor, B. (1991). Women and the law: challenging or expanding legal categories? *Legal Services Bulletin*, 16, 301–2.

Laster, K. and Taylor, V. (1994). *Interpreters in the Legal System*. Sydney: Federation Press.

Law Reform Commission of Victoria (1991). *Rape: Reform of Law and Procedure. Interim Report and Appendices, Report 42*. Melbourne: Law Reform Commission of Victoria.

McGregor, H. and Hopkins, A. (1991). *Working for Change: the Movement against Domestic Violence*. North Sydney: Allen and Unwin.

Maher, L. (1992). Reconstructing the female criminal: women and crack cocaine. *University of Southern California Review of Law and Women's Studies*, 2 (1), 131–54.

Mukherjee, S.K. and Scutt, J.A. (1981). *Women and Crime*. North Sydney, NSW: George Allen and Unwin.

Naffine, N. (1987). *Female Crime: the Construction of Women in Criminology*. London: George Allen and Unwin.

Naffine, N. (1992). Children in the Children's Court: can there be rights without a remedy? *International Journal of Law and the Family*, 6, 76–97.

Naffine, N. (1994a). A struggle over meaning: a feminist commentary on rape law reform. *Australian and New Zealand Journal of Criminology*, 27, 100–104.

Naffine, N. (ed.) (1994b). *Gender, Crime and Feminism*. Aldershot: Dartmouth Press.

National Committee on Violence against Women (1993). *National Strategy on Violence against Women*. Canberra: National Committee on Violence against Women.

Naylor, B. (1990). Media images of women who kill. *Lagal Services Bulletin*, 15, 4–8.

NSW Bureau of Crime Statistics and Research (1992). *Domestic Violence in NSW: a Regional Analysis*. Sydney: NSW Bureau of Crime Statistics and Research.

Ollis, D. and Tomaszewski, I. (1993). *Gender and Violence*. Position paper, Department of Employment, Education and Training. Canberra: Australian Government Publishing Service.

O'Malley, P. and Carson, K. (1989). Contemporary Australian criminology. *Australian and New Zealand Journal of Sociology*, 25, 333–55.

Oxley, D. (1991). Women transported: gendered images and realities. *Australian and New Zealand Journal of Criminology*, 24, 83–99.

Payne, S. (1993). Aboriginal women and the law. In P.W. Easteal and S. McKillop (eds) *Women and the Law*, pp. 65–75. Canberra: Australian Institute of Criminology.

Phillips, D. (1991). A nation of rogues? Recent writings on crime, law and punishment in Australian history. *Australian and New Zealand Journal of Criminology*, 24, 161–7.

Sam, M. (1992). *Through Black Eyes: a Handbook of Family Violence in Aboriginal and Torres Strait Islander Communities*. Melbourne: Secretariat of the National Aboriginal and Islander Child Care.

Scutt, J. (1980). Crime and sexual politics. In E. Windschuttle (ed.) *Women, Class and History: Feminist Perspectives on Australia 1788–1978*, pp. 531–51. London: Fontana Books.

Scutt, J. (ed.) (1988). *The Baby Machine*. Melbourne: McCulloch Publishing.

Scutt, J. (1990a). Invisible women? *Aboriginal Law Bulletin*, 2 (46), 4–5.

Scutt, J. (1990b). *Even in the Best of Homes: Violence in the Family*. North Carlton, Victoria: McCulloch Publishing.

Smart, C. (1990). Feminist approaches to criminology or postmodern woman meets atavistic man. In L. Gelsthorpe and A. Morris (eds) *Feminist Perspectives in Criminology*, pp. 70–85. Milton Keynes: Open University Press.

Strang, H. (1992). *Homicides in Australia 1990–1991*. Canberra: Australian Institute of Criminology.

Stubbs, J. (1991a). The sentencing of young offenders in Canada: a question of principle? *Current Issues in Criminal Justice*, 3(2), 219–36.

Stubbs, J. (1991b). Battered women syndrome: an advance for women or further evidence of the legal system's inability to comprehend women's experience? *Current Issues in Criminal Justice*, 3, 267–70.

Stubbs, J. (1994). Introduction. In J. Stubbs (ed.) *Women, Male Violence and the Law*, pp. 1–13. Sydney: The Institute of Criminology Monograph Series No. 6.

Stubbs, J. and Tolmie, J. (1994). Battered women syndrome in Australia: a challenge to gender bias in the law? In J. Stubbs (ed.) *Women, Male Violence and the Law*, pp. 192–226. Sydney: The Institute of Criminology Monograph Series No. 6.

Summers, A. (1994). Feminism on two continents: the women's movement in Australia and the United States. In N. Grieve and A. Burns (eds) *Australian Women: Contemporary Feminist Thought*, pp. 53–9. Melbourne: Oxford University Press.

Wallace, A. (1986). *Homicide: the Social Reality.* Sydney: NSW Bureau of Crime Statistics and Research.

Wilczynski, A. (1991). Images of women who kill their children: the mad and the bad. *Women and Criminal Justice,* 2, 71–89.

Women's Coalition against Family Violence (1994). *Blood on Whose Hands? The Killing of Women and Children in Domestic Homicides.* Brunswick, Victoria: Women's Coalition against Family Violence.

3

Agenda-ing gender: feminism and the engendering of academic criminology in South Africa

DESIRÉE HANSSON

Introduction

In most Western countries today, feminism is facing an organized, androcentric backlash. Feminist changes wrought over the past century are now under attack and some have already been undermined severely (Faludi 1991). One of the feminist responses to this backlash has been an internal stock-taking of gains and losses in various spheres. Feminist scholars in particular have begun evaluating the extent to which feminism has reshaped androcentric knowledge in different academic disciplines (e.g. Crowley and Himmelweit 1993; Kramarae and Spender 1993). Debates about whether it is worth continuing to engender certain academic discourses, like criminology and law, and if so, how best this can be accomplished, are central to contemporary feminist assessments.

This book is part of the current stock-taking trend and the specific focus here is the comparative analysis of the impact of feminism on *criminology*, including criminal justice policy, in different countries. In this chapter I explore the nature and extent of feminist transformations to academic criminology in *South Africa*. This analysis is based on my experience as a South African feminist working both in feminist organizations and in academic criminology. Since South Africa differs in many ways from most Western nations and is currently undergoing rapid and major socio-political change, I have compared aspects of the South African situation to circumstances in other countries to facilitate an international perspective. My starting point is an overview of some of the main developments in, and characteristics of, South African feminism and academic criminology. Against this background I examine what I consider to be the main engendering effects of feminism on various aspects of academic criminology and I conclude with a discussion of some of my concerns and speculations about the future of feminism in the context of the new, post-apartheid, democratic South Africa.

South African feminism in context

In South Africa, as in most countries, the very meaning of feminism is contested (Purvis 1994). At the most general level, however, South African feminists seem to agree that feminism is a political activity (Smith 1982), the core goal of which is to eliminate the systematic social injustice that females suffer because of their sex (Richards 1980). South African feminism differs from Western feminism of the post-1960s era. Most evidently, we do not have an established, national feminist organization akin to those in Australia, Canada and the United States. Furthermore, organized feminism has only had a significant impact within mainstream South African politics in the past five years, and in political practice sexism is still treated as secondary to both racism and classism. In view of the dominance of the racism issue in politics and the many deep divisions among women, it is a brand of socialist feminism aimed at ending *all* social relations of domination, without privileging any form of oppression *a priori*, which is most popular among feminists in South Africa today (Hansson 1995).

Political organization and activism against racism (apartheid), and to a lesser extent classism (capitalism), have long and internationally renowned traditions in South Africa. Until recently, there has been hostility towards feminism by those in progressive politics, since racism has been constructed as *the* oppression and feminism has been viewed as a divisive element (Charman *et al.* 1991). Race, ethnic and class-based conflicts of interest have thus impeded the development of a powerful, national, feminist organization in South Africa (Hansson 1991a,b). Instead, what we have is the Women's National Coalition (WNC), a temporary, national alliance of eighty women's organizations[1] from across the political, racial, social and religious spectrum, which is estimated to represent at least two million women (Women's Coalition: Western Cape 1994). The WNC was established in April 1992 to produce a document that would represent the concerns and demands of as wide a range of South African women as possible. The resulting text, the Women's Charter for Effective Equality, was ratified by the WNC in June 1994, and is currently being used to lobby the interim government for changes in the status and material conditions of South African women.[2]

Furthermore, and in contrast to most Western countries, South Africa does not have nationally organized, politically powerful anti-rape (rape crisis) or anti-battery (shelter)[3] movements. The first Rape Crisis centres were opened in the late 1970s and are the longest-standing explicitly feminist organizations in the country (Mayne 1990). However, these few centres have operated in a political climate of civil war against apartheid and antipathy to feminism. Rape Crisis centres have been located in large urban areas and have been staffed largely by white, economically privileged women. Since the majority of women in this country are black and economically oppressed and have been forced to live far from urban centres,[4] Rape Crisis organizations have been criticized for being unrepresentative of, and inaccessible to, black women, as well as for failing to take sufficient account of their experiences. Over the years black women have thus established their own organizations in the field of patriarchal force, or male violence against women and girls (Caputi 1987: 3). It was not until the mid-1980s that firm links were systematically forged between organizations in black townships and Rape Crisis centres in white, urban areas. More specifically, it was the two largest Rape Crisis centres in the country[5] that launched programmes to assist in the development of black women's organizations. The production of resources for training was central to this endeavour and by 1989 Rape Crisis organizations had produced educational materials on a wide range of issues (e.g. Rape Crisis 1989a–m). Importantly, this writing boosted the production of feminist discourses in the field of patriarchal force. Overall, then, in South Africa Rape Crisis organizations have provided *some* sexually abused women with a much-needed service, and have been an important feminist voice on issues of patriarchal force. They have not, however, constituted a representative or powerful political voice for the majority of South African women.

The production of discourses that, ideally, challenge the androcentrism of dominant knowledges is central to the feminist endeavour. Historically, it is feminist organization that has stimulated the production of feminist discourses, both within and outside of academia. The long absence of a powerful, national feminist organization in South Africa has stunted the production of feminist discourses, and relatively little feminist knowledge was produced within academia before the 1990s. In 1988, however, the ANC Women's League succeeded in having an anti-sexism clause included in the draft constitutional guidelines of the ANC. This seemed to catalyse a political focus on women's issues, for once the ANC, South Africa's largest political organization, backed women, other political actors began to follow suit, although in different ways and to varying degrees. Today, most political parties and trade unions have women's sectors, or positions with regard to a range of women's issues.

Since 1990, when the negotiation of a new constitution was formally initiated, the terrain of rights has been hotly contested by a wide range of groups, including feminists, all struggling to have their particular interests framed in this country's first bill of rights. In the past four years, discourses on constitutional and human rights, including women's rights, have flourished. Ferment around women's rights in mainstream politics has produced a marked increase in the demand for discourses on women.

Consequently there has been an extremely sudden and rapid growth in the production of feminist and non-feminist discourses on women, most notably in the previously barren terrain of academia. It is only very recently, then, that the issue of sexism, or gender oppression, has been accorded sustained political attention.

In South Africa, as in most countries, feminism is not an institutionalized academic discipline like criminology, sociology or law. A handful of women's studies units have been established in universities over the past few years, but even the work of these units has not been consistently feminist. Indeed, academic feminist discourses are somewhat fragmented across subjects and disciplines, although a few foci are now beginning to crystallize and planned interdisciplinary links are being forged. Today, more than ever before, feminists from different academic disciplines and from organizations outside of the academy are working together. Feminists, like most other progressives, are approaching the current restructuring of the South African state as a temporary window of opportunity. Since 1990, the energies of the majority of feminists, both academic and otherwise, have been mobilized in policy-oriented work such as the Charter Campaign, projects to frame constitutional rights against sexism and rape reform initiatives. Contemporary feminist discourses are thus strongly policy-oriented, with analyses of rights, law and the legal system as sites for struggle against gender oppression predominating.

South African academic criminology in context

Unlike feminism, criminology is a specialized discipline in South African academia and most universities have departments of criminology. However, the production of criminological discourses is not limited to this academic discipline. Like feminist discourse, knowledge relevant to criminology is produced from a wide range of sites, both within and outside of the academy. It is criminological discourse produced within academia (academic criminology), however, that is the focal concern of this chapter.

A state-aligned, politically conservative and correctionalist discourse has dominated academic criminology since the establishment of the discipline in South Africa over fifty years ago. It is this criminology that has been taught in the vast majority of universities, including those in the so-called independent black states. It has also shaped teaching in secondary schools and the training of state employees. This mainstream discourse has been dubbed Afrikaner nationalist criminology, owing to its close alignment with the politics of the Nationalist state (van Zyl Smit 1989). The latest variant is self-titled 'fundamental criminology' (Hansson 1992), and although it began as a relatively atheoretical form of individualistic, multifactorial positivism, more recently it has taken on a strong right-realist flavour. More specifically, the major focus of fundamental criminology has shifted from the positivist priority of identifying the causes of crime to the right-realist goal of controlling crime directly.

Afrikaner nationalist criminology was not systematically challenged until the late 1970s, when a university-based, counter-hegemonic discourse began emerging.[6] The mainstay of this counter-discourse was a critique of Afrikaner nationalist criminology, in particular the contradiction between its racist politics and its claim to scientific objectivity and political neutrality (Davis and Slabbert 1985). Originally, South African counter-hegemonic criminology was shaped along the lines of British critical criminology (Taylor *et al.* 1975). During the past decade, however, this discourse, which is now termed progressive-realism, has been consciously styled in the British left-realist mould (e.g. Young 1986).

Generally speaking then, the history of South African academic criminology during the 1980s has been that of contestation between two politically polarized discourses – one anti-apartheid and subordinate, the other pro-apartheid and dominant. However, particularly since 1990, when the dismantling of apartheid was formally announced, fundamental criminology has begun to slip from dominance and progressive politicians have drawn increasingly upon progressive-realist academic criminology in re-constituting discourses on crime, punishment and justice. Close working relations have developed between academics in progressive-realist criminology and the ANC. Progressive-realist criminology is thus no longer a counter-hegemonic discourse, for it is rapidly replacing fundamental criminology as the dominant criminological discourse in South Africa.

Feminism and academic criminology

An overview

Although organized feminism is more than one hundred years old, it is only during the past twenty-five years that feminist discourses have begun shaping academic criminologies in Western countries (Schwendinger and Schwendinger 1991). During this quarter of a century, feminist scholars in the United States, Britain and Canada have been systematically exposing the androcentrism of criminological discourses across the political spectrum. In South Africa, where nationally organized feminism is less than five years old, feminist discourses are even later arrivals to the domain of academic criminology, and feminist scholars have not yet produced methodical deconstructions of the androcentrism of dominant or subordinate criminological discourses.

Women in conservative academic criminology have remained largely invisible, both as subjects and as practitioners. The subject domain of Afrikaner nationalist criminology has been limited to crime, crime control and, more recently, the victims of crime (Hansson 1992). In effect, this way of defining academic criminology has obscured women, girls and gender issues within Afrikaner nationalist criminology. Since the vast majority of those arrested, tried, convicted and incarcerated in South Africa are male, females have hardly featured as *subjects* of criminological research.

The visibility of women as practitioners in conservative academic criminology as well as in the legal and penal systems has been little better. Indeed, the only place where women and girls have been conspicuous is as *victims* of crime in the field of victimology, which is a relatively new sub-discipline of fundamental criminology (Hansson 1992). However, the mere presence of females, as practitioners and subjects, has not engendered academic victimology. Instead, mainstream constructions of women and girls as victims of crime, and particularly of sexual violence, have simply reinforced sexist gender stereotypes (e.g. Labuschagne and van der Hoven 1988; Schurink 1992). Fundamental academic criminology thus remains a thoroughly androcentric discourse.

Even with the growth in feminist scholarship in recent years, feminists have chosen to pay little attention to this declining conservative discourse, and have instead concentrated on engendering progressive-realist criminology. This is understandable since progressive-realism is becoming the dominant criminological discourse in South Africa, and is also politically more resonant with feminism.[7] Additionally, unlike fundamental criminology, the subject domain of progressive-realist criminology has *not* been defined in a way that necessarily excludes women, girls and gender issues. To the contrary, it is progressive-realism's unusual lack of disciplinary closure that has facilitated feminist enquiry *within* this otherwise androcentric academic discipline. In fact, focusing on the engendering of more progressive criminological discourses seems to have become something of a feminist strategy in many Western countries.

In South Africa, gender relations have been *formally* recognized within academia as an important analytical ingredient of social analysis. As yet, however, this recognition remains somewhat superficial in its effect on the discipline of progressive-realist criminology. Despite feminist efforts to engender this discourse, in general women and feminist concerns are still marginalized. The first feminist critiques of androcentrism within counter-hegemonic criminology were published in the mid-1980s (e.g. Durbach 1985). The substance of these objections was that women and girls were being neglected as subjects of research and that gender was not being taken into account in criminological analyses. The subsequent tendency in academic writing in this field has been to mention the relative dearth of work on women and girls, and to remark on the need to engender criminological analyses. To date only two texts, both edited collections, have been published on counter-hegemonic criminology in South Africa (Davis and Slabbert 1985; Hansson and van Zyl Smit 1990). The earlier book contains a single feminist piece on women in prison (Durbach 1985), while feminist analyses are absent from the latter. The amount of feminist writing published in the field of progressive-realist criminology is relatively small, although feminist work on some specific topics is now accumulating. Thus, while feminist discourses have succeeded to some extent in introducing women and girls as worthy subjects of knowledge production and gender as an analytically important construct, it seems that feminist issues are not yet *integral* to the production of progressive-realist criminological discourse in South Africa.

Women are also not particularly visible as producers of knowledge in the academic field of progressive-realist criminology. White men have long dominated as teachers and researchers, although there is now a growing trend towards hiring more black men. Not only do men outnumber women, they also tend to hold positions of higher authority and status. There has been very little change in the number or position of women academics in the discipline even over the past decade. Since much the same trend is evident in the postgraduate student population, it seems unlikely that the gender ratio among academic knowledge producers in progressive-realist criminology will change significantly in the short term.

Progressive-realist criminological discourse thus continues to be constructed largely by men, for men and about men. Gender relations continue to be accorded scant attention and women are still outnumbered and 'outweighed', both as knowledge producers and as subjects of enquiry in the discipline. Overall, the engendering effect of feminism on the discipline of progressive-realist criminology *as a whole* seems somewhat negligible. Nevertheless, feminist activity *has* managed to bring about significant, though smaller-scale, changes to *specific* aspects of the discipline. Feminist scholars have introduced gender issues into some important fields of criminological research and teaching; we have opened up new research fields within progressive-realist criminology; we have rejuvenated, and in some cases colonized, certain criminological fields; and we have been centrally involved in developing new teaching methods and research practices.

Transformations to research practice

Like most mainstream knowledges, Afrikaner nationalist criminology has been grounded in an epistemology in which knowledge producers are constructed as impartial recorders who bear no responsibility to local or global communities for the impact of the knowledge that they produce (Kramarae and Spender 1993). Criticism of Afrikaner nationalist criminology's epistemological position and, in particular, the claim to political neutrality and objectivity in knowledge production has been the crux of counter-hegemonic criminologies in South Africa (Hansson 1992). By contrast, the production of progressive-realist criminological discourses rests upon a declaration of political interest in oppressed groups. Thus, the development of an alternative research practice has been viewed as something of a priority within progressive-realist criminology. Significantly, it is mainly feminist scholars who have both initiated and developed the democratic, participatory and action-oriented approach to research that has come to distinguish progressive-realist criminology (e.g. Hansson *et al.* 1989; Sloth-Nielsen *et al.* 1992; Hansson 1993a). The main impetus behind this development has been concern over the hierarchical nature of knowledge production in general, which originated in feminist practice outside of academia. Indeed, feminists had long been experimenting with ways of democratizing research practice and eradicating the power imbalance between researchers and those who are researched. Progressive-realist criminology, which was on the look-out for more democratic approaches to research, thus provided fertile academic soil for the incorporation and cultivation of feminist experience in this arena. The feminist contribution to the transformation of progressive criminological research practice is, however, seldom acknowledged and is a clear example of feminist knowledge being absorbed by an androcentric discourse.

Today progressive-realist criminology is characterized by an innovative research approach which is grounded in the following principles: (a) non-exploitation of those who are researched or affected by research; (b) active sharing of resources, skills and information between researchers and researched, including direct assistance to the researched where appropriate; (c) accountability of researchers to the researched; (d) active participation in the research process by those who are researched, particularly through democratic consultation about what is to be researched, how it is to be investigated and what is to be done with the knowledge that is produced; (e) the placement of researchers on the same analytical plane as the researched.

Developments in teaching

At present, progressive-realist academic criminology is taught largely at the postgraduate level to students of law and social science. When the teaching of counter-hegemonic criminology was started in the late 1970s, the student population was predominantly male and white. However, female and black students have been actively recruited in the past few years, since universities have adopted equal opportunity policies. Slowly the student population in criminology is changing, but it is the ratio of black to white students, rather than female to male students, that is altering most noticeably.

Over the past decade, feminist academics have also wrought changes to *what* is taught in the field of progressive-realist criminology. After much debate, feminist scholars at a number of universities decided that the aim of engendering progressive-realist criminology would be better served by introducing gender issues into mainstream courses, rather than by establishing a separate course, vulnerable to marginalization. Thus, there is no subject or course known as 'feminist criminology'. Instead, gender issues are consistently raised along with race issues in many of the compulsory courses comprising postgraduate degrees in criminology and criminal justice. In addition, specialized, though optional, courses on women and the legal system have been introduced, mainly in law faculties. One of the important consequences of the introduction of feminist issues in academic teaching has been a marked increase in student research on gender-related topics.

Feminist scholarship has shaped not only the content, but also the *methods* of teaching on progressive-realist criminology. The changes feminists have made to teaching methods are reminiscent of feminist developments in criminological research practice. In essence, the main teaching methods used today are small-group techniques designed to encourage critical thinking and active participation by students, while reducing the hierarchical power relations among students and between students and teachers. Once again, while we feminist academics cannot claim sole credit for developing these teaching methods, our awareness and commitment have been central to their design and implementation.

The expansion of subject boundaries

Feminist scholars may not have transformed the general androcentricity of progressive-realist criminology, but we have managed to stretch the subject boundaries of the discipline. While the subject domain of progressive-realist criminology has always extended well beyond the traditional criminological limits of criminal law and the criminal justice system, feminist research has expanded these boundaries by introducing a range of new sites where social conflict is constructed and managed: for example, the mental health system (Offen 1986); the family (Hansson 1991c,d; Russell 1991); sexuality and intimate relations (van Zyl 1988; Retief 1993); and culture or tradition (Chinkanda 1992; Nhlapo 1992). In this sense, then, feminists not only have put gender on the criminological agenda, we have expanded the boundaries of the progressive criminological agenda.

The engendering of key fields

The most noteworthy existing criminological field into which feminists have injected gender issues is the key arena of policing. Policing has been the most rapidly expanding research field in progressive-realist criminology in the past decade, and the overarching focus here has been the restructuring of the South African Police force (SAP) from a white, Afrikaner-dominated, repressive agent of the apartheid state to an accountable, impartial community service, which is representative of the population in general. Progressive-realist reform proposals have centred on eradicating racism in the SAP, especially through the increased hiring of black police officers and anti-racism training programmes (e.g. Scharf 1993a). Building on the progressive-realist policing principles of impartiality and representivity, feminists have successfully argued the importance of eradicating sexism along with racism, and of hiring women along with black people, in restructuring the SAP (e.g. Rauch 1991, 1994). At present, then, gender is being taken into account more systematically in this, a particularly male-dominated and eminent field of contemporary progressive-realist criminology.

The introduction of new research fields

Feminist scholars have recently established two new fields of research which fall within the ambit of progressive-realist academic criminology, namely women's rights and gender oppression in the legal system. A substantial proportion of feminist knowledge production has been concentrated in these two fields.

The overall objective of feminist work in the field of women's rights has been to evaluate whether, and if so how, different legal mechanisms can best be used to protect women from gender oppression and to improve their subordinated position in different spheres, such as marriage, the family, work, the criminal justice system and government (e.g. Bazilli 1990; Hansson 1991e; Hansson and Hofmeyr 1992; Murray 1993; O'Regan and Murray 1993). Due to the fact that a new constitution has been in the making, assessments of the utility of a constitutional right to non-sexism have been treated as an exigency. The central debates have hinged on whether feminists should aim for equality or special treatment for women, and how gender oppression should be treated in relation to other oppressions. A great deal of feminist energy has been spent on debating and framing an optimal constitutional clause, and on injecting feminist constructions into the constitutional negotiations that preceded the general election in April 1994. It now seems that we feminists have firmly entrenched non-sexism as a constitutional principle, at least in writing. The provisional constitution (Act 200 of 1993), which is to operate until the interim government enacts a final constitution, contains two specific gender-related clauses. The preamble states *inter alia* that there shall be 'equality between men and women', and the section on fundamental rights specifies further that: 'No person shall be unfairly discriminated against, directly or indirectly, and, without derogating from the generality of this provision, on one or more of the following grounds in particular: race, gender, sex, ethnic or social origin, colour, sexual orientation, age, disability, religion, conscience, belief, culture or language' (Section 8(2) of Act 200 of 1993). However, the practical impact of such a constitutional right on women's lives remains to be seen.

Gender oppression in the South African legal system is the second new research field which feminists have introduced to progressive-realist criminology. The main aim of feminist research in this area has been to establish whether and how women and girls are disadvantaged in different parts of the legal system. For example, there has been work on: matrimonial property settlements in contested divorces (O'Sullivan n.d., a); damages awards in delictual cases (O'Sullivan n.d., b); the secondary victimization of rape complainants in the criminal justice system (Hansson 1994; Lochrenberg and Stanton n.d.); and the sexist nature of the law itself – the way in which offences are defined (Hall 1988), rules of evidence (Hansson 1991e), available defences and jurisprudential assumptions (Albertyn 1993).

The colonizing and development of research fields

Patriarchal force, or male violence against women and girls, has been a focal concern, and at times *the* key issue, for Western feminism since 1960

(Caputi 1993). Although it took South African feminism another decade to raise this issue politically, it is in the field of patriarchal force that feminism has had its greatest engendering impact to date. Indeed, this is the subject which has the longest feminist herstory in South Africa (Mayne 1990; van Zyl 1990). It is also the only field in contemporary academic criminology in which feminists have successfully dislodged androcentric authorities.

In 1993, a feminist colleague and I conducted a rigorous search of the South African literature on patriarchal force, spanning the thirty-three year period from 1960 to 1993[8] (Hansson and Russell 1994). I have used the quantitative findings from this search here, to give a more concrete picture of the feminist contribution to writing in the field of patriarchal force in South Africa.

During the 1970s the majority (56 per cent of writings in the field were non-feminist, legalistic analyses of rape which were produced mainly in the discipline of law (e.g. Labuschagne 1972; van der Westhuizen 1977; Salmon 1980). It was the establishment of Rape Crisis organizations in the country, starting in 1977, that stimulated the production of feminist discourse on patriarchal force, both inside and outside of academia. Over the past sixteen years Rape Crisis organizations have been the motor force behind feminist work in this arena. From the outset there has been a close inter-relation between the work of academic feminists and feminist activists on patriarchal force. Feminists in academia, both students and teachers, were instrumental in establishing Rape Crisis centres, and have subsequently comprised the majority of the membership of these organizations. Further-more, for researchers in this field, Rape Crisis centres have provided the sole access to survivors of patriarchal force, especially since the SAP and the criminal justice system have been resistant to academic research and particularly to feminist work.

Before the 1980s, patriarchal force or sexual crime/violence, as the subject was then defined, was not a particularly active or significant research arena in any academic discipline in South Africa. In fact, only 3 per cent of the writing in this field was produced in the decade of the 1970s, as compared to 50 per cent during the 1980s and 47 per cent in the first three years of the 1990s. Notably, the feminist contribution to this field has increased consistently over time: from 44 per cent between 1970 and 1980 to 55 per cent between 1980 and 1990 and 69 per cent between 1990 and 1993. In less than two decades, then, feminists turned a rather insignificant topic of research into a sizeable and thriving research field, which now includes the following range of subject areas: patriarchal force in general, rape, battery, intimate murders, sexual harassment, pornography and intra- and extra-familial child sexual abuse. Although the discourse in all these areas was non-feminist to begin with, feminists have colonized five of the seven subject areas. It is only in the areas of child sexual abuse and intimate murders that non-feminist writings now outnumber feminist analyses. Feminist discourse has thus succeeded in revealing 'the immense scope and complexity of phallic violence as a diverse set of practices both individual and institutional' (Caputi 1993: 340).

South African feminists began expanding their writings beyond the topic of rape during the 1980s. The first feminist pieces on battery began emerging from 1981 onward, followed by analyses of patriarchal force in general, intra- and extra-familial child sexual abuse and sexual harassment from 1987, and, most recently, work on the issue of pornography.[9] Over time, the amount of writing, both feminist and non-feminist, has varied in the seven subject areas listed above. In the past three years, for example, rape has attracted the highest proportion (29 per cent) of writing in the field, and this topic has been followed by child sexual abuse (25 per cent), patriarchal force in general (17 per cent), battery (15 per cent), sexual harassment (9 per cent), pornography (3 per cent) and intimate murders (2 per cent). In each of the subject areas feminist writings have addressed a similar range of themes, although not in any set sequence: the breaking of the silence around an issue, thus making it visible; the reconstruction of a type of sexual violence as a social, rather than just a personal, problem; the location of a particular type of patriarchal force within gender oppression more generally; and critiques and policy proposals regarding available services, the law and the legal system.

Rape is the subject area that has attracted, and continues to attract, the greatest proportion of writing in the field of patriarchal force. However, rape is not only the biggest of the subject areas, it is also the oldest topic. The first writings in the field of patriarchal force were focused on the issue of rape, although these were non-feminist analyses (e.g. Labuschagne 1972). It was from 1977 onward that feminist writings on rape began to emerge and gradually to proliferate. During the 1970s the main themes of feminist writings on rape were the effects of rape on survivors, or rape trauma syndrome (e.g. Mayne and Levett 1977; Anderson 1981), and the secondary victimization of rape complainants in criminal trials (Waller 1977). Throughout the 1980s a range of themes was added, including evaluations of the services available to survivors (e.g. Levett 1981), in-depth critiques of the androcentrism of the law and legal practice around rape (Hall 1988) and, most significantly, the issue of marital rape (e.g. Kaganas and Murray 1983; Kaganas 1986). The particularly sexist response of the Law Commission, which was set up in 1985 to assess whether rape in marriage should be criminalized, drew feminist attention to this issue. Over the next five years, feminist writing on this topic proliferated, and today marital rape constitutes the largest sub-issue in the area of rape.

With the exception of date, or acquaintance, rape (Kaplan 1992; Russell 1993), few new topics have been added in feminist writings on rape in the 1990s. Instead, over the past four years feminists have increased their focus on issues first raised in the 1970s, in particular the inadequacy of support services and the secondary victimization of rape survivors by state agencies. Although Rape Crisis organizations have been actively campaigning for rape reform over the past sixteen years, the feminist impact on state policy in this area has been very limited and somewhat fragmented. Where gains have been made they have generally taken the form of local, informal changes in the practice of certain state agencies. It is true to say that the Nationalist state was particularly resistant to feminist reform initiatives, and there has thus been little engagement between feminists and state agencies. It is only recently, in the nationwide climate of reform, that the state has begun to work directly with feminist organizations on policy reform around rape. Renewed feminist attention to rape issues is thus a response to unprecedented opportunities that are now opening up for policy reform in the state's management of rape.

The most noteworthy of the current reform initiatives is the Cape Attorney General's Task Group on Rape. In late 1992, representatives from the Cape Attorney General's office, feminist and non-feminist non-governmental organizations and individual academics working in the field of rape joined forces for the first time ever. The resulting Task Group has been established as a long-term structure with the overall objective of initiating interventions aimed at ending the secondary victimization of rape survivors and improving the treatment they are afforded, in particular that received at the hands of the police, hospital staff, district surgeons, prosecutors and judicial officers. More specifically, the role of the Task Group is to identify problem areas, assess ways of overcoming these shortcomings and then instigate the introduction and monitoring of interventions within the appropriate agencies. Since the inception of the Task Group a wide range of reforms have been initiated in the Western Cape region, including the legal recognition (in case law) of rape trauma syndrome in the Cape Supreme Court, the establishment of the first specialized rape court in the country,[10] the opening of a rape unit in a local hospital[11] and the development of training programmes for medical staff, police officers and prosecutors (Hansson 1994). Although the Cape Task Group is a regional initiative,[12] it has prompted work on rape reform in other parts of the country, and the government announced in 1994 that new legislation to protect women and children from all forms of violence was to be passed by the end of the year (*Argus* 20 January 1994).

Rape reform issues are now also attracting increased research attention and much of this work falls within the ambit of progressive-realist criminology (e.g. Hansson 1991e, 1993b, 1994; Cowling 1994; Rauch 1994; Reddy 1994; Swikkard 1994). Of special note is the research currently being conducted to evaluate the new sexual offences court and related services (Lochrenberg and Stanton n.d.).

While feminism has successfully colonized the field of patriarchal force, particularly in the discipline of academic criminology, dominant feminist constructions have been, and continue to be, contested by androcentric discourses. More specifically, since the late 1980s most androcentric, often victim-blaming, analyses of sexual violence have been developed from victimology (e.g. Faul and Muller 1990; Schurink *et al.* 1992). Nevertheless, today feminist constructions of patriarchal force continue to predominate in academic discourse. To a large extent, then, South African feminism has succeeded in 'the naming of sexual violence as a systematic form of patriarchal oppression' (Caputi 1993: 340).

Feminist shortfalls

There has *not* been a feminist *revolution* in progressive-realist criminology. However, feminism is gradually eroding the androcentric foundation on which this academic discipline rests. Over a relatively short space of time, we feminists have infiltrated and changed many aspects of the discipline. We have indeed made the vital step of agenda-ing gender, by putting gender relations and feminist issues on the agenda of progressive-realist criminology in South Africa. With regard to knowledge production, feminists have stretched the subject boundaries, added new research fields, injected feminist issues and constructions into existing fields of research and teaching, and transformed research practices and teaching methods. While this is no mean feat, particularly since it has been achieved in the space of a decade, in my opinion feminist engendering has fallen short in a number of ways.

Feminist scholars in South Africa have not systematically deconstructed the androcentrism of the range of criminological discourses; nor have we developed general theories to counter androcentric constructions of social conflict and its management. The fact that law-making, law-breaking and law enforcement are male-dominated realms where conflicts of interest between men (usually from differing social positions) are constructed and managed has not been theorized from a feminist perspective. Furthermore, since most feminist analyses have concentrated on women, the construction of masculinities and gender *relations* have been neglected. In addition, in South Africa relatively large numbers of black youths are processed by the legal and penal systems, both as law-breakers and as victims of crime. To date, most feminist work has been focused on adult women. There are thus few feminist analyses of the gendering of social control and conflict in relation to children and youths. Broadly speaking, as South African feminist scholars we need to begin consciously and methodically dissolving women/girls and criminal justice issues within an interrogation of gender relations and social justice more generally (Carlen 1991).

While feminist analyses have been strong on theorizing gender from the perspective of femininities, as yet these discourses are not sufficient for constructing integrated analyses of multiple oppressions. Although socialist feminist theorists have attempted to theorize the contradictions and simultaneity of interrelated oppressions, such as colonialism, racism, classism and sexism, there has often been a rather uncritical reliance on non-feminist discourses in the formulation of these constructions.

It is noteworthy that as feminist scholars we have largely neglected women and girls in law-making, law-breaking and law enforcement. Although there has been some research conducted on women as so-called political offenders,[13] there has been very little work done on women and girls as 'ordinary' law-breakers, with the exception of offences relating to sex work. While we have introduced female *victims* as worthy subjects of criminological analysis, this focus may, ironically, have served to reinforce the feminine gender stereotype of women and girls as passive rather than active social agents.

Concerns and predictions

In closing this chapter I will discuss some of my concerns and speculations about future directions for feminism, particularly in relation to progressive-realist criminology in the context of the new post-apartheid, democratic South Africa.

The current phase of societal restructuring in South Africa is a critical stage for feminism. In view of the widespread and serious poverty in this country, economic development and redistribution are priorities for the new government. Thus, race and class interests are likely to continue dominating mainstream politics, with gender interests remaining subordinated. At the same time women are better placed in government than ever before. The speaker and 106 of the 400 members of parliament are women. Nevertheless, there are only two women in the thirty-member cabinet, three female deputy ministers, sixteen women among the ninety senators and no women among the premiers of the nine regions (*Speak* 1994: 21). At this stage, then, it seems only safe to say that women have 'a foot in the door'. However, once the final constitution, including a right to non-sexism, is in place and the law has been purged of the most evident sexism, concern with women's issues in mainstream politics could well diminish, as it has done in other countries, unless feminism can keep up sustained political pressure on the new government. In this context it is crucial that the South African feminist movement be developed into a large, militant and politically powerful force. Furthermore, the production of feminist discourses in all spheres remains imperative. At present, feminist scholars in this country cannot afford to adopt a disengaged or separatist stance in any arena.

Some Western feminists have argued that academic criminology is so fundamentally androcentric that it cannot be engendered. More specifically, the ways in which the subject domain and problematics of the discipline are defined exclude and negate gender issues, particularly those issues of central relevance to women and girls. For this reason, it has been argued, feminist scholars should not bother attempting to engender criminological discourses. To date, this argument has not held water in the South African context, as progressive-realist criminology has not 'shut feminism out'. Indeed, its pliable subject boundaries have facilitated the passage of feminist concerns into this field. Thus, while resistance to engendering within progressive-realist criminology should not be underestimated, neither should it be exaggerated. In my opinion, South African feminism has managed to bring about significant changes to this androcentric academic discipline in a short space of time. In view of the persisting androcentrism of progressive-realist criminology, for feminist scholars to desist from attempting to engender such discourses is to ensure that androcentric constructions, policies and practices will be perpetuated and reified. In the context of contemporary South Africa, non-interventionism is not an ethical option, especially for privileged academics. Socialist feminist scholars and progressive-realist criminologists have more than an overall commitment to social justice in common; we also share a commitment to interventions that provide short-term relief to those who are most affected by social conflict and social control mechanisms, including the criminal justice and penal systems.

Historically, progressive-realist criminology has not been constrained by many of the limitations of an academic discourse. The subject boundaries and problematics of this criminological discourse have remained relatively open and flexible. The discourse has been continually invigorated because it has been produced from a variety of different and often disparate sites, both in and outside of academia. To date, the academic discipline of progressive-realist criminology has been used as an important organizational site for theorizing and intervening in the field of the construction and management of social conflict. These characteristics, which are unusual in an academic discipline, have developed to a large extent out of the counter-hegemonic role played by progressive-realist criminology in the South African context. Most importantly, it is the malleability of the subject domain that has enabled the engendering of progressive-realist criminology. However, this once subjugated discourse is currently rising to dominance and its counter-hegemonic character is thus changing. My concern for feminism is that, once it is dominant, progressive-realist criminology will become a closed academic discipline, thus limiting future opportunities for engendering.

Progressive-realist criminology has been raised as a counter-hegemonic discourse, closely aligned with the politics of the anti-apartheid movement. Over the past few years of transition the ANC has relied increasingly upon progressive-realist criminological ideas in designing new policies and structures with regard to law-making, law-breaking and law enforcement. It has been argued that Afrikaner nationalism and apartheid have shaped a highly conflictual (criminogenic) society, which the new government will be unable to remedy significantly in the near future. The majority of the South African population have not only been racially oppressed for many years, they have been, and remain, economically oppressed. The enstatement of a largely black government, almost overnight, has bred high expectations of rapid improvement in the material position of these people. Swift change on such a wide scale is, however, unlikely. The new government is being confronted with demands for expensive reform in all areas of society, but the South African economy has not yet recovered from almost two decades of economic sanction. The hopes of the masses are thus largely unrealistic and disappointment is likely to breed conflict. Predictions are that law-breaking, and particularly violence, will not decrease markedly in the short to medium term in South Africa (Scharf 1993b). Since progressive-realist criminology is the most substantial and established source of progressive discourse on the management of social conflict, the influence of this discourse on government policy is likely to strengthen over the next five to ten years. The question is whether progressive-realist criminology, as a dominant discourse, will be able to distance itself critically from the new government. If not, the danger is that the dominant criminological discourse will be dictated solely by political contingencies, so forceclosing the pursuit of theoretical deconstruction.

The 'refusal to abandon the space of politics should not also entail an abandonment of a principled theoretical commitment to calling into question all already-known explanations' (Carlen 1991: 118). Political commitment to social justice and short-term progressive interventions are only two of the three 'voracious gods' (Cohen 1990: 24) academics in this field ought to serve. The third is intellectual scepticism, or ongoing theoretical deconstruction. In the prevailing frenzy of social reconstruction in South Africa, academics in progressive-realist criminology, both feminist and non-feminist alike, run the very real risk of abandoning the pursuit of theoretical deconstruction in favour of political pragmatism. This is likely to result in the production of closed and reified discourses limited entirely by political contingencies. However, criminological scholars need not find integration between intellectual scepticism and political commitment. Instead, we should seek to identify and articulate the tensions resulting from the pursuit of these frequently contradictory objectives. The goal should be to seek 'that loss of authorship which, in the production and recognition of new knowledge, renders the *politically* important signifiers "feminist" and "realist" irrelevant' (Carlen 1991: 119).

Acknowledgements

Parts of this chapter are based on Hansson (1993a). My loving thanks go to M.G. for her patient listening, good humour and encouragement. Thanks are also due to Rona Cochrane and Jennifer Radloffe, and special thanks are due to my friend Margot Lochrenberg for keeping me updated across the miles.

Notes

1 The African National Congress (ANC) Women's League is the largest single women's organization in the country, and also the most influential grouping within the WNC. It is a section of the ANC, which is also the majority party in the coalition government.
2 Research has been the core of the Charter campaign. Throughout the country women's views have been surveyed and a national database of work on women's issues is being established.

3 At present there are a handful of shelters for battered women, some of which are run by feminists, and a few regionally organized coalitions such as Coordinated Action for Battered Women in the Western Cape.
4 Under apartheid legislation such as the Group Areas Act and laws relating to influx control.
5 The centres located in Cape Town and Johannesburg.
6 The first site for the sustained production of this counter-hegemonic discourse was the Institute of Criminology at the University of Cape Town. Today this institute is one of the most important sites for the teaching and production of progressive-realist criminology in South Africa.
7 At present there is a large degree of overlap between the political aims of socialist feminism and progressive-realist criminology in South Africa, namely working for social justice in the long and short term and the current focus on legal reform.
8 The review turned up 319 works on the subject, 196 (61 per cent) of which were explicitly feminist analyses.
9 Under Nationalist rule South Africa had strictly enforced censorship laws. Thus, unlike in the USA, for example, pornography has not been a priority for feminism in South Africa. Feminist interest in pornography has now been sparked owing to constitutional debates on freedom of speech.
10 Formerly known as the Sexual Offences Court at the Wynberg Magistrates Courts.
11 Victoria Hospital.
12 Limited to the Western Cape area.
13 Mainly for violating influx control and public safety regulations.

References

Albertyn, C. (1993). Women and the criminal justice system: defined (out) by men. Paper presented at the Women and the Criminal Justice System conference, Centre for Criminal Justice, University of Natal at Pietermaritzberg.
Anderson, P. (1981). The rape trauma syndrome and the experience of rape. Paper presented at the Law Student–Teacher conference, Faculty of Law, University of Natal at Durban.
Bazilli, S. (ed.) (1990). Putting Women on the Agenda. Johannesburg: Ravan.
Caputi, J. (1987). The Age of Sex Crime. London: Women's Press.
Caputi, J. (1993). To acknowledge and heal: 20 years of feminist thought and activism on sexual violence. In C. Kramarae and D. Spender (eds) The Knowledge Explosion: Generations of Feminist Scholarship. London: Harvester Wheatsheaf.
Carlen, P. (1991). Women, feminism and realism. Social Justice, 17, 106–23.
Charman, A., De Swardt, C. and Simons, M. (1991). The politics of gender: a discussion of the Malibongwe conference papers and other current papers within the ANC. Paper presented to the Women and Gender in Southern Africa conference, University of Natal at Durban.
Chinkada, E. (1992). Victimization of women: some cultural features. In W. Schurink, W. Snyman, I. Krugel and W. Slabbert (eds) Victimization, Nature and Trends. Pretoria: Human Sciences Research Council.
Cohen, S. (1990). Intellectual scepticism and political commitment: the case of radical criminology. First Bonger Lecture, University of Amsterdam.

Cowling, M. (1994). A critical overview of criminal procedure and the adversarial system in relation to rape trials. In P. Swikkard, S. Jagwanth and B. Grant (eds) *Women under the Criminal Justice System in South Africa*. Pretoria: Human Sciences Research Council.

Crowley, H. and Himmelweit, S. (eds) (1993). *Knowing Women: Feminism and Knowledge*. Milton Keynes: Open University.

Davis, D. and Slabbert, M. (eds) (1985). *Crime and Power in South Africa: Critical Studies in Criminology*. Cape Town: David Philip.

Durbach, A. (1985). Reforming women: a case study of disintegration. In D. Davis and M. Slabbert (eds) *Crime and Power in South Africa: Critical Studies in Criminology*. Cape Town: David Philip.

Faludi, S. (1991). *Backlash: the Undeclared War against American Women*. New York: Crown.

Faul, A. and Muller, R. (eds) (1990). *The Development of a Crisis-intervention Programme for Victims of Rape*. Pretoria: Human Sciences Research Council.

Hall, C. (1988). Rape: the politics of definition. *South African Law Journal*, 105, 67–79.

Hansson, D. (1991a). The patchwork quilt of power relations: a challenge to South African feminism. In K. Daly, M. Bertrand and D. Klein (eds) *Proceedings of the International Feminist Conference on Women, Law and Social Control*. Montreal.

Hansson, D. (1991b). A brief synopsis of the historical development and nature of some of the contemporary divisions among women in South Africa. In K. Daly, M. Bertrand and D. Klein (eds) *Proceedings of the International Feminist Conference on Women, Law and Social Control*. Montreal.

Hansson, D. (1991c). We the invisible: a feminist analysis of the dominant conception of street children in South Africa. Occasional paper 1–91, Institute of Criminology, University of Cape Town.

Hansson, D. (1991d). 'Strolling' as a gendered experience: a feminist analysis of young females in Greater Cape Town. Occasional paper 2–91, Institute of Criminology, University of Cape Town.

Hansson, D. (1991e). Working against violence against women: recommendations from Rape Crisis (Cape Town). In S. Bazilli (ed.) *Putting Women on the Agenda*. Johannesburg: Ravan.

Hansson, D. (1992). Broadening our vision: a challenge to South African mainstream victimology. In W. Schurink, W. Snyman, I. Krugel and W. Slabbert (eds) *Victimization, Nature and Trends*. Pretoria: Human Sciences Research Council.

Hansson, D. (1993a). Feminist scholarship and progressive realist criminology in contemporary South Africa: preferred relations and future directions. Paper presented to the British Criminology conference, University of Cardiff.

Hansson, D. (1993b). Rape trauma syndrome: a psychological assessment for court purposes. Occasional paper 2–93, Institute of Criminology, University of Cape Town.

Hansson, D. (1994). Interim reflections on the Cape Attorney General's Task Group on Rape. In P. Swikkard, S. Jagwanth and B. Grant (eds) *Women under the Criminal Justice System in South Africa*. Pretoria: Human Sciences Research Council.

Hansson, D. (1995). South African feminism and the patchwork quilt of power relations. *Women's Studies*, 6(1).

Hansson, D., Carolissen, R. and Prinsloo, R. (1989). Progressive participatory research: stress factors in Manenberg. *Critical Health*, 28, 59–65.

Hansson, D. and Hofmeyr, B. (1992). Women's rights: towards a non-sexist South

Africa. *Developing Justice* series, no. 7, Institute of Criminology, University of Cape Town.

Hansson, D. and Russell, D. (1994). A bibliography on patriarchal force in South Africa. In P. Swikkard, S. Jagwanth and B. Grant (eds) *Women under the Criminal Justice System in South Africa*. Pretoria: Human Sciences Research Council.

Hansson, D. and van Zyl Smit, D. (eds) (1990). *Towards Justice? Crime and State Control in South Africa*. Cape Town: Oxford University Press.

Kaganas, F. (1986). Rape in marriage: developments in South African law. *International Journal of Law and the Family*, 4, 318.

Kaganas, F. and Murray, C. (1983). Rape in marriage: conjugal right or criminal wrong? *Acta Juridica* (annual volume), 125.

Kaplan, B. (1992). Date rape: an in-depth pilot study of the experiences of six white, female students at the University of Cape Town. Honours dissertation, Institute of Criminology, University of Cape Town.

Kramarae, C. and Spender, D. (eds) (1993). *The Knowledge Explosion: Generations of Feminist Scholarship*. Hemel Hempstead: Harvester Wheatsheaf.

Labuschagne, I. and van der Hoven, A. (1988). Victim experience. In C. Cilliers (ed.) *Victimology*. Pretoria: Haum.

Labuschagne, J. (1972). The South African rape law: a penal-comparative investigation. Doctoral dissertation, University of Potchefstroom.

Levett, A. (1981). Considerations on the provision of adequate psychological care for the sexually-assaulted woman. Masters dissertation, Department of Psychology, University of Cape Town.

Lochrenberg, M. and Stanton, S. (n.d.). A critical evaluation of the Wynberg Sexual Offences Court and related services. Research in progress, Institute of Criminology, University of Cape Town.

Mayne, A. (1990). Feminism and the anti-rape movement. In D. Russell (ed.) *Lives of Courage: Women for a New South Africa*. Cape Town: David Philip.

Mayne, A. and Levett, A. (1977). The trauma of rape: some considerations. *South African Journal of Criminal Law and Criminology*, 1, 163–82.

Murray, C. (1993). What place could a new constitution give to women? In M. Lessing (ed.) *South African Women Today*. Cape Town: Maskew-Miller Longman.

Nhlapo, T. (1992). Culture and women abuse: some South African starting points. *Agenda*, 13, 5.

O'Regan, C. and Murray, C. (1993). Women's rights. In N. Boister, K. Ferguson-Brown and C. Scott (eds) *South African Human Rights Yearbook 1992, Volume 3*. Cape Town: Oxford University Press.

O'Sullivan, M. (n.d., a). Women in delict. Research in progress, Department of Public Law, University of Cape Town.

O'Sullivan, M. (n.d., b). Women in the Supreme Court. Research in progress, Department of Public Law, University of Cape Town.

Offen, L. (1986). The female offender and psychiatric referral: the medicalisation of female deviance. *Medicine and Law*, 5, 1–18.

Purvis, J. (1994). Hidden from history. In *The Polity Reader in Gender Studies*. Cambridge: Polity Press.

Rape Crisis (1989a). *Introduction to Counselling Skills*. Training manual 2. Cape Town: Rape Crisis.

Rape Crisis (1989b). *Rape and the Law*. Training manual 4. Cape Town: Rape Crisis.

Rape Crisis (1989c). *Medical Information (Rape)*. Training manual 5. Cape Town: Rape Crisis.

Rape Crisis (1989d). *Rape.* Training manual 6. Cape Town: Rape Crisis.

Rape Crisis (1989e). *Child Sexual Abuse.* Training manual 7. Cape Town: Rape Crisis.

Rape Crisis (1989f). *How to Deal with Child Sexual Abuse.* Training manual 8. Cape Town: Rape Crisis.

Rape Crisis (1989g). *Rape.* Violence against women pamphlet 1. Cape Town: Rape Crisis.

Rape Crisis (1989h). *Battery.* Violence against women pamphlet 2. Cape Town: Rape Crisis.

Rape Crisis (1989i). *Guidelines for the Treatment of Rape Survivors.* Violence against women pamphlet 4. Cape Town: Rape Crisis.

Rape Crisis (1989j). *What Kind of Men Rape?* Violence against women pamphlet 5. Cape Town: Rape Crisis.

Rape Crisis (1989k). *Incest and Child Abuse.* Violence against women pamphlet 6. Cape Town: Rape Crisis.

Rape Crisis (1989l). *The Rape Law.* Women using the law pamphlet 7. Cape Town: Rape Crisis.

Rape Crisis (1989m). *Reporting Rape or Assault.* Women using the law pamphlet 8. Cape Town: Rape Crisis.

Rauch, J. (1991). Deconstructing the SAP. Paper presented at the Association of Sociologists of South Africa conference, Cape Town.

Rauch, J. (1994). The impact of training on the police response to rape. In P. Swikkard, S. Jagwanth and B. Grant (eds) *Women under the Criminal Justice System in South Africa.* Pretoria: Human Sciences Research Council.

Reddy, M. (1994). A feminist perspective on the substantive law of rape in South Africa. In P. Swikkard, S. Jagwanth and B. Grant (eds) *Women under the Criminal Justice System in South Africa.* Pretoria: Human Sciences Research Council.

Retief, G. (1993). Policing the perverts: an exploratory investigation of the nature, extent and social impact of police action towards lesbians and gay men in South Africa. Research report 2–93, Institute of Criminology, University of Cape Town.

Richards, J. (1980). *The Sceptical Feminist.* Harmondsworth: Penguin.

Russell, D. (1991). Rape and child sexual abuse in Sowetu. An interview with community leader Mary Mabaso. *South African Sociological Review,* 3, 62–83.

Russell, D. (1993). The story of Lulu Diba: acquaintance rape at a rural university. *Agenda,* 16, 67.

Salmon, O. (1980). Judicial discretion in sentencing in the Supreme Court: a computerized survey in the Durban and Coast local divisions, 1970–1979. *Natal University Law Review,* 2, 580–92.

Scharf, W. (1993a). *Policing in Transition.* Cape Town: Institute of Criminology, University of Cape Town.

Scharf, W. (1993b). Crime and violence. Paper presented to the Contemporary Social Realities in South Africa conference, The Urban Foundation, Johannesburg.

Schurink, E. (1992). Rape victimization. In W. Schurink, W. Snyman, I. Krugel and W. Slabbert (eds) *Victimization, Nature and Trends.* Pretoria: Human Sciences Research Council.

Schurink, W., Snyman, I., Krugel, W. and Slabbert, W. (eds) (1992). *Victimization, Nature and Trends.* Pretoria: Human Sciences Research Council.

Schwendinger, H. and Schwendinger, J. (1991). Feminism, criminology and complex variations. In B. MacLean and D. Milovanovic (eds) *Directions in Critical Criminology.* Vancouver: The Collective Press.

Sloth-Nielsen, J., Hansson, D. and Richardson, C. (1992). *'Chickens in a Box': a Progressive Participatory Study of Lwandle Hostel Residents' Perceptions of Personal Safety*. Pretoria: Human Sciences Research Council.

Smith, B. (1982). Racism and women's studies. In G. Hull, P. Scott and B. Smith (eds) *All the Women Are White, All the Blacks Are Men, but Some of Us Are Brave*. New York: Feminist Press.

Speak (1994). Women in power. *Speak*, August, 21.

Swikkard, P. (1994). A critical overview of the rules of evidence relevant to rape trials in South Africa. In P. Swikkard, S. Jagwanth and B. Grant (eds) *Women under the Criminal Justice System in South Africa*. Pretoria: Human Sciences Research Council.

Taylor, I., Walton, P. and Young, J. (eds) (1975). *Critical Criminology*. London: Routledge & Kegan Paul.

van der Westhuizen, J. (1977). Rape. *South African Journal of Criminal Law and Criminology*, 2, 286.

van Zyl, M. (1988). A victimological study of women in the Western Cape. Research report 5-88, Institute of Criminology, University of Cape Town.

van Zyl, M. (1990). Rape Crisis in South Africa: overview of a decade. Paper presented to the Rape Crisis conference, Cape Town.

van Zyl Smit, D. (1989). Adopting and adapting criminological ideas: criminology and Afrikaner nationalism in South Africa. *Contemporary Crises*, 15, 227-51.

Waller, L. (1977). Victim on trial. *South African Journal of Criminal Law and Criminology*, 1, 147-62.

Women's Coalition: Western Cape (1994). Women for a new South Africa: the creation of the Women's Charter. *Women's National Coalition News*, May, 1-2.

Young, J. (1986). The failure of criminology: the need for a radical realism. In R. Mathews and J. Young (eds) *Confronting Crime*. London: Sage.

Part II
Europe

4

Feminist perspectives and their impact on criminology and criminal justice in Britain

FRANCES HEIDENSOHN

Introduction

Criminologists in Britain were among the first to contribute to the development of feminist critiques and perspectives within the subject. They have played a significant pioneering role, and continue to take part, in national and international debate. More recently, feminist writers have produced key studies, notably analysing aspects of the criminal justice and penal systems. Others have focused on victims and victimization and emphasized the gendered nature of much personal crime in their writings. There has been some, albeit mixed, feminist impact on criminology and criminal justice agencies in Britain.

The history of feminism in criminology in Britain most nearly resembles that in the USA in its length and variety. There are, however, several peculiarly local aspects to this story. These derive from characteristics of British academic life and policy processes. In this chapter I shall outline the main features of developments in Britain and try to assess their effects.

In the following pages I outline a journey, which is both personal and shared by many others. Partly this has been a voyage of exploration and discovery, but it has also had elements of conflict, as in sea battles, as well as passages of comfort and conviviality more akin to periods on a cruise ship. In the first section I set the compass with an outline of key definitions and debates. Next, I describe the change in the geoposition of feminist criminology. The third and longest piece charts developments in feminist criminology in Britain while the final one shows not the end of the excursion, but some future directions that may be followed. In imposing even such a loose framework on work in Britain, I am aware that some distortion and omission will occur. Britain is notable for the diversity and individuality of its feminist criminologists. We are few in number, scattered and have no central organization.

Setting the compass: definitions and debates

Among the most distinctive aspects of the British contributions to this field have been discussions of the nature and possibilities of feminist perspectives in criminology. This is a product of three key features of the situation in Britain: the very early origins and form of feminist perspectives here; the position of the British participants and their partners and colleagues in such debates; and the parallel developments in British criminology during this period.

In my article 'The deviance of women: a critique and an enquiry' (Heidensohn 1968) I outlined key questions which merited further enquiry and discussion. Women were much less likely than men to be convicted of crimes; far fewer were in prison. While this was a robust and stable finding it had attracted little attention from criminologists. What research and writing there had been on female deviance misrepresented and distorted it, and the sex crime ratio was similarly neglected. There was a need to remedy these deficiencies by intensive study of female crime and of gender differences in criminality.

These topics have remained central to much subsequent feminist writing in this area. Yet I had not approached them through a modern feminist perspective; indeed, that was not then familiar to me. The language in the article is not, therefore, that of modern feminist writing. I was very conscious then, and for some years afterwards, that my concerns did not resonate with anyone else's. I published two other papers (Heidensohn 1969, 1970) based on this research. Only the latter can be said to bear any traces of modern feminist influence and this was because of what I had learnt through media coverage of events in the USA and not through any academic links in Britain at that time.

It was not until Carol Smart published her *Women, Crime and Criminology* in 1977 that feminist perspectives really achieved any recognition in criminology in Britain. Awareness of feminism had been growing in this country, especially in sociology, and several major conferences had been held and papers and texts published (Mitchell 1971; Oakley 1972; Leonard *et al.* 1976). The study of crime and deviance had scarcely been touched by these trends. Smart introduces her book with her awareness

> of the overwhelming lack of interest in female criminality displayed by established criminologists and deviancy theorists . . . it became obvious to me that, as a first step at least, what was required was a feminist critique of existing studies of female criminality.
>
> (Smart 1977: xiii-xiv)

Smart's book presents just such a thorough and detailed critique; indeed, six of its seven chapters are concerned with this. Only in the final chapter does she approach the question of an alternative. She does so, however, in a most tentative and qualified way, proposing 'perhaps a feminist criminology ... because the new criminologies fail to address the question of women it might seem that we should ourselves formulate a feminist criminology ... or ... a feminist sociology' (Smart 1977: 182). Smart goes on to suggest that further work on women and crime is necessary, but that a mere critique of sexism will not of itself constitute a new theoretical approach (Smart 1977: 183).

In her later work, Carol Smart has come to reject the notion of feminist criminology (Smart 1990). This is not inconsistent with her pioneering study. What this involved (as mine had done on a much smaller scale) was primarily a critical review of existing work, precisely and rigorously conducted. The task was not necessarily to found a new theory.

Several American writers have also produced critical reviews of criminology from a feminist perspective (e.g. Klein 1973; Leonard 1982). What distinguishes the debate in Britain is the way in which the doubts and debates raised by Smart in her early work have continued to be elaborated, and not only by her. Carlen has usefully summed up the stage this debate had reached at the start of the 1990s as

1 Whether the development of a feminist criminology is a possible theoretical project (Cousins 1980; Carlen 1985).
2 Whether the focus on women lawbreakers is a 'proper' concern of 'feminism' (Allen 1988; Smart 1990).

(Carlen 1990b: 107–8)

Three of the authors cited by Carlen are British and the concerns she notes have continued to surface in much British work. Carlen (1990b: 111) herself observes: 'I have hoped that my work might contribute to – or at least not obstruct – some feminist projects ... I have never called myself a feminist "criminologist".' Gelsthorpe and Morris (1988, 1990) also express anxiety about the scope, definition and possibilities in this field, while Maureen Cain has attempted to set out the qualities required for what she headlines as 'feminist criminology?' and clearly sees as a difficult enterprise: 'a theory for feminists and criminologists which accepts ... and opens a way to live with and create uncertainties' (Cain 1990: 140).

A range of other British writers have challenged or opposed the notion of feminist criminology. Worrall studied women offenders and the 'experts' who dealt with them and concluded that 'certain women are united within the criminal justice system ... [They] resist such construction' (Worrall 1990: 163). Young, in her analysis of media coverage of the women protesters at Greenham Common Peace Camp, is much more radically deconstructive, rejecting alliances of feminism with criminology. Although her work is 'produced as part of a commitment to feminism ... [it] is with the deconstruction of the category of "Woman" that the women's movement will find its liberation' (Young 1990: 170–1). She calls the result 'this ragged collection of fractured explanatory notes'.

There is considerable diversity among these approaches and some contradiction. Thus Smart and Carlen both argue against the possibility or desirability of feminist criminology; Smart does so from a strongly anti-criminology position, which Carlen (1992: 54) finds unacceptable. Carlen advocates a feminist alliance with 'left realism' (a distinctively British contribution to criminology of the 1980s; Matthews and Young 1992). While these approaches are quite distinctive, they can almost all be summarized under the title of a paper by Betsy Stanko (who is an American living and working in Britain): 'Feminist criminology: an oxymoron?' (Stanko 1993).

This discussion reflects, I believe, the history of feminist perspectives in Britain. These had their origins in the academic world, among academic criminologists interested in intellectual questions. In order to advance their concerns they needed to present reasoned critiques of existing approaches, and this characterized the early work described above. These critiques did not resolve the problems of finding new understandings, although analysis and debate is now considerably more sophisticated. Much of the argument in this debate is *between* feminist participants and thus restricted to them alone. Until comparatively recently, it was possible to argue, as I did in a paper published in 1987, that 'criminology is poorer in all its forms' because of the failure to use 'the insights and knowledge gained from the study of women and crime' (Heidensohn 1987: 27). Gelsthorpe and Morris (1988), in an article on feminism and criminology in Britain, agreed that their review showed that ' "Gender" has not become a critical issue on the criminological agenda' (p. 232). It is possible in the mid-1990s to reassess these conclusions and consider whether feminist debates have yet influenced mainstream criminology.

From Falklands to Shetlands: the evolution of feminist criminology

Writing of female criminality a decade ago, I characterized the topic as suffering from the Falklands factor. It seemed remote, unvisited and ignored, as the British dependency in the South Atlantic had been, and attention and exploration might prove unwelcome and lead to conflict (Heidensohn 1985: 124). This is what happened to the Falkland Islands in the South Atlantic when Britain and Argentina clashed over them in the early 1980s. That prediction has not entirely been fulfilled. Far more interest had certainly been devoted to female criminality and, indeed, to a longer feminist agenda. However, in the criminological globe, while feminism is no longer perhaps located in the Falklands, it is in British terms still only in the position of the Shetland Islands. (For those less familiar with British geography, it should be explained that the Shetlands, although part of the British Isles, are usually represented on maps in a box which separates them and also reduces the distance between them and the rest of the country.)

It is extremely hard to assess impact and influence in an academic discipline. Before doing so I need to explain several distinctive features of criminology in Britain. Criminologists here were very much influenced by American developments of the 1960s in the sociology of deviance: an experience of paradigm shift often called the 'big bang'. This and the expansion of universities and social research organizations increased career opportunities. There are several useful instruments to help us with regard to past and recent developments in criminology in Britain. Paul Rock (1988, 1994) has published two papers based on surveys of practising criminologists in Britain. In the first of these he outlines the characters of British criminology and its exponents. He depicts it as a relatively modern enterprise, concentrated in a few universities and the Home Office, involving a small number of scholars, many of whom belong to a 'fortunate generation' recruited in the 1970s. In the second paper Rock addresses questions of gender and of feminism. He notes a sex ratio of four men to one woman among his respondents and that 'gender certainly affected work and interest' (Rock 1994: 137). No men, but over a third of women, had studied a problem affecting women. Only a quarter of the women, but fewer than one in forty of the men, claimed to be feminists (Rock 1994: 138). The second paper lists key influences on criminological thought and it is clear that the so-called 'big bang' of the 1970s, the impact of the conceptual revolution introducing the 'new deviancy' of Marxism and interactionism, is still dominant (pp. 140–1). It formed the fortunate generation who continue to hold many key posts in the field, although their research is 'monopolized by an interest in the institution of law enforcement' (p. 146). What they continue to teach is overwhelmingly 'theorizing about crime', which is 'what they inherited from the 1970s when their discipline was institutionalized in the universities' (p. 146). Rock concludes by observing that 'Criminology is a masculine discipline, and the other big idea of the 1970s, feminism, has not spread far within it (p. 147).

In texts and major journals published in Britain in the past decade what is apparent is that the *recognition* factor for feminism has increased in recent years. In the same volume in which Rock's first article appeared, Jock Young insisted that 'The importance of feminist work in the recent development of radical criminology cannot be overestimated . . . The contribution of *feminist victimology* has been profound' (Young 1988: 301, emphasis added). In outlining 'recent paradigms in criminology', however, Young (1994) has very little to say about feminist influences. Ironically, Rock in other work acknowledges the impact of feminist work: the second edition of his *Understanding Deviance* (his joint work with David Downes) contains a chapter on 'feminist criminology' (Downes and Rock 1988). Mainstream texts and sets of reading often acknowledge the feminist critique of the absence of gender and record the contribution to topics such as studies of victims (e.g. Downes and Rock 1988; Jupp 1989; Roshier

1989; Stenson and Cowell 1991; Maguire *et al.* 1994). Acknowledgement is not usually accompanied by incorporation. Feminist approaches remain *outside* the main criminological enterprise, although there is now both considerably more awareness of them and response to them. With the possible exception of a founding role in left realism, they are not integrated.

This situation, as well as the state of criminology in Britain, helps to explain the continued concern with definitions and boundaries of feminism I outlined above. Criminology in Britain is much influenced by its links to the 'big bang' of the 1970s paradigm shift when the current forms of the subject were laid down. Reframing of feminist discourses reflects and adds to this situation. Feminists in Britain have also had to engage with certain peculiar local factors. Within criminology, the rise of left realism has been one of these, but another has been the relative decline, charted by Rock, of opportunities in academic social sciences during the 1980s: 'Faults in the line of succession have interfered with the smooth transmission and expansion of feminism' (Rock 1994: 139). It is all the more surprising then that so much work has been achieved, even though it still awaits full recognition.

Lonely, uncharted seas

Writing of the study of gender and crime in the 1960s, I was able to claim that

> at present we barely possess the basic components for an initial analysis ... we lack, for this area, the rich resources of past documentation and research that one can call upon in studying male juvenile delinquency or alcoholism, we have no equivalent of *The Jackroller, The Professional Thief*, still less is there a *Delinquent Girls* ... what seems to be needed in the study of female deviance is a crash programme of research which telescopes decades of comparable studies of males.
> (Heidensohn 1968: 170–1)

Decades have now passed and it is possible to look back and see how this challenge has been taken up in Britain and, even more importantly, in what direction the torch will be carried in the future.

In a summary chapter it is hard to do justice to all that is available. Notable work which I shall cover includes studies of female offenders and victims, women and justice and social control. I also indicate the considerable responses to this work from various bodies.

In earlier work I have described developments in British feminist work as having two phases, of pioneering and consolidation (Heidensohn 1994a). I also suggested that it demonstrates the key characteristics of female offenders (Heidensohn 1987). As I noted above, pioneering work involved critical evaluations of conventional criminology and more modern approaches. It is important to stress that almost all these early studies were of female criminality and its comparative neglect and distorted treatment in the literature. Smart did consider the position of rape victims in rape trials, but the first thrust of empirical studies in Britain focused on women offenders, turning particularly to look at women in the criminal justice system and women in prison. A second area of research, with a largely distinct group of researchers, is that of victim or survivor studies.

Studies of women offenders in Britain have certainly charted the lonely seas, although the map is made up of many small-scale studies with some particular clusters. Carlen (1983, 1988, 1990a) has, for example, presented a series of documentations and analyses of the lives of female offenders, which emphasize certain features of their careers, such as the interaction of what she calls the gender bind and the class bind. Yet she stresses that as far as the topic of women and crime is concerned, she does not believe 'there is a distinctly feminist theoretical conceptual system' of exploration (Carlen 1990a: 112). While several studies include interviews with various groups of women, such as prostitutes (McLeod 1982; Edwards 1984), young gang members (Campbell 1981) and drug couriers (Green 1991), these are relatively exceptional in British work. What does distinguish it is the recording and analysis of women's encounters with the criminal justice system in the courts and in prison.

Comparatively small numbers of women come before British courts because of their low levels of recorded crime and the greater likelihood that they will be cautioned (dealt with by an official warning but no court process: 90 per cent of young female offenders are handled in this way). Yet the operation of the courts has drawn considerable interest from British feminist scholars. Eaton (1986) studied a London magistrate's court and its respective treatment of male and female defendants, observing that familial ideology played a key role in the disposal of both sexes. Edwards (1984) has also observed court treatment of prostitutes. Allen (1987) compared the handling of male and female serious violent offenders. She found a much greater tendency for women's actions to be explained in psychopathological terms and for them in consequence to be less harshly treated than men.

The small group of women who are sent to prison in Britain have been extensively studied in recent years in a very clear example of a feminist-inspired 'catching-up'. In the 1980s, several major research studies examined prison regimes for women. Two of these (Carlen 1983; Dobash et al. 1986) examined the same (and sole) Scottish secure institution and remarked on the close confinement women experienced and the gender stereotypes it reinforced. Mandaraka-Sheppard (1986) and Genders and Player (1986, 1987) compared women's experiences in several British gaols. These studies noted the many contradictions in the regimes enforced on women, usually owing to their being subject to rules and systems designed for men, and the consequent tensions and conflicts. Several other researchers (Morris and Wilkinson 1988; Casale 1989; Padel and Stevenson 1989) have studied particular groups such as remand prisoners. Eaton (1993) published an analysis of the strategies which women used to adapt and survive after being imprisoned.

Gelsthorpe (1989) conducted one of the few enquiries which explored treatment of girls and boys in different agencies: an assessment centre, a police juvenile bureau and a secure remand centre. She concluded that to attribute the treatment of young females wholly to institutional sexism was misleading (pp. 147–53). Many other factors mediated what happened to them.

All these studies help to mark out the map, but only some sections of the map are illuminated in this way. Notable above all is the common theme of how women are *treated* by courts, prisons and other agencies, how they experience them, react to them and overcome them. Few British feminist researchers (apart from those noted above) have looked at women's *actions*. This is in tune with the second major theme of British work I have already identified: women (and children) as victims and survivors of violent, sexual and other crimes.

This motif dominates much modern work in Britain. To some degree, while there are parallel approaches and shared work (and workers), feminist safety and security studies can be distinguished from other criminological work. The first stimulus to such enquiries in Britain came through care and campaign work. The modern 'rediscovery' of wife-battering happened in London (Pizzey 1973) and led to a network of women's aid shelters being set up (Lupton 1994). American influence later led to the founding of Rape Crisis, and to the provision of help and support for survivors of rape and sexual assault (Hanmer *et al.* 1989; Walklate 1989; CASU 1993; Lupton and Gillespie 1994).

Feminist work in this field in Britain has had greater impact than in any other. First, it has been the most productive. In a survey of literature recorded on major databases and through writing to an extensive range of writers and researchers, Marisa Silvestri and I located more titles and more contributors under this heading than any other (Heidensohn 1995). Not only is its volume notable, 'feminist victimology' has had a significant impact both on criminological theory and on criminal justice policy in Britain. Its influence on left realism 'has been profound' and is acknowledged (Young 1988: 301). Lowman and McLean (1992: 8) suggest that 'gender was the central category of analysis in the Islington Crime Survey' (Jones *et al.* 1986), one of the key surveys from the realist school.

The direct influence of feminist thinking is sometimes acknowledged. For example, a very senior police officer described clearly how he researched the topic of marital violence under the supervision of feminist researchers. His conscious aim was to established police 'ownership' of the issue so that changes in practice could be brought about more quickly. (Bourlet 1990: x–xi).

It is, however, for their impact on policy that these feminist activities are most notable. The greatest shifts have been in public debate:

feminists have achieved a good deal of success in terms of heightening public awareness, and subsequently shaping support services, for women and children in the context of men's violence . . . policymakers in . . . health and social services, housing, the police and the criminal justice system more generally have responded . . . to the demands made by feminists.

(Lupton and Gillespie 1994: 4–5)

Not all feminists would be as confident as these authors. What can be agreed is that as moral entrepreneurs, feminists have had success in stimulating public debate in Britain.

The voyage of discovery of victimization has gone further and into darker and more dangerous waters. Feminist work on victims is sometimes presented as distinct from and even antithetical to the original concerns with female offenders, which were the starting point for feminist perspectives in criminology. It is certainly true that some writers have concentrated on women's victimization and survival in relation to men's violence, while others have written about female criminality or supplied a critique of conventional criminology. A further complexity is added because some of the most prominent groups campaigning on behalf of women offenders have used variations of the battered wife's defence (Southall Black Sisters 1990) to promote their causes.

Work undertaken from these perspectives may seem less concerned with problems of definition and identity. As Liz Kelly, who has produced key studies on sexual violence (1988) and child abuse (CASU 1993), succinctly puts it in a thoughtful account of her own research career: 'Feminist research investigates aspects of women's oppression while seeking at the same time to be part of the struggle against it' (Kelly 1990: 107). It is perhaps understandable that there should be fewer signs of anxiety in feminist debates about violence to women than when women are perceived as perpetrators of violence. Nevertheless, these themes do intertwine and sections on each of them can be found in many collections of British studies (see e.g. Hanmer and Maynard 1987; Hanmer et al. 1989; Lupton and Gillespie, 1994). In both empirical and campaign activities British strength lies less in work on women's actions and more in work on their reactions to and treatment by the criminal justice system.

Women and social control

In a key early theoretical paper, Jalna Hanmer (1978) made significant links between women's experiences of violence and of social control. A small – but rapidly developing – area of work in Britain has focused on gender and social control, particularly women's participation in informal social control (Heidensohn 1985) and, increasingly, in formal agencies. In part this results from changes caused, at one remove, by feminism. In the 1970s British police forces, like many of their counterparts in the USA,

abolished separate spheres for female police officers and introduced integrated policing. In consequence, women officers had to manage routine
police activities including violence and disorder (Heidensohn 1994b). Some
work on this topic is obviously either not feminist (e.g. Carrier 1988) or
merely operational (Southgate 1981), but feminist interest has grown
(Radford 1987, 1989) along with particular public concerns about women
officers' mistreatment by their male colleagues (Halford 1993). While these
studies reveal near universal experiences of harassment (Jones 1986; Silvestri
1993), they also provide a firm sense of agency in the lives of female
officers and clear evidence of their survival skills and coping strategies
(Heidensohn 1992).

Further illumination on this topic comes from the contribution made by
historians from feminist viewpoints. Mahood (1990), for instance, illustrates the way in which liberal reforms of the laws on prostitution had a
'net widening' effect. In a major historical study of women's nineteenth-
century custodial experiences in Britain, Zedner (1991) explores the regimes of Victorian prisons for women and two attempts at penal 'reform'
for women, which both failed. She concludes by noting 'how little understanding of female crime has altered in the intervening years when compared to interpretations of male criminality' (Zedner 1991: 300). She also
shows that women were subject to distinctively gendered forms of social
control, and also to common regimes. Both these historians apply insights
of modern feminist criminology in order to explore their historical subjects.

In an assessment of the impact of feminism on this subject in Britain, it
is important to include spheres of influence other than the purely academic.
The largest criminal justice research unit in Europe is (up to the time of
writing) run by the Home Office. I wish, therefore, to look in the following
sub-sections at responses at an official level from pressure groups and the
media to indicate the effectiveness of feminism.

Official responses

Between 1968 and 1973 the British Home Office published a series of
Bulletins on Female Offenders (Home Office Research Unit 1968–1973).
They contained a few reports of research, accounts of visits to prisons
abroad, lists of forthcoming lectures and regular appeals for contact and
communication. At this time several small-scale studies of the female inmate population had been carried out (Goodman and Price 1967; Gibbens
1971). It might seem that the careful and conservative Department of State
was in the forefront of awareness in the earliest days of the flowering of
feminist criminology. In fact, although these bulletins are worth some
further study (see Heidensohn 1994b), this interest then lapsed and the
official response in Britain has been mixed and muted. As I have already
indicated, the police have responded to challenges to their policies on
handling rape and domestic violence cases. However, women's understanding and experience of crime and criminal justice are often still ignored. As

Genders and Player (1987: 175) point out, 'there has never been a major review of the women's prison system' in Britain. Official reviews of the penal system still tend to ignore women and their needs. In 1990 riots and disturbances at several British prisons led to the Woolf Inquiry. The inquiry team produced a major report proposing significant changes. However, Lord Justice Woolf decided it would 'not be right to investigate or make findings about problems which solely relate to women prisoners, none of whom was involved in the disturbances' (HMSO 1991: section 2.18).

This reason for sidelining women cannot be sustained in relation to the Royal Commission on Criminal Justice (HMSO 1993). This formidable body, the first such set up for twelve years, had its origins in the government's response to a series of widely publicized miscarriages of justice which threatened the reputation of the British criminal justice system. Several women were involved in these cases (Kennedy 1992: 239), yet the Royal Commission refused to hear evidence on gender-related matters (Dobash 1992) and commissioned no relevant research.

On the other hand, there are a few signs of feminist impact on officialdom in Britain. As a consequence of requirements in section 95 of the 1991 Criminal Justice Act, more gender-related data on the criminal justice system have to be published, and this provides useful material for researchers. It is clear that Home Office researchers are becoming engaged in the feminist-led debates about discrimination in the criminal justice system. Smith (1988) had already produced a review of the evidence on the 'chivalry' debate. A recent research finding, for example, addresses the assertion made by some feminists (although the paper names none) 'that the criminal justice system in England and Wales routinely discriminates against women. This paper . . . concludes that the weight of evidence is against this claim' (Hedderman and Hough 1994). The paper also picks up claims that women are more likely to be imprisoned than men for domestic murder, and argues that the opposite is the case. This is clearly a response to the very vocal campaigns mounted on behalf of several women who were found guilty of murdering their husbands in the 1980s and 1990s and sentenced to life imprisonment.

Pressure groups and activism

Universities, government departments and research institutes are elite and august institutions, especially in Britain. They are thus less susceptible to innovating influences and can be slow to be swayed by new trends and fashions. Feminism in various forms has contributed to just such a series of trends since the 1970s. These have had most effect on newer and more fashion-conscious bodies. The new wave of pressure groups is one example where feminist perspectives on crime and gender have been quickly appreciated and assimilated.

Both established penal lobby groups and newly formed single-issue outfits have taken on board messages about the comparative neglect of female offenders. When the Woolf inquiry largely excluded women from its terms of reference (see above) the National Association for the Care and Resettlement of Offenders published a report detailing how the Woolf proposals could be implemented for women (NACRO 1991). This built on their own Women Prisoners' Resource Centre as well as initiatives they had assisted for women in prison. Their recent activities and publications clearly show awareness and assimilation of aspects of feminist agendas, as in *Opening the Door: Women Leaving Prison* (NACRO 1993).

The Howard League for Penal Reform has also campaigned on behalf of women offenders and with an increasingly sophisticated approach. In 1986 it published proposals for penal policy for women, which included coeducational prisons. Its more recent work aims both at improving conditions for women in prison and at stressing a near-abolitionist approach: 'the majority of women are sent to prison unnecessarily. The system is desperately in need of change' (Howard League 1993). It has stressed particularly the damaging effects of custody on prisoners' children, family ties and ethnic minority offenders (Howard League 1991, 1993, 1994). Perhaps the most 'establishment' body to show traces of feminist influence was the Women's National Commission, which published a thorough and moderately radical report, *Women and Prison* (Cabinet Office 1991), with the blessing of its two chairs, both Conservative government ministers.

Much more radical, but commanding far fewer resources, are the multiplicity of campaigns and pressure groups which grew and developed in Britain in the 1980s. They had their roots in particular political circumstances: the combination of a strong Conservative government, a weak and divided opposition in Parliament and a flowering of 'rainbow' politics, fostered by local authorities outside. In London especially, subsidies from the now-defunct Greater London Council encouraged these activities (Women's Equality Group/London Strategic Policy Unit 1986). Other authorities funded women's units and police monitoring committees. During this period, many groups were founded or received a major boost from these sources. Most combined campaigning with some form of service provision, in refuges, client work etc. The history of Southall Black Sisters (founded in 1979) exemplifies this.

In 1983 Greater London Council funding produced a bonanza for the voluntary sector. Southall Black Sisters were among the beneficiaries ... Funding changed the nature of the group. Before, women had taken part in a number of campaigns, but ... now 'case work' ... takes up the majority of our time ... When we were first established we had to demand the right to exist and be heard ... Now we are recognised as a legitimate autonomous women's group. The problems we face now relate to the co-opting of the debate about domestic violence and the appropriation of autonomous activity by the Council and other bodies.

(Southall Black Sisters 1990)

Since they published this report, Southall Black Sisters, although still struggling to survive on tiny resources, have achieved considerable success with their campaign for the release of Kiranjit Ahluwalia, sentenced for the murder of her husband after years of abuse and violence.

Besides Southall Black Sisters, there are many groups affiliated to the refuge movement (Crime Concern 1993). British experience with both women's refuges from domestic violence and rape crisis centres is distinctive. Each has retained a feminist ethos, despite backlash and other great difficulties. Rape crisis centres have 'a proven track record as the frontline providers of distinctively feminist support services for female survivors of sexual violence' (Gillespie 1994: 36). It is easy to list a dozen or so groups that offer services and action on behalf of women offenders and clearly have feminist roots. Women in Prison, founded in 1984, is among the most typical, run by ex-prisoners and providing services, advice and consultancy, as well as firm criticism of policy proposals (WIP 1994). Its influence on the new agenda of the established pressure groups has been significant. These groups live with constant funding crises and sometimes go under. The climate in which they struggle is well documented in articles by Lupton and Gillespie (1994). The contradictions are exemplified in Southall Black Sisters' review of themselves:

> as well as being the child of both the black and feminist movement, albeit a rebellious one, Southall Black Sisters is also in a sense a child of Thatcher . . . As individuals we have not been conventional wives or mothers, as political beings we have not confined our discourse within acceptable boundaries.
>
> (Southall Black Sisters 1990: 4)

The media

The success of campaigns such as that which led to the release of Kiranjit Ahluwalia would have been impossible without the skilful use of the media, both print and broadcast. In this they resemble the even more determined and long-term actions which finally brought freedom to several groups wrongly convicted of terrorist and other crimes. But there are ways in which feminists' agendas have shaped media representation of some aspects of crime and criminal justice in the 1980s and 1990s. Britain has important local newspapers and radio stations, but most British media have national coverage. They are also, as numerous studies testify, extremely obsessed with crime stories.

Systematic research on such vast outpourings is still relatively modest. In a short summary I shall select three kinds of development: focus on feminist crime concerns, equity stories and gendered revelations. What becomes clear is that, while the media have become the most responsive audience for feminists working in this field, they also provide the forum for challenge and debate, and that a dialectical process is encouraged by them. Sometimes this becomes a backlash.

Feminist crime concerns

The most popular television programmes in Britain are mass audience drama serials, still called 'soap operas'. They have in recent years featured episodes involving rape, domestic violence and sexual abuse. These are not the only social problems they present: racism, mental illness, AIDS and unemployment have also been included. It is clear, however, that these presentations have usually been handled with an awareness of feminist approaches and criticisms. When the rape of a women by an acquaintance was portrayed in the London-based *EastEnders* series, the Metropolitan Police and the producers quickly reacted to public disquiet over the 'harsh' treatment of the victim. The programme was obviously seen as educative and influential.

Fictional presentations of certain feminist concerns have been particularly strong and effective in introducing issues in wider debates. The three *Prime Suspect* (La Plante 1991, 1992, 1994) television mini-series, for instance, which have won numerous awards, present concerns about crime and about gender and social control in the police force. The stories are known to be based on the career of a real-life woman detective. They have featured a serial sex killer, a long-concealed murder in which racism is involved and a paedophile ring. The macho culture of the police is very deliberately exposed in each one and is explicitly linked to failures in policing. In *Prime Suspect III* organized sexual abuse of young boys is concealed by high-ranking police officers because one of them is implicated in it. (But see Eaton (1995) for a critical appraisal of the way in which policewomen have been portrayed as less powerful.)

Equity stories

Maureen Cain has described what she calls 'equity studies' as one of the major themes of feminist criminological work. Notions of equity and discrimination are also among the commonest and most comprehensible that the media and public opinion can grasp. While the media, especially tabloid newspapers, are always ready to claim 'real' sex differences as support for inequality, they have featured many accounts which can be summed up under the headline 'Is it fair?' Reactions, for example, to the treatment of rape victims in various trials or to battered wives who 'battered back' and were sentenced to life for murder have often been relatively sympathetic. As I was preparing this chapter, highly adverse publicity was given to the case of a woman prisoner who had been forced to give birth in hospital while still handcuffed to a prison officer.

Gendered revelations

The most controversial feminist issues taken up by the media are those based on the revelation of the gendered nature of many forms of crime.

Wife beating, rape and sexual abuse of children are not 'new' offences, but they have all been presented and defined in different ways since the rise of modern feminism. Feminists have argued, for instance, that wife beating is widespread, and not confined to particular social groups, that rape is often committed by a man known to the woman and that child abuse is much more common that generally acknowledged. All these views have been widely featured in the media. They have also been criticized and rejected.

Two episodes from recent times illustrate this process. The Cleveland child sex abuse scandal (as it is often described) concerned local disquiet, which then became national through the media, about diagnoses of sexual abuse made by paediatricians in Cleveland in the north of England. Ultimately a major inquiry under Justice Butler Sloss (1988) was held. In the meantime, a large outcry alleging 'witch hunts' was built up in the mass media (Campbell 1988; Morgan and Zedner 1992; CASU 1993).

The other episodes concerned allegations of ritual and organized child sexual abuse. Much of the concern that has led to a form of moral panic about 'satanic' abuse actually stems from fundamentalist religious groups, but the media have over-simplified the issues and have contributed to the disbelief and backlash which is now under way (Boyd 1992; CASU 1993). The danger is that genuine forms of gendered crime may be ignored or caricatured.

It is clear that a popular audience for feminist-inspired perspectives on crime and criminal justice exists. Once again, the recognition quotient is high. When, as I noted above, 'The deviance of women' was published in 1968, none of my academic colleagues responded. On the appearance of the first edition of *Women and Crime* in 1985, although it was a scholarly, not a popular, book, there was widespread media interest and I was interviewed by journalists and even appeared on radio phone-ins. More significantly, whereas 'shadow criminologies' of women hardly existed ten years ago, or only of a voyeuristic kind, there is now a whole genre. These range from *Eve Was Framed* (Kennedy 1992), by a leading woman Queen's Counsel who indicts the whole of British justice for its treatment of women, to MacDonald's (1991) account of interviews with female terrorists and various accounts of female violence (Kirsta 1994) and aspects of criminal justice (Reynolds 1991).

Towards conclusions

In introducing a series of papers similar to the present collection with a British focus half a decade ago, Gelsthorpe and Morris (1990: 4) described 'feminist perspectives in criminology [as] *a project under construction*' (original emphasis). That description still applies, although the construction is more advanced and has received more setbacks than the two editors hoped. Perhaps an apter term would be a partially postmodern project. By that I mean that feminist influences are fragmented and diverse; their greatest force lies in the questions they pose and hence their deconstructive capacity. Postmodernism, however, suggests no history, and that is certainly not the case.

In this final section I shall cover three themes by way of summarizing feminist impact and influences in Britain: an account of achievements thus far, an explanation of developments in Britain and some prospects for the future.

Achieving uncertainty

If feminist perspectives have any themes in common in criminology, especially in Britain, they are surely inquiries and interrogations. Feminists of all persuasions have persisted in asking questions; in asking why questions had not been addressed they have continued to query and challenge. They persist in active deconstruction, targeting ever more precisely on concepts and topics. Originally concerned with the gender ratio and the generalizability questions, they will now take nothing for granted, least of all their own subject and discourse. Nothing should be excluded from this process, least of all such highly charged concepts as 'gender'.

These preoccupations they share with colleagues in other countries, although the tendency is particularly striking in British work, especially when compared, as in this book, with others. (Although the notion of 'British' is of course only a heuristic one. There is rather an Anglo-American universe of discourse based on a common language and partially shared histories. Cain (1986, 1989, 1992) has taught in the West Indies for many years, and Stanko in England. Shaw works in Canada, Campbell has done so in the USA and has returned to Britain. Morris currently heads the Institute of Criminal Justice in New Zealand.)

'Feminist criminology' does not exist in Britain, not at least in the ways that realist criminology does or as interactionism and critical criminology did. That is, there are neither people nor organizations clearly and closely so identified. There is, however, a loose near-network of scholars, campaigners, project workers and policy-makers who share certain common interests and perspectives. It could be said that they are few enough to recognize each other, but numerous enough to have made some kinds of impact.

Their impact has been mixed and interpreting it is a matter of judgement. Benchmarks are hard to find and depend on the area one is assessing. In the academic criminological world, it is quite clear that feminism has near-universal recognition. If we take the old rule of thumb – 'Are women mentioned in the literature?' – a review of recent handbooks, texts and readers show that they now include gender, although their coverage and understanding of gender issues is usually limited. If we use more sophisticated measures, such as whether gender perspectives are fully integrated, the outcomes are much more limited. Feminist perspectives may now be present, but confined within their own little box.

Nevertheless, feminism can be said to have contributed to major shifts in debates about criminal justice in Britain and to changing the agenda of discussions about policing, law enforcement and the treatment of victims of crime. These changes have had most effect in the practical worlds of policy and politics. There, coalitions of activists have campaigned and some professionals have listened – the police, for example – while others, such as the judiciary, have remained immune. Feminists have managed to alter the crime agenda in a number of ways. They are still not in positions where they can write or keep the records and use them to change the world.

Many, activists especially, express concern and disappointment at this situation (e.g. Stanko 1993), although others (Carlen 1990b) set out clear and pragmatic policy programmes. British feminists are notable for their great diversity, even their contradictions, and many (e.g. Smart) reject the possibility of meaningful change within current systems.

What do stand out are the qualities of the work produced from feminist perspectives. Criminology is generally perceived to be in crisis in Britain. Feminist work is striking for its scholarship and also for its liveliness and engagement.

Explaining Anglo-Saxon attitudes

At some point in a collection like this, one has to address the question of explaining national differences in a comparative context. I have already suggested that the British contribution is distinguished by its early origins, its considerable academic achievements and its stimulus to reflection and debate about gender and crime. Why have things taken this course in Britain? I think the answer lies in a combination of interaction and social structural context.

The first feminists in criminology had to be academic entrepreneurs. We needed to act as change agents. Feminist ideas offered criticisms, challenges and questions. It was important to be inside the academy (even if only just). Next there was a gradual amplification of the notions about deviance from feminism. This was a long, slow process and acted via the wider impact of feminism on social science, culture and public opinion. It was assisted by the expansion of British higher education and later the funding of pressure groups. These were features of particular times, places and politics. Many factors were inimical to these developments. Modern Britain has experienced economic decline and with this public sector cutbacks.

Two typical features from British history characterize the nature and impact of feminism here: morality and the market. Moral enterprises recur throughout modern British history. Feminists have played leading roles in many campaigns to do with moral crusades. In the nineteenth century and early twentieth century first-wave feminists threw themselves into temperance and anti-vice campaigns and fought for the right to be police officers, as well as founding purity and peace movements. In many ways, modern feminist analyses and activities share some of these concerns and aims. It is always easier to attain success in Britain through appeal to tradition rather than change. Part of the feminist achievement has been to do both.

The market has been a major preoccupation in Britain in the 1980s and 1990s under a Conservative government influenced by the New Right. One of the features of feminism is that it sells. Feminist books sell and feminism has been fashionable. This is an over-simplification of course, but it does convey a key point. Feminism focused attention on certain aspects of crime and criminal justice which struck chords: fear of crime, sexual harassment, inequities in law and justice. What is perhaps most typically British in all this is that we are good at discussing matters – our parliamentary debates attract foreign TV viewers – and ineffective at implementing change.

If I were to try to summarize the position of feminism in criminology in Britain in the 1990s, I should do so with a simple diagram. It is still too soon for us to map the oceans and draw a full marine chart. A modest algorithm rather like the London underground map would be more appropriate. Linked along the lines with feminism and criminology are a series of features: recognition, research, riches and relations. Further along, we can find debate and dialogue of a rigorous and serious kind, although these do not halt either diffusion or dilution of the key concepts and ideas. Finally, as is characteristic of many aspects of life in Britain, the major end-points are policy, politics and pragmatism.

Back to the future

If feminism is still under (postmodern) construction in criminology, it follows that we do not yet know what the completed structure will look like. I think it will remain unfinished, although still being re/deconstructed. I think feminists' tasks are to question and challenge and to join others in doing so. It is also important to interrogate and challenge one's own work and practices, and this will/should happen more in the future.

While I do not deny the possibility of a feminist criminology, or define it as an oxymoron, I do believe that feminists will be increasingly adventurous in the future. Exploring issues of gender and social control will lead them into more work with diverse ethnic groups, with welfare agencies and informal mechanisms of control.

British researchers have written extensively on the courts and prisons. Less has been heard about non-custodial penalties for women, about women and violence, and about other serious offences. These might prove to be areas to explore, but they may remain neglected.

One very important new topic is already on the agenda: masculinity. A number of journalistic accounts, reflecting feminist influences (Campbell 1993; Phillips 1993) have already focused on the problem of masculinity and crime, especially juvenile delinquency. Other studies are under way (e.g.

Newburn and Stanko 1994). Of course, studying this topic poses major problems for feminists. Can it be approached from a feminist standpoint? Who should carry out the research? Yet, in one sense, it is in this direction that much feminist work has always pointed. And that same sign points out a central paradox for feminist perspectives in criminology. This is particularly pertinent in Britain where feminism is established, recognized but not yet integrated in mainstream criminology. Suppose it were fully absorbed? Would there still be a need for these approaches? Or would success lead to surcease? While the struggle continues, the questions stand.

If emphasis on gender is a key aspect of feminist work, then the further study of masculinity must be vital. Without it there will be no progress in understanding the violence women experience at the hands of men, or in exploring male criminality, which still remains the significant problem for criminology and for society.

Acknowledgements

I am most grateful to Marisa Silvestri and Martin Heidensohn for their help and advice in preparing this chapter, and to Mary Eaton for her comments on an earlier draft.

References

Allen, H. (1987). *Justice Unbalanced*. Milton Keynes: Open University Press.
Allen, J. (1988). The masculinity of criminality and criminology: interrogating some impasses. In M. Findlay and R. Hogg (eds) *Understanding Crime and Criminal Justice*. Sydney: Sydney Law Book Co.
Bourlet, A. (1990). *Police Intervention in Marital Violence*. Milton Keynes: Open University Press.
Boyd, A. (1992). *Blasphemous Rumours*. London: Prism.
Butler Sloss (1988). *Report of the Inquiry into Child Abuse in Cleveland 1987*. Cmnd 412. London: HMSO.
Cabinet Office (1991). *Women and Prison*. London: Women's National Commission.
Cain, M. (1986). Realism, feminism, methodology and law. *International Journal of the Sociology of Law*, 14, 255–67.
Cain, M. (ed.) (1989). *Growing up Good*. London: Sage.
Cain, M. (1990). Realist philosophy and standpoint epistemologies or feminist criminology as a successor science. In L. Gelsthorpe and A. Morris (eds) *Feminist Perspectives in Criminology*. Milton Keynes: Open University Press.
Cain, M. (1992). Fractured identities, standpoints and social control: (yet) another essay in realist philosophy. In M-A. Bertrand, K. Daly and D. Klein (eds) *Proceedings of the International Feminist Conference on Women, Law and Social Control*. Quebec: Mont Gabriel.
Campbell, A. (1981). *Girl Delinquents*. Oxford: Basil Blackwell.
Campbell, B. (1988). *Unofficial Secrets. Child Sexual Abuse. The Cleveland Case*. London: Virago.
Campbell, B. (1993). *Goliath*. London: Methuen.

Carlen, P. (1983). *Women's Imprisonment*. London: Routledge and Kegan Paul.

Carlen, P. (ed.) (1985). *Criminal Women*. Cambridge: Polity Press.

Carlen, P. (1988). *Women, Crime and Poverty*. Milton Keynes: Open University Press.

Carlen, P. (1990a). *Alternatives to Women's Imprisonment*. Milton Keynes: Open University Press.

Carlen, P. (1990b). Women, crime, feminism and realism. *Social Justice*, 17(4), 106–23.

Carlen, P. (1992). Criminal women and criminal justice . . . In R. Matthews and J. Young (eds) *Issues in Realist Criminology*. London: Sage Publications.

Carrier, J. (1988). *The Campaign for the Employment of Women as Police Officers*. Aldershot: Avebury.

Casale, S. (1989). *Women Inside. The Experience of Women Remand Prisoners in Holloway*. London: Civil Liberties Trust.

CASU (Child Abuse Studies Unit) (1993). *Abuse of Women and Children*. London: University of North London Press.

Cousins, M. (1980). Men's rea: a note on sexual difference. Criminology and the law. In P. Carlen and M. Collison (eds), *Radical Issues in Criminology*. Oxford: Martin Robertson.

Crime Concern (1993). *Inspirations for Action*. London: Crime Concern.

Dobash, R.E. (1992). Personal communication.

Dobash, R.P., Dobash, R.E. and Gutteridge, S. (1986). *The Imprisonment of Women*. Oxford: Blackwell.

Downes, D.M. and Rock, P.E. (1988). *Understanding Deviance*, 2nd edn. Oxford: Oxford University Press.

Eaton, M. (1986). *Justice for Women?* Milton Keynes: Open University Press.

Eaton, M. (1993). *Women after Prison*. Buckingham: Open University Press.

Eaton, M. (1995). Is it a fair cop guv? Media, masculinity and police sub-culture. Unpublished paper.

Edwards, S.M. (1984). *Women on Trial*. Manchester: Manchester University Press.

Gelsthorpe, L. (1989). *Sexism and the Female Offender*. Aldershot: Gower.

Gelsthorpe, L. and Morris, A. (1988). Feminism and criminology in Britain. *British Journal of Criminology*, 28(2), 93–110.

Gelsthorpe, L. and Morris, A. (eds) (1990). *Feminist Perspectives in Criminology*. Milton Keynes: Open University Press.

Genders, E. and Player, E. (1986). Women's imprisonment. The effects of youth custody. *British Journal of Criminology*, 26(4), 357–71.

Genders, E. and Player, E. (1987). Women in prison: the treatment, the control and the experience. In P. Carlen and A. Worrall (eds) *Gender, Crime and Justice*. Milton Keynes: Open University Press.

Gibbens, T.C.N. (1971). Female offenders. *British Journal of Hospital Medicine*, 6.

Gillespie, T. (1994). Under pressure: rape crisis centres, multi-agency work and strategies for survival. In C. Lupton and T. Gillespie (eds) *Working with Violence*. Basingstoke: Macmillan.

Goodman, N. and Price, J. (1967). *Studies of Female Offenders*. London: Home Office Research Unit Report.

Green, P. (1991). *Drug Couriers*. London: Howard League for Penal Reform.

Halford, A. (1993). *No Way up the Greasy Pole*. London: Constable.

Hanmer, J. (1978). Violence and the social control of women in G. Littlejohn *et al.* (eds) *Power and the State*. London: Croom Helm.

Hanmer, J. and Maynard, M. (eds) (1987). *Women, Violence and Social Control*. London: Macmillan.

Hanmer, J., Radford, J. and Stanko, E. (eds) (1989). *Women, Policing and Male Violence International Perspectives*. London: Routledge.

Hedderman, C. and Hough, M. (1994). *Does the Criminal Justice System Treat Men and Women Differently?* London: Home Office Research Findings, No. 10.

Heidensohn, F.M. (1968). The deviance of women: a critique and an enquiry. *British Journal of Sociology*, 19(2), 160–75.

Heidensohn, F.M. (1969). Prison for women. *Howard Journal*, 281–88.

Heidensohn, F.M. (1970). Sex, crime and society. In G.A. Harrison (ed.) *Biosocial Aspects of Sex*. Oxford: Blackwell.

Heidensohn, F. (1985). *Women and Crime*. London: Macmillan and New York University Press.

Heidensohn, F.M. (1987). Women and crime: questions for criminology. In P. Carlen and A. Worrall (eds) *Gender, Crime and Justice*. Milton Keynes: Open University Press.

Heidensohn, F.M. (1992). *Women in Control? The Role of Women in Law Enforcement*. Oxford: Oxford University Press.

Heidensohn, F.M. (1994a). Gender and crime. In R. Reiner, R. Morgan and M. Maguire (eds) *The Oxford Handbook of Criminology*. Oxford: Oxford University Press.

Heidensohn, F.M. (1994b). 'We can handle it out here'. Women officers in Britain and the USA and the policing of public order. *Policing and Society*, 4(4), 293–303.

Heidensohn, F.M. (1994c). From being to knowing. Some reflections on the study of gender in contemporary society. *Women and Criminal Justice*, 6(1), 13–37.

Heidensohn, F.M. (with the assistance of M. Silvestri) (1995). *Women and Crime*, 2nd edn. Basingstoke: Macmillan.

Her Majesty's Stationery Office (1991). *Woolf Report. Report of an Inquiry into the Prison Disturbances, April 1990*. Cmnd 1546. London: HMSO.

Her Majesty's Stationery Office (1993). *The Royal Commission on Criminal Justice. Report*. Cmnd 2263. London: HMSO.

Home Office Research Unit (1968–1973). *Research Bulletins on Women Offenders*, Nos 1–15. London: Home Office.

Howard League (1986). *Imprisonment of Women*. London: Howard League.

Howard League (1994). Women and criminal justice. *Criminal Justice*, 12(2).

Howard League (1991). *Drug Couriers*. London: Howard League.

Howard League (1993). *The Voice of a Child – Impact on Children of Mothers' Imprisonment*. London: Howard League.

Jones, S. (1986). *Policewomen and Equality*. London: Macmillan.

Jones, T., Maclean, B. and Young, J. (eds) (1986). *The Islington Crime Survey*. London: Gower Press.

Jupp, V. (1989). *Methods of Criminological Research*. London: Unwin Hyman.

Kelly, L. (1988). *Surviving Sexual Violence*. Cambridge: Polity Press.

Kelly, L. (1990). Journeying in reverse: possibilities and problems in feminist research on sexual violence. In L. Gelsthorpe and A. Morris (eds) *Feminist Perspectives in Criminology*. Milton Keynes: Open University Press.

Kennedy, H. (1992). *Eve Was Framed. Women and British Justice*. London: Vintage Press.

Klein, D. (1973). The aetiology of female crime: a review of the literature. *Issues in Criminology*, 8(2): 3–30.

Kirsta, A. (1994). *Deadlier than the Male*. London: Harper Collins.

La Plante, L. (1991). *Prime Suspect*. London: Mandarin.

La Plante, L. (1992). *Prime Suspect II*. London: Mandarin.

La Plante, L. (1994). *Prime Suspect III*. London: Mandarin.

Leonard, E.B. (1982). *A Critique of Criminology Theory: Women, Crime and Society*. New York and London: Longman.

Barker, D. Leonard and Allen, S. (1976). *Sexual Divisions and Society: Process and Change*. London: Tavistock.

Lowman, J., McLean B.D. (eds) (1992). *Realist Criminology: Crime Control and Policing in the 1990s*. Ontario: University of Toronto Press.

Lupton, C. (1994). The British refuge movement: the survival of an ideal. In C. Lupton and T. Gillespie (eds) *Working with Violence*. Basingstoke: Macmillan.

Lupton, C. and Gillespie, T. (eds) (1994). *Working with Violence*. Basingstoke: Macmillan.

MacDonald, E. (1991). *Shoot the Women First*. London: Fourth Estate.

McLeod, E. (1982). *Women Working: Prostitution Now*. London: Croom Helm.

Maguire, M., Morgan, R. and Reiner, R. (eds) (1994). *The Oxford Handbook of Criminology*. Oxford: Oxford University Press.

Mahood, L. (1990). The Magdalene's friend: prostitution and social control in Glasgow 1869–1890. *Women's Studies International Forum*, 13(1/2), 49–61.

Mandaraka-Sheppard, A. (1986). *The Dynamics of Aggression in Women's Prisons in England*. Aldershot: Gower.

Matthews, R. and Young, J. (1992). *Issues in Realist Criminology*. London: Sage Publications.

Mitchell, J. (1971). *Women's Estate*. Harmondsworth: Penguin.

Morgan, J. and Zedner, L. (1992). *Child Victims: Crime, Impact and Criminal Justice*. Oxford: Oxford University Press.

Morris, A. and Wilkinson, C. (eds) (1988). *Women and the Penal System*. Cambridge: University of Cambridge Institute of Criminology.

NACRO (1991). *A Fresh Start for Women Prisoners*. Implications of Woolf Report. London: NACRO.

NACRO (1993). *Opening the Doors: Women Leaving Prison*. London: NACRO.

Newburn, T. and Stanko, E. (eds) (1994). *Just Boys Doing Business: Masculinity and Crime*. London: Routledge.

Oakley, A. (1972). *Sex, Gender and Society*. London: Temple Smith.

Padel, U. and Stevenson P. (1989). *Insiders*. London: Virago.

Phillips, A. (1993). *The Trouble with Boys*. London: Pandora.

Pizzey, E. (1973). *Scream Quietly or the Neighbours Will Hear*. Harmondsworth: Penguin.

Radford, J. (1987). Policing male violence – policing women. In J. Hanmer and M. Maynard (eds) *Women, Violence and Social Control*. London: Macmillan.

Radford, J. (1989). Women and policing: contradictions old and new. In J. Hanmer et al. (eds) *Women, Policing and Male Violence*. London: Routledge.

Reynolds, A. (1991). *Tight Rope*. London: Sidgwick and Jackson.

Rock, P. (1988). The present state of criminology in Britain. *British Journal of Criminology*, 28(2), 58–69.

Rock, P.E. (1994). The social organization of British criminology. In M. Maguire et al. (eds) *The Oxford Handbook of Criminology*. Oxford: Oxford University Press.

Roshier, B. (1989). *Controlling Crime*. Milton Keynes: Open University Press.

Silvestri, M. (1993). Communicating the message of equal opportunities in the police service, with reference to gender. Unpublished MA thesis, Brunel University.

Smart, C. (1977). *Women, Crime and Criminology*. London: Routledge & Kegan Paul.

Smart, C. (1990). Feminist approaches to criminology or post-modern woman meets atavistic man. In L. Gelsthorpe and A. Morris (eds) *Feminist Perspectives in Criminology*. Milton Keynes: Open University Press.

Smith, L.J.F. (1988). Images of women – decision-making in courts. In A. Morris and C. Wilkinson (eds), *Women and the Penal System*. Cropwood Conference Series. Cambridge: Institute of Criminology.

Southgate, P. (1981). Women in the police. *The Police Journal*, 54(2).

Southall Black Sisters (1990). *Against the Grain. A Celebration of Struggle and Survival*. Nottingham: Russel Press.

Stanko, E. (1993). Feminist criminology: an oxymoron? Paper presented to British Criminology Conference, Cardiff.

Stenson, K. and Cowell, D. (eds) (1991). *The Politics of Crime Control*. London: Sage.

Walklate, S. (1989). *Victimology*. London: Unwin Hyman.

Women in Prison (1994). Annual Report. London: WIP.

Women's Equality Group/London Strategic Policy Unit (1986). *Breaking the Silence*. London: WEG/LSPU.

Worrall, A. (1990). *Offending Women*. London: Routledge.

Young, A. (1990). *Femininity in Dissent*. London: Routledge.

Young, J. (1988). Radical criminology in Britain: the emergence of a competing paradigm. *British Journal of Criminology*, 28(2), 289–313.

Young, J. (1994). Incessant chatter: recent paradigms in criminology. In M. Maguire *et al.* (eds) *The Oxford Handbook of Criminology*. Oxford: Oxford University Press.

Zedner, L. (1991). *Women, Crime and Custody in Victorian England*. Oxford: Oxford University Press.

5

Feminist politics, crime, law and order in Italy

TAMAR PITCH

Introduction

When I was asked to provide reflections on the impact of feminism on Italian criminology, I felt I couldn't do it. Feminism has been flourishing in Italy both politically and theoretically. It has had an impact on policy and theoretical questions traditionally of interest to criminology (namely abortion, rape, family violence, sexual harassment and incest). Yet while I can easily identify trends in the disciplines of history,[1] philosophy, psychoanalysis and even, to a lesser extent, literary studies, sociology and economics that are clearly influenced by feminist thought and practices, such trends are hard to see in 'criminology'. This might appear to be a paradox, because feminism was the driving force in the reconstitution into public issues of the 'problems' mentioned above and of others, such as child abuse. I then found myself pleading for a somewhat different subject for my contribution. And I did find another, but I must attempt to explain the apparent paradox.

First, I shall give an overview of Italian 'criminology'. Then I shall describe how feminism, from both political and theoretical points of view, reframed a number of questions of (potential) interest to criminology. Third, I shall look into the political impact this reframing of questions had, not only at the level of institutional responses, but also at the more general social level, and argue that the way other questions came to be posed and other collective actors acted may be related to the impact of feminist thought and practices. I shall then consider in more detail one specific area, organized crime. Whereas studies on this issue were not produced by feminist *criminologists*, they were produced by feminists (journalists, sociologists, politicians), just as some innovative practices emerging within this area may be imputed to the diffusion of a feminist 'common sense'.

Italian 'criminology'

Law and order have been central concerns in Italian politics since Italian reunification (1860) and even before then: John Davis (1989) shows how these concerns have not changed much since, and how they have continued shaping the political debate well into the twentieth century.[2]

However, the importation of sociological treatments of deviance and social control is a recent phenomenon in Italy and comes up against two well established traditions: jurisprudence and clinical criminology. If the object of study of the former is more the system of criminal law and procedure than the criminal justice system, the object of the latter is the 'criminal'. Italian criminology is in fact forensic psychiatry, or investigation aimed at the reconstruction of the psychological dynamics of individual offenders (that is, obviously, individuals who have been arrested, tried and sentenced). In recent years Italian criminology has also taken account of tendencies in the criminology of other countries, largely of a sociological orientation (see, for example, the past fifteen years of the journal *Rassegna di Criminologia*). Yet what still prevails is a focus on the single individual, seen as the 'end-product' of processes and conditions which can indeed be 'social', but which are of interest predominantly to 'explain' or situate the behaviour of the single individual. This is what is meant by the term 'criminology' in the academy, in criminal justice institutions and in the media. That is to say, not only questions having to do with social control and social problems, but also those relating to, say, organized crime or terrorism, are only marginally touched by 'criminologists', who by and large still have a predominantly medical or psychological background. General and political sociologists, political scientists, historians, social psychologists and legal students have dealt with aspects of these questions.

The legacy of the rather short-lived experience of a critical criminology was taken up by law students and sociologists of law, and its contribution to established 'criminology' limited itself to the diffusion of more sociologically oriented approaches.

Critical criminology did not emerge from the ranks of academic criminology. When, in 1975, the journal *La questione criminale* was first published, its contributors were legal students, historians, cultural anthropologists, philosophers of law and sociologists, who for a time collaborated in the attempt to provide a new – to Italy – approach to the study of the 'criminal question'. This project had a strong political and ideological component. Curiously, though, it was never felt necessary to address a demistifying critique to established Italian criminology. Rather, critiques were addressed to dominant criminal policies and their underlying rationales. In fact, a few academic criminologists were later co-opted on to the journal. What that produced at the level of academic criminology was perhaps a few more sociologically oriented younger criminologists. But the protagonists remained outside the field of criminology proper.

Now, on the one hand it may be argued that, if certain topics are being studied, it does not matter whether or not they are studied under the label 'criminology'; one can still establish if the manner in which they are tackled is influenced by feminism. On the other hand, however, the existence of a recognizable body of literature, of established practices, of a network of institutions and relationships is rather more amenable to reflection and, above all, self-reflection than a widely scattered number of studies employing different methods, having different aims and lacking a network of mutual communication. To be sure, criminology is such a subject, and it is certainly possible to ascertain the influence of feminism upon it. I am of the opinion, however, that this would be of little interest, criminology being rather marginal in contemporary political and cultural debates, and not too concerned with either major general social questions or issues of interest to feminists. Naturally, there have been researches on rape, on women criminals and on women's prisons by academic criminologists, and certainly some of them may be said to have been stimulated by the interest these questions were receiving from the feminist movement; but neither their methodology nor the hypotheses they choose to test much reflect the contemporary feminist debate. Still less can feminism be said to have contributed to a major reconstruction of the discipline.

This state of affairs has another consequence. Very little empirical research has been conducted on questions of relevance to criminology by feminists.[3] Thus, we lack reliable data on most areas (rape, sentencing of offenders, prison treatment etc.). Those that exist have been gathered and discussed separately, each set within its own area of interest. The researchers did not, in general, communicate and produce feedback to each other.

For these reasons, no description of research done and data gathered is given here. There has been no impact on one discipline, and, being dispersed over many fields of study, the research cannot be reflected upon collectively as a body of literature amenable to a unitary project.

Feminism and 'social problems'

Despite what has been said above, it is quite possible to analyse how a number of 'criminological' and 'law and order' questions have been (re)framed by feminist thought and practice.

First, of course, feminism was instrumental in the construction into public problems of previously hardly debated or non-existent (in public debate and awareness) issues, namely rape, sexual harassment and family violence. The way in which these problems were constructed was significantly different not only from the way in which the related issues were studied (when they, rarely, were) by criminologists, but also from the general frame in which issues were approached by critical criminologists and, in general, by the left.

Critical criminologists, and the cultural and political left, had imported the Anglo-American notion of social control, but had ended up by eliminating its potential richness by reducing it within a dualistic framework that unduly emphasized its 'repressive' connotations. In contrast, feminism used the notion of social control as a weapon in conflict, to de-naturalize the world, make the taken for granted problematic, the obvious 'unjust'. 'Social control' was not equated with repression. Rather it came to signify those ongoing processes by which femininity was constructed, in language, sexual and social relationships and law as much as in the world of the market or of politics. The awareness that the imputation of social control was made from within a political process of self-conscious identity construction helped avoidance of falling into the trap of dualism: 'authentic' womanhood, as something which lay hidden and repressed by 'social control', was never postulated. Rather, feminism's role in the imputation process and in its consequences, namely the construction of new social problems, was usually acknowledged, and responsibility was taken for the ambivalent results this might lead to. Thus, feminists tended to view themselves, and women in general, as actors, rather than merely acted upon, and very early on rid themselves of the oppression paradigm, which they had at first used in analogy with the 'working class'.

Thus, on the one hand, a number of new questions were reframed as public problems. Some of them were reframed as mainly criminal problems (problems whose 'solution' appeared to reside in criminal justice), others as mainly social problems (problems whose 'solution' lay in social and psychological services). To be sure, feminism was a powerful instrument in this.

On the other hand, the innovative use of the notion of social control, though harder to document, may be seen to have influenced large sectors of social service workers and school teachers (both of whom are mainly women), and to have been the implicit tool of the challenge brought by many citizens' groups to the ways private and (especially) social service institutions dealt with their problems. In the first case, we may notice a widespread acknowledgement of one's control responsibilities together with the recognition of one's clients' active status. In the second case, the clients' or their relatives' (again, mainly women) refusal to be passive recipients of 'solutions' defined and managed by social service institutions shows acknowledgement of the social control side of these solutions and at the same time its use as a double-edged resource (see De Leonardis 1990; Pitch 1995).

Feminism, criminal justice and the law

The rape campaign signalled a turning point in Italian feminism and its relationships with the law and legal institutions. The earlier abortion campaign, resulting in the legalization of abortion (1978), had been conducted

– not without internal conflicts and polemics (Pitch 1992) – by consciously refraining from providing explicit reform proposals. Feminists asked for 'free, on demand and publicly subsidized' abortion. They did not draft their own law proposal, and exhibited an attitude of distance from both the parliamentary discussion and the political forces engaged in it. Preference was given to legalization rather than to simple decriminalization (which had its supporters even at the time), even though the ambivalent consequences of increased state control over the private sphere were recognized, because of two main considerations: legalization was seen as more adequate protection against the risks of a 'free abortion market', and as more clearly symbolizing the principle of women's reproductive freedom.

Two contrasting attitudes towards the law may be seen to have been coexisting in this majority feminist position. One attitude, traditional within the Italian left, saw *more* law both as a useful instrument to curb arbitrary and discretionary power and as symbolically legitimizing demands. Consistent with this attitude was the construction of reform requests as privileged terrains of struggle. Another attitude more in tune with the anti-institutional climate of the early 1970s viewed not only institutional political activities but also their main objectives and terrains of struggle, laws, with suspicion. Feminist experience and reflection gave a new turn to this suspicion. It was not so much the distrust against reform politics as such that fuelled it as the recognition of the inevitable connotations of control the extension of public intervention had.

The rape campaign appeared to adopt more clearly the first attitude (see Pitch 1985, 1995), to the abandonment of the second. The difference is that here it was a criminal law that was being requested, and therefore criminal justice that was being endorsed. Feminists drafted a law proposal and actively lobbied for it. As I have argued more extensively elsewhere (Pitch 1994), the terrain of criminal justice was exploited for its symbolic potential. In the draft proposal, and in subsequent discussions, two main principles were being forwarded, one explicitly, i.e. the construction of women as 'persons' (the existing rape law defines rape as a crime against 'morality') and one implicitly, i.e. the construction of rapists as wilful and responsible actors. The oppression paradigm definitively gave way to a victim paradigm (see also Pitch 1990). What I believe to be important in the deployment of this paradigm is that it constructs reality in terms of the interaction of conscious and wilful actors: while responsibility for the victimizing action is firmly attributed to such actors, responsibility for this attribution is assumed by the imputing actors. This entails a simplification, in that actors are constructed as merely possessing consciousness and will; and it entails a risk that the imputing actors, once they have successfully gained the recognition of their demands, will be reduced to merely 'victims'. Moreover, the interaction loses all ambivalence and takes the shape of a simple, and stark, adversarial interaction.

While, generally, the shift towards a more diffuse assumption and attribution of individual responsibility was not (and is not) contested, the notion of 'victim' and the adversarial shape of interactions came increasingly under attack. Feminist criticisms of both, already strong during the rape campaign, are even more vocal today in the context of the newly discovered problem of sexual harassment. Resistance was voiced against a specific law, advocated by feminists active in the unions,[4] on many grounds: the refusal to delegate once again to a (criminal) law the management of relationships; the necessary simplification of the issue such delegation implies; the construction of women as always and inevitably 'victims' and therefore 'weak subjects' in need of protection; and the subtle endorsement of an ever-spreading vision of sex and sexuality as dangerous, menacing and evil (see, for example, Zuffa 1993).

The two main attitudes to the law that I have described as existing within feminism have been ascribed recently to two different trends in feminism itself. The first is 'institutional', and allegedly endorsed mainly by women active in the institutions – political parties, parliament, unions, local governments – who consider the terrain of legal reforms as the privileged terrain of struggle, and law itself as an instrument of further emancipation and/or protection. To these feminists we owe, for example, the approval (1991) of the law on positive actions within the labour market, the approval (1992) of a norm establishing a fifty per cent quota of women in the lists of candidates for local and general elections, and the draft of a proposal on a global redefining of the borders between leisure, care and work times – plus the proposal of a law against sexual harassment within work situations.

The other trend contends that women's freedom has little to do with (more) law on two different, though connected, grounds: political subjectivity, they say, can neither be reflected within law nor be constructed through struggles aimed to change or gain laws; 'too much' law can be shown to be detrimental rather than helpful in the development of women's individual and collective autonomy (which, here, regains the meaning of self-production of norms) and reinforces the idea of women's constant 'secondariness' and weakness.[5]

Actually, the two camps are not so clearly separated, and cannot be distinguished empirically on the basis of working or not within 'institutions'. The growing interest in 'delegalization' (for example, in the case of abortion, where the demand for simple decriminalization is gaining support, in part because of the unintended consequences of the 1978 law;[6] but also in the case of rape, where there is a widespread feeling that though a new law is necessary, it should be as 'light' a law as possible) does not testify to an abandonment of the terrain of law, especially as far as the symbolic potential of law is concerned,[7] but rather to a different idea of which political practices are more conducive to 'women's freedom' (see, on all these questions, Pitch et al. 1993).

The existence of women's institutions and practices that exhibit considerable flexibility in their use of laws and in their relationships with state institutions must also be noted. These not only must be an object of study and reflection but are themselves engaged in a process of self-study and self-reflection. An example is the anti-violence 'homes', now present in many cities, which are partly financed by local governments but totally autonomous in their guidelines and mode of operation. They appear to engage in relationships with public agencies – social services, juvenile and adult courts, psychiatric services, police – which produce innovations in the latter. Women working in the homes – some are paid, most are voluntary – explicitly acknowledge their control function and authoritative role *vis-à-vis* their women clients, and try to use it as a resource to help them make an autonomous decision about their lives.[8] A fundamental part of their work is reflection on their own practices. They are also gathering material on the cases they deal with.

Sexual difference and criminal justice

I shall describe here in more detail what I think are the major theoretical insights that were produced through feminist politics and by feminist self-reflection on these politics and their results.

To be sure, the 'maleness' of criminal justice, both at the level of the penal code (Virgilio 1987) and at that of actual court proceedings and sentencing (especially in cases of rape and domestic violence), was one of the first 'discoveries' of feminism. The maleness of the penal code was seen to reside not only in the interests and rights being protected, nor only in the way certain crimes are defined, but rather in an overall discourse whereby gender appears, and is relevant, only in reference to women. Gender, then, is something that applies to women and, specifically, characterizes them in that it is a determinant of their condition. Juridical 'persons' are 'neutral'; then there are gendered beings and these are women, who, therefore, are not really 'persons'. This is a familiar critique of legal discourse, which has given way to an ample debate on the opportunity, feasibility, modalities and consequences of strategies geared to 'gendering the law'. Much of this debate may be subsumed under the equality versus difference controversy.

In Italy, however, this critique was elaborated in a context characterized by a particular interpretation of sexual difference and sexual difference politics. Sexual difference was interpreted not as a given but rather as a politics of construction and assertion of a female subjectivity. The site of this politics was indicated in dual relationships characterized by the practice of 'entrustment'.[9] I shall not analyse here the various implications of this practice, which has been widely discussed from both a political and a philosophical point of view (see, instead, Libreria delle donne di Milano, 1983; De Lauretis, 1991). Suffice it to say that it implied the construction of asymmetrical relationships, one woman 'entrusting' herself to another who was thereby recognized as in possession of qualities, capacities or professional abilities desired by or useful to the first. In the context of criminal justice, it came to mean the construction of 'meaningful relationships' between women clients, women lawyers and women judges in court proceedings. The symbolic appearance of a female subjectivity within criminal justice was thus entrusted to this practice, and its consequences in court, rather than to projects designed to change legal norms and procedures.

Whatever its real impact, this notion of sexual difference has two consequences at the level of theory. First, it connects indissolubly penal norms with criminal proceedings, inverting the hierarchy of relevance usually assumed by critical legal students, at least in Italy. The symbolic potential of criminal justice can thus be assessed not just at the point where norms are produced, but at the point where they are enacted. But this has an implication which is also political: the letter of norms is not that important; criminal proceedings may be used 'alternatively', bent to signify something other than what appears to be prescribed.

Second, it signals the appearance on the scene of criminal justice of a new and unexpected subject. The standard subject of criminal *law* is an abstract subject only connoted by the capacity 'to understand and want', as the Italian law recites. Exceptions are minors and mentally handicapped persons and, to a certain extent, women, whose capacity to understand and want is undermined, determined, by age, illness and gender. In criminal *proceedings*, however, what makes everyone what he or she is reappears – age, even if adult, social and economic condition, profession or lack thereof, ethnic and cultural background. They reappear as what determines and undermines one's capacity to understand and want, and lead to different attitudes on the part of judges, different sentences and different ways in which punishments are enacted.

The appearance of an explicitly gendered subject on this scene is potentially very innovative: exceptions reveal themselves as the rule, one's singular characteristics – what makes one what one is – are nominated not as simply 'determinations' subtracting from one's 'freedom' (the capacity to understand and want), but precisely as what is constitutive of individuality and subjectivity. Potentially, then, a sexual difference discourse opens up avenues for rethinking both the way criminal law constructs its standard subject and the way in which criminal justice concretely operates, differentiating between formally equal subjects by taking account of differences only as what undermine one's freedom. It could open up avenues for bridging the gap between formal equality and substantial inequality without undermining – but reinstating – the legal safeguards that ought to inform both criminal norms and criminal procedures (and sentence execution), precisely because it introduces a standard subject who is neither neutral nor abstract, and whose 'freedom' should be viewed as deriving from – rather than being undermined by – what he or she is.

Such a view is already being tested in the context of our latest penitentiary reform law (1986). This reform introduces or extends a number of benefits to well-behaved prisoners, such as leaves, work outside the prison, partial freedom and early release. In short, the reform introduces flexible sentences in our system, contravening the principle of certainty of the law and expanding the discretionary power not only of judges of execution, but also of administrative personnel. On the other hand, it does soften prison regimes and offer 'hope' to prisoners.

The reform is structurally ambivalent. On the one hand it legitimates its innovations as tools of the 're-education' that our Constitution poses as the aim of 'punishment', and on the other hand it conceives of them not as rights of each prisoner, but rather as privileges to be granted on the basis of 'successful participation in the re-education project'. This concretely means good prison behaviour and the possession of a series of characteristics – both personal and social – that make you, in the eyes of prison personnel and judges of the execution, trustworthy (see the data in Mosconi and Pavarini 1993).

This is evident not only in respect of how gender works, but also, specifically, in the case of women prisoners (see Campelli *et al.* 1993). A virtuous circle was shown to exist between being given access to the (very few) prison resources (work, educational courses) and being granted leaves, early releases etc. Access to prison resources was mostly given to women deemed trustworthy, and in turn trust was given to older women without a history of drug addiction[10] and with more stable and predictable links outside the prison.

What this amounts to is that another selective process adds itself to the selective processes operating at the level of the criminal code (which, or perhaps whose, goods, rights and interests are protected), at the level of criminal justice agencies (who is denounced, arrested and brought to court and for which crimes) and at the level of criminal proceedings (who is sentenced, for which crimes and for how long). This selective process does differentiate on the basis of what one is, but on a discretionary basis, attributing to personal and social characteristics a determining influence (it matters not whether interpreted favourably or otherwise). This would be true even if the reform law were implemented 'correctly', i.e. even if it were possible to link the concession of benefits to a 'successful re-education'.

A 'sexual difference' approach would lead to a different interpretation of the penitentiary law. It would emphasize its 'rights' side, down-playing the stress on 're-education' and the link between re-education and concession of benefits. If what one is does not determine what one does and will do, but is only the context of one's action, then leaves of absence, permission to work outside etc. should be considered rights of each prisoner that personnel inside and outside the prison should strive to implement, by working with the prisoner to use and augment the resources – relational, social, economic – of that context itself. Similar critiques of the penitentiary reform law have come from legal students and critical criminologists (Ferrajoli 1989; Mosconi and Pavarini 1993). Legal students have directed their critiques especially towards those aspects which blatantly contradict the principles and safeguards of criminal justice; critical criminologists have shown the way the law actually works and the ample discretionary powers it gives to administrative personnel. A 'sexual difference' approach takes on board both preoccupations, balances them with the desires and interests of prisoners, who are outspokenly in favour of the law, and explores the concrete avenues for an extensive implementation geared to achieve a 'complex' equality. The equality claimed by the legal theorists critical of the law means only the recognition and respect of individual differences: it is on this basis that 're-education' ideas are rejected. Flexible sentences, moreover, produce inequality in punishment. The relationship between the two is, from this point of view, doubly suspect.

However, if we transform benefits into rights and turn individual differences into potential resources – rather than 'determinations' or, vice versa, 'identities' that must be simply 'respected' (i.e. not be tampered with) – 're-education' could be interpreted as the right of each prisoner to have her life project taken seriously and to obtain help in having it implemented outside the prison. This could appear a rather small achievement, if not in practice, then from a theoretical point of view. But a strong feature of a 'sexual difference' approach is the methodological and structural link between practice and theory. And a practice informed by the ideas I have delineated would be revolutionary in the Italian context, and would surely produce new theoretical insights.[11]

A much more complicated issue from a sexual difference perspective is whether and how to deal with the penal code. On the one hand the overall package and hierarchy of goods and interests protected by criminal law may be seen to be extremely important at the symbolic level, as it may be conceived as the result of a 'pact' among citizens regarding what they deem to be universally worth being protected by criminal law. If we assume two differently gendered subjectivities, we might want a penal code that reflects this difference, both in the type of offences it sanctions and in the way they are defined. We might argue that it would not be enough to 'neutralize' the norms by ridding criminal texts of reference to 'homunculi' of whatever sort (for example, the assumption of a 'good father of family'; on this, see Fiandaca 1991), insofar as type of offences, and their hierarchy, reflected only the point of view of a male subject.

In a way, the politics of those women engaged in the attempt to change abortion, rape and sexual harassment norms might be interpreted as a rewriting of the penal code to accommodate the point of view of the female gender. However, even if we acknowledged the possibility and opportunity of translating the point of view of the 'female gender' into the penal code – which I would disagree with, women not being conceivable as a social group with identifiable common interests and needs – this would neither 'gender' criminal law nor make a noticeable impact in the language and logic of criminal law. If we take the two main criminalizing requests so far, rape and sexual harassment, we see that they merely add two new crimes to the list, whose victims are mainly women. Apparently, the point of view of women regarding important spheres of life is assumed by criminal law.[12] Yet when this point of view is translated into norms it becomes neutralized. These crimes lose their gendered characteristic (rape even loses its sexual one): they become crimes imputable by anyone against anyone.[13] The addition does not subvert the hierachy of goods to be protected; nor does it make an impact on the language and logic of criminal law. It could be argued that it reinforces its legitimacy. Neither, I think, could we easily circumvent this problem by merely explicitly gendering authors and victims, as, after all, the neutrality of the standard subject of law is, in criminal justice, a fundamental safeguard against a discriminatory and discretionary use of the power to limit people's freedom.

Norms, however, are messages whose meaning may change, just as their application may change. Thus, I would renounce, at least for the time being, the project of rewriting the penal code, or even that of introducing new norms in it, and would delegate both the question of a new 'pact' and that of 'gendering law' to the 'entrusting' practices in court proceedings that have been described. It is really only within court proceedings that the meaning of norms and the way they are used and applied – including how important they are assumed to be in the hierarchy of goods protected by criminal law – may be tackled from a 'sexual difference' point of view, by endeavouring to let a gendered subjectivity emerge in such a way that gender is not taken to be only a specification of the female sex, or merely one of the many *determining* variables of one's actions.

In contrast, the decriminalization of abortion assumes a different meaning, because it affirms that in this area the state cannot legislate. The existence of two differently gendered subjects would be here acknowledged by a recognition that all that has to do with procreation pertains to individual women's sphere of sovereignty.

The construction of social problems: the impact of feminism?

The women's movement was certainly instrumental in the problematization of the so-called private sphere. Personal and intimate relationships became an object of scrutiny and an issue of public debate and intervention. Intra-family violence became an object of investigation, child abuse assumed the status of a public problem and became the object of a fully fledged symbolic crusade. But I would like more generally to relate feminist practices and experiences to two tendencies visible in the Italian contemporary culture of public problems. Both relate to method rather than content, though content is all but irrelevant.

In the 1980s a new phenomenon became visible in Italy: the activism of groups of 'citizens', associating on the basis of their perception of having suffered a personal wrong which they thought required public recognition and public redress. What was new was that these citizens acted personally, refusing both delegation to and affiliation with traditional political parties; that they claimed legitimation for this activism as *private* citizens, members of families (mothers, fathers, relatives etc.), whose personal grievance had gained or must gain general significance. These groups are many and diverse in composition, type of grievance, modes of action and institutions they engage with (see Pitch 1994). Most, especially at the beginning, were led by, and mainly composed of, women. I refer to groups such as the so-called Mothers Courage of Naples, active on the question of heroin addiction of their children, who, similarly to analogous groups of 'mothers' in other cities, set up help activities, drove pushers (for a time) out of their neighbourhoods and at the same time campaigned for a more repressive drug law. Other groups included relatives of victims of terrorism, relatives of mental patients, relatives of victims of the Mafia and women against organized crime (see Turnaturi 1991). There are various connections between these types of groups and feminism. The first, more obvious one, is the prevalence of women in all of them, testifying to a diffuse women's protagonism, a diffuse feeling both of women's strength and women's desire to take charge and become visible, unthinkable in preceding years. To be sure, these women usually act not as women, but, more traditionally, as mothers, wives or sisters. Yet they interpret this traditional role in a totally untraditional way, in that they act as individuals, as 'citizens' whose rights have been wronged, rather than as representatives of 'families'. Another connection may be traced in the culture of 'starting from oneself' that they express. Certainly this was (and is) among the more significant traits of feminist political culture: one should start from and keep close to one's individual experience, at the same time searching for its universalizing aspects while not sacrificing its individual, differentiating ones.

The second tendency is the increasing recourse to criminal justice to formulate problems and voice requests. In a way, this tendency is present within the first. Criminal justice may be one, or the main, institution addressed by citizens' groups. The appeal of criminal justice is three-fold: it translates individual or collective grievances into universal ones; it translates grievances into wrongs imputable to identifiable actors; it legitimizes the collective protagonism of those who name the grievances. However, once grievances are translated into crimes, the grievances' namers are re-translated from actors into victims and the grievances themselves are reduced and rigidified within the language and logic of criminal justice. This, as I have already said, may be seen to have happened with women.

There is a third consequence: because one delegates to criminal justice the legitimation of one's status as actor, when a request has been accepted and that status has been turned into that of victim, one may be compelled to turn yet again to criminal justice with another grievance in order to regain actor status. To use a metaphor that Resta (1992) has used to interpret law, criminal justice may be seen as working as a *pharmakon*, that is as at the same time poison and cure, cure of its own poison. This leads to a multiplication of questions being translated into criminal problems. We might read in this way the emergence of the sexual harassment issue within feminism, after the rape campaign. But we might also read in this vein the adversarial turn the campaign against child abuse took in the 1980s in Italy, the way in which many environmental issues have been voiced and, last but not least, the delegation of politics to the criminal courts, which brought about the demise of an entire political class and the regime it had instituted.[14]

The two tendencies coexist, sometimes within the same struggles, and both are visible and present within feminism. They have in common the desire to be and be recognized as protagonists – full status citizens – but whereas the first goes in the direction of keeping the problem near to those who voice it and leads to an ongoing engagement with it, which transforms both the problem and those who voice it (De Leonardis 1990; Turnaturi 1991), the second separates the problem from its advocates and turns them, perversely, into passive victims, which leads to a renewed recourse to criminal justice, in a spiralling way.

It would certainly be inappropriate to impute all this to feminism. All the same, I am convinced that feminism was a factor in this process, at the same time that, paradoxically, it offered perhaps the best tools to understand and criticize it.[15]

Feminism and the Mafia

I shall explore the influence of feminism on the phenomenon of organized crime from two connected sides: on the one hand, the emergence of women's voices and women's groups against the Mafia; on the other hand, the reflections this emergence gave rise to, which have stimulated new ways to look at the phenomenon itself.

There have been a few cases of individual women rising against the Mafia before (Levi 1979; Pegna 1992; Siebert 1994): mothers of men assassinated by Mafiosi, fighting (usually in vain) to obtain justice from the state, outspokenly indicating complicities, sometimes engaging in the types of activities that had led to the assassination of their relatives. But in recent years two different phenomena have emerged. The first is apparently more in continuity with the past: relatives of Mafia victims – wives, mothers, sisters – form networks, communicate with and help each other, and organize themselves to transform their private suffering into a public and political issue, by speaking in public meetings and on TV, by working with and sometimes against police and judges, by being present and vigilant in trials etc. After the assassination of Judge Falcone and his police guards (1992), this process increased and accelerated. During the solemn official funeral in Palermo Cathedral, the ritual was shockingly subverted by Rosaria Schifani, the young wife of one of the policemen assassinated. She was to recite a prepared text. She couldn't. On national TV (the funerals were broadcast), her voice rose to accuse: 'Because here too there are Mafiosi . . . I forgive you, but you must kneel down . . . But they do not want to change, they do not change . . . too much blood, there is no love here, there is no love here, there is no love at all' (quoted in Siebert 1994: 274).[16] Rosaria's story is in a way emblematic of the process I have indicated. Before her husband's assassination, she was just a 'normal' girl. She married early, and her first vacation was her honeymoon. She was pregnant when her husband was killed. But after that, she changed. She wanted to understand and she wanted to fight. In a few months, she became an expert on the Mafia. She went to other relatives of Mafia victims, asked questions, wondered with them what she, and they, could concretely do (Schifani and Cavallaro 1992). She, and others like her and with her, are an expression of what has been termed 'moral familism' (Turnaturi and Donolo 1988): family members, deeply touched in their most intimate affections, act as *individuals* who, in the name of a family tie, of an offended and violated love, fight for justice, fight for their injury to be recognized as a universal one. Not unlike women in the early women's groups, there is here a process of moral growing that gives way to new forms of political presence.

The second phenomenon is more directly related to feminism and the women's movement. It is the emergence, in Sicily and Calabria, of women's groups against the Mafia, women who organize themselves as women to engage in a struggle to change the culture and social relationships within which the Mafia thrives, and which the Mafia deeply conditions. On the one hand, the emergence of these groups is a symptom of a more diffuse rebellion by sectors of civil society, especially in urban Sicily.[17] On the other hand, though, these groups are something more, both because their anti-Mafia activism is undertaken within a more profound and general engagement with the deep structures of southern Italian culture and society, traditionally inimical to women's freedom, and because, complementarily, they signify the assumption of responsibility of southern women towards their own transformation into individuals. As the Mafia, as we shall see, both uses and distorts traditional family relationships, based on specific and rigid roles for women, women's organized activism and challenge is doubly subversive (Cascio and Puglisi 1986a,b; Puglisi 1990; Crisantino 1991; Bertuglia 1993; Bonavita 1993; Fondazione Marisa Bellisario 1993; Lanza, 1993).

Women's new protagonism, women's political activism and more generally women's increased visibility are at the roots of the recent interest in the relationships between women and the Mafia. This interest takes three main directions: the life of women of the Mafia and their role and attitudes; the enquiry into women who, for one reason or another, fight the Mafia or break with it; and analyses of the Mafia from a feminist point of view. Three other recent developments may be seen to be behind this flurry of studies of women and the Mafia. The first is the acknowledgement, on the part of judges, but also of those Mafiosi who decided to collaborate with them, of the influence of wives in this decision (Arlacchi 1992; Madeo 1994). The second is the increased number of female relatives of Mafiosi who break with the Mafia, denouncing the killers of their husbands, brothers and sons (De Stefani 1991; Montemagno 1992). The third is the changing role of women in the Mafia itself, their increasing direct involvement in its economic affairs (Pino 1988).

A recent book tries to tackle all these questions together (Siebert 1994). Renate Siebert, born in Germany, has for a long time taught sociology at Calabria University. Her interest in southern Italian life and especially southern Italian women had already led her to publish a book on the processes of persistence and change in southern women's lives and attitudes.

For her exploration of the Mafia she explicitly – and repeatedly – chooses the situatedness of a woman's point of view. From this vantage point she looks at the culture and organization of the Mafia, at women's role in it, at the way women are organizing against it. I shall here give a brief account of her main points on the first two issues.

The Mafia, she says, is an obsessively masculinist organization. Initiation rites, leisure activities such as hunting and constant reference to a violent and bloody mythology reveal and reinforce its reliance on strong male bonding. Although she doesn't equate masculinist identity with Mafioso identity, she claims that the latter stresses elements of the former. Her hypothesis is that the Mafia can be seen as offering a 'mistaken' answer to the fragility of the male condition. She sees this fragility as structural, having to do with the male anxiety of confronting the dilemma of whether to accept their feminine aspects. Siebert insists on the 'radical ambivalence' typical of this male bonding towards all that is female.

The Mafiosi's brotherhood emerges and is perceived as a revolt against the 'law of the father': historically, the barons' and big landowners' power; today, the state's. At the same time, it adopts and internalizes its very culture, its arrogance, its violence. The 'law of the father' is then assumed by the Mafiosi as their own law. Siebert argues that the object for whose possession and defence the brotherhood was created is the mother, who symbolizes the possession of the land. The mother is fantasized as all that is good, and must be preserved from external attacks. Thus an exclusively male group, kept together (also) by an emphasis on aspects of the male identity revealing fear and scorn towards all that is female, at the same time unites in the name of the defence of the mother.

The same ambivalence is shown to exist towards the family. On the one hand, the Mafia rests on family networks, and the family offers the organizing model of its criminal activities and its legitimating ideology. Yet family networks and family feelings are manipulated and instrumentally used to the point of being sacrificed to the superior interests of the organization. At the moment of joining the Mafia, the new member promises to put the interests of the Family above those of the family even if that requires killing one's own closest relatives. The Mafia poses, on the outside, as a defender of traditional family values, but inside these values are used instrumentally and cynically. Family ties are used to increase the power of the organization, often through matrimonial strategies. Alliances are created through marriages, whereby women's role appears as central. Women are, in these strategies, a fundamental exchange commodity. The influence of

the Family on the family can be shown in the actual disruption of traditional southern family relationships. In the south, though women were
formally powerless, they had *de facto* great power within the family. But
in the Mafioso family, women are denied this power at the same time that
they are denied access to the formal equality of the bourgeois family.

Siebert stresses the gap between appearance and reality, however. A
rigid normative formalism prevails in the Mafia, especially concerning the
rules regulating family relationships, which can be shown to reveal the
distance between the traditional patriarchal family the model stresses and
a much more complex and troublesome reality. Siebert argues not only
that the difference between the family and the Family has been overlooked
by students of the Mafia, but that this has led them to miss the strains and
tensions which occur between the two. After all, whereas the family is
based on heterosexual relationships, the Family is based on strictly homo-
social bonds. Here, Siebert thinks, lies a line of stress as yet insufficiently
explored.

How are women perceived, and what is supposed to be their role in the
Mafioso culture? Women, who are excluded from even the knowledge of
criminal activities, none the less play a central role, not only as exchange
commodities in matrimonial strategies, but as producers of sons (it is
mainly as 'mothers' that women are extolled) and custodians of the Mafiosi's 'honour'. Mafia's mythology stresses women as the men's cherished
and protected possession, and at the same time prescribes scorn, spite and
often violence towards outside women and one's own misbehaving women.
Siebert stresses the Mafioso's diffidence towards women, his own included.
It is this diffidence, she claims, that explains their exclusion from criminal
activities and the rule prescribing their very ignorance of them, rather than
a lack of emancipation on their part. Women cannot be trusted: their
knowledge not only could be dangerous for them (that is the main reason
given by Mafiosi for the existence of this rule), but could give them a
power they might exercise to the detriment of the men's.

Siebert then explores how women actually live and perceive themselves
in the Mafia context. We know very little of them: those still inside do not
talk, those who split, usually because their sons or husbands have been
killed, tell only of their rage and their desire for revenge. From court
proceedings, interviews and confessions Siebert draws the hypothesis that
Mafia women oscillate between distance and complicity. Mafia women are
at the same time deprived of individual rights, subordinated to their men,
and granted not only material rewards but also symbolic recognition as
women of powerful men.

Siebert stresses women's complicity. Notwithstanding the rule, she claims,
women know a lot of their men's affairs. Not only that: as these affairs
become larger and more complicated, they increasingly assume an active
role, acting as mediators, keepers of communication networks, especially
when their men are held in prison, and figureheads to whom different
possessions are entrusted. Siebert claims that the judges' culture colludes

with Mafia ideology when Mafia women are discharged or even not pro-
secuted on the grounds of women's traditional exclusion from the men's
criminal activities. This, she says, may become a useful screen behind
which women may hide, sometimes even to themselves, their actual responsibility and concrete complicity in Mafia affairs.

Women are often the weak link in the Mafia. Precisely because they do
know, precisely because they often do participate in their men's activities,
they become dangerous when they want out. Many women have been
recently killed for this very reason. And they may want out because their
desire for a 'normal' life is stronger than their men's, because their attach-
ment to their sons and husbands proves stronger than fear or loyalty to the
Family and its values.[18] The line of stress between the family and the
Family is thus walked over by Mafia women, and this line deepens as both
families change and their distance increases.

I have referred at some length to this book because, though it is not the
only recent study exploring the link between women and the Mafia (see,
for example, Fiume 1990), it is the first attempt to bring together different
reflections on the Mafia from the standpoint of a woman. It focuses on
rarely and unsystematically studied aspects of this peculiar phenomenon of
organized crime, and has the merit of indicating the usefulness of exploring more fully women's role in it, as women may prove to be a disruptive
element, both of its sustaining ideology and of its organization. The presence of women's groups against the Mafia, in the same territory governed
by the Mafia, testifies to and intensifies profound changes in the general
culture and social texture in which the Mafia has its roots, and offers
stronger female models than the traditional emancipatory ones to women
in the Mafia themselves. The drive towards 'individuation' – the process
of becoming an individual – which leads women to assume responsibility
as women towards their own life, symbolized by Rosaria Schifani and
many others like her, cannot be not felt by women in the Mafia. And
individuation is dangerous to the present Mafia ideology and organization.

Conclusion

An Italian feminist criminology does not exist. But I hope I have indicated
how the women's movement and feminist practices and theories may be
seen to have influenced both the actual shape of social problems and
studies concerning some of them.

As I have always had serious doubts about the viability of criminology
as a distinct discipline, its present non-status within Italian feminist studies
does not worry me; nor am I unduly concerned by the lack of interest of
feminists in the criminology that does exist, since this criminology is scarcely
present in public debate and uninfluential on major policy decisions. Women,
however, and many of them are feminist, are increasingly dealing with and
reflecting on questions dealing with social control, law and criminal justice,
urban security (see the journal *Sicurezza e territorio*[19]) and organized crime.

What we may be missing is a site, such as a field of studies could furnish, where these reflections could be linked together and confronted. Criminology cannot be it. Present political practices and experiences, though fragmented, possibly converge on such a field as 'law and social problems'. The new political scene may indeed require intensified action and reflection on this theme, to contrast successfully with the initiatives the new government will no doubt attempt to take.

Notes

1 There is a growing historical literature exploring the relationships between women and the law, including criminal law, from a feminist point of view (see, for example, Graziosi 1993; Calvi 1994; Groppi 1994).

2 If, until the 1970s, and again during the 1980s, (criminal) justice and criminal justice questions have been 'used' as tools in political battles and as instruments to gain political consensus, now politics has been defeated and replaced by (criminal) justice. An entire regime has collapsed under the counter-corruption activities of criminal judges. But more ominous is that the language of politics has been replaced by the language of justice.

3 See, among them, Campelli et al. (1993) on women in prison and Ventimiglia (1987) on reported rapes and (1991) on sexual harassment.

4 The first research on sexual harassment was commissioned by the Modena CGIL (General Confederation of Italian Workers, a large left-wing union) (see Ventimiglia 1991).

5 The limited impact of the law on positive action is, for example, imputed by these feminists to the little use women have made of it, which, they contend, cannot be attributed to ignorance, but rather to lack of interest and implicit resistance to constructing themselves as 'weak' and in need of it. On the other hand, many men have made use of it.

6 The relative difficulty, especially in certain regions, of obtaining legal abortions, which can be had only in state or state-subsidized hospitals where most doctors plead conscientious objection, is one. Another is the constant danger of a restriction of legal abortion, if an anti-abortion majority was to be present in Parliament. Many anti-abortion forces argue against a state pronouncement of the legality of abortion. They would probably not contest simple decriminalization. In the demand for decriminalization strong symbolic components are also present, namely the idea that an abortion law subjects women's decision to the scrutiny and approval of 'society', rather than recognizing their full autonomy on procreation matters. On this, see Boccia (1990) and Cavarero (1992).

7 It is precisely among those feminists demanding less law that discussion and reflection are growing about changing some principles of our supreme law, the Constitution.

8 A woman's recognition of another woman's authority (in the sense of 'authoritativeness') – more generally of a legitimated and explicitly acknowledged female authority – is seen as a step towards conferring value on oneself as a woman (see also note 9). Acknowledgement of one's control functions, on the other hand, is fundamental in that it makes them explicit, a terrain of conflict and negotiation with 'clients' who are thereby constructed as potential actors, rather than passive recipients of pre-prepared recipes for their future well-being.

9 Recently, this practice was said by one of its theorists, lawyer Lia Cigarini, to have been originated precisely through the particular relationships between lawyers and clients (see Cigarini 1992, 1993). Relationships between psychoanalysts and patients have similar characteristics. The important elements here, from a political point of view, are the acknowledgement by one woman of another's authority and competence in a particular field and the use of these to gain whatever the first desires. 'Disparity' and 'putting another woman between me and the world' are the two key concepts.

10 Over 70 per cent of women prisoners were found to be addicts and to have been convicted for crimes directly related to addiction (Campelli *et al.* 1993).

11 When we argue in the context of women prisoners, we may be much more radical and specific. Most women (more than men) nowadays enter prison for drug-related offences: an abolitionist policy would reduce their number by 70–80 per cent. They are young, get sentences up to three years, come and go from the prison. Even without decriminalization, most of them, if the reform law operated along the principles I described above, could spend their sentences outside the prison.

12 Here, for simplicity, I leave out the problem of what 'women' means, as of course 'feminists' does not mean 'women', and self-acknowledged feminists are by no means in accord about these requests.

13 I leave out other important issues, such as the opportunity, from a political and cultural point of view, to present ourselves as victims, or even worse the opportunity to make recourse to criminal justice in order to voice and define social and political issues. I shall return to this problem.

14 With its corollary: the contempt towards politics and especially party politics as such, and the victory of a right-wing coalition led by a TV tycoon, which called for 'honesty', 'novelty' and 'entrepreneurship', and in a well intentioned way, tried to put a stop to the judges' dangerous activism by devising measures to limit the independence of public prosecutors.

15 It must be noted that many feminists not only were very critical of the use of criminal justice in the case of rape and in that of sexual harassment (Campari and Cigarini 1989; Dominijanni 1992; Zuffa 1993), but have been among the few cautioning against the wholehearted endorsement on the part of the left of the so-called 'political revolution' brought on by the judges' onslaught on political and administrative corruption.

16 Incidentally, some detained Mafiosi watching her on prison TV later claimed to have decided to collaborate with the judges because they were moved by her.

17 Of which women are anyway in the forefront. After Falcone's assassination a 'sheets committee' was organized in Palermo thanks to the initiative of a few women, which inaugurated a new form of showing the city's revolt against the Mafia by hanging white sheets outside windows and balconies (Alajmo 1993).

18 Liliana Madeo (1994), a journalist, draws a few portraits of women in the Mafia, and reaches the same conclusions.

19 This is a new terrain for Italy, but potentially very interesting, as it could offer the possibility of linking together different strains of experience and study, such as those of the anti-violence women's homes, prostitution, the criminalization of immigrants and gypsies, women's fear of crime etc.

References

Alajmo, R. (1993). *Un lenzuolo contro la mafia*. Palermo: Gelka.
Arlacchi, P. (1992). *Gli uomini del disonore*. Milan: Mondadori.

Bertuglia, S. (1993). *Le digiune*, video. Palermo: Zizzania.
Boccia, M.L. (1990). Aborto, pensando l'esperienza. In Coordinamento Nazionale Donne per i Consultori *Storie, menti e sentimenti di donne di fronte all'aborto*. Rome: Eliograf.
Bonavita, P. (1993). *Donna Sicilia*. Pfaffenweiller: Centaurus.
Calvi, G. (1994). *Il contratto sessuale. Madri e figli nella Toscana moderna*. Bari: Laterza.
Campari, M. and Cigarini, L. (1989). Fonti e principi di un nuovo diritto. In Libreria delle donne di Milano *Un filo di felicità, Sottosopra*, January.
Campelli, E., Faccioli, F., Giordano, V. and Pitch, T. (1993). *Donne in carcere*. Milan: Feltrinelli.
Cascio, A. and Puglisi, A. (eds) (1986a). *Con e contro. Le donne nell'organizzazione mafiosa e nella lotta antimafia*. Dossier 4, CSD, Palermo.
Cascio, A. and Puglisi, A. (1986b). Intervista a Maria Benigno, Centro Siciliano di Documentazione 'Giuseppe Impastato', unpublished manuscript.
Cavarero, A. (1992). Sovrane. *Via Dogana*, 5.
Cigarini, L. (1992). Sopra la legge. *Via Dogana*, 5, 3–4.
Cigarini, L. (1993). Libertà femminile e norma, in Pitch *et al*. Diritto sessuato? *Democrazia e diritto*, 2–3, 95–8.
Crisantino, A. (1991). *La città spugna*. Palermo: Centro siciliano di documentazione 'Giuseppe Impastato'.
Davis, J. (1989). *Conflict and Control. Law and Order in 19th Century Italy*. London: Macmillan.
De Lauretis, T. (ed.) (1991). *Libreria delle donne di Milano, Sexual Difference. A Theory of Social Symbolic Practice*. Bloomington: University of Indiana Press.
De Leonardis, O. (1990). *Il terzo escluso*. Milan: Feltrinelli.
De Stefani, L. (1991). *La mafia alle mie spalle*. Milan: Mondadori.
Dominijanni, I. (1992). Un progetto di legge si aggira da tredici anni. *Via Dogana*, 5 and 6, 14–16.
Ferrajoli, L. (1989). *Diritto e ragione*. Bari: Laterza.
Fiandaca, G. (1991). Concezioni e modelli di diritto penale tra legislazione, prassi giudiziaria e dottrina. *Questione giustizia*, 1, 35–43.
Fiume, G. (1990). Ci sono donne nella mafia? *Meridiana*, 7–8, 293–302.
Fondazione Marisa Bellisario (1993). *Donne e mafia: dentro, contro, fuori*. Palermo: Premio Marisa Bellisario.
Graziosi, M. (1993). Infirmitas sexus. La donna nell'immaginario penalistico. *Democrazia e diritto*, 2–3, 99–143.
Groppi, A. (1994). *I conservatori della virtù. Donne recluse nella Roma dei Papi*. Bari: Laterza.
Lanza, A. (1993). Visibilità e invisibilità delle donne del digiuno. *Nosside*, 7–8.
Levi, C. (1979). *Le parole sono pietre*. Turin: Einaudi.
Libreria delle donne di Milano (1983). Più donne che uomini. *Sottosopra* (special issue).
Madeo, L. (1994). *Donne di mafia*. Milan: Mondadori.
Montemagno, G. (1992). *Il sogno spezzato di Rita Atria*. Palermo: Edizioni della Battaglia.
Mosconi, G. and Pavarini, M. (1993). *Flessibilità della pena in fase esecutiva e potere discrezionale. Sentencing penitenziario: 1986–1990*. Associazione CRS, Centro di studi e iniziative per la riforma dello Stato.
Pegna, V. (1992). *Tempo di lupi e di comunisti*. Palermo: La Luna.
Pino, M. (1988). *Le signore della droga*. Palermo: La Luna.
Pitch, T. (1985). Critical criminology, the construction of social problems and the question of rape. *The International Journal of the Sociology of Law*, 13, 35–46.

Pitch, T. (1990). From oppressed to victims. In A. Sarat and S. Silbey (eds) *Studies in Law, Politics and Society, vol. 10.* JAI Press.

Pitch, T. (1992). Decriminalization or Legalization? The Abortion Debate in Italy. in C. Feinman (ed.) *The Criminalization of a Woman's Body.* New York: The Haworth Press.

Pitch, T. (1994). *Limited Responsibilities.* London: Routledge.

Pitch, T. *et al.* (1993). Diritto sessuato? *Democrazia e diritto,* 2–3 (special issue).

Puglisi, A. (1990). *Sole contro la mafia.* Palermo: La Luna.

Resta, E. (1992). *La certezza e la speranza* Bari: Laterza.

Schifani, R. and Cavallaro, F. (1992). *Lettera ai mafiosi – vi perdono ma inginoc-chiatevi.* Naples: Pironti.

Siebert, R. (1994). *Le donne, la mafia.* Milan: Il Saggiatore.

Turnaturi, G. (1991). *Associati per amore.* Milan: Feltrinelli.

Turnaturi, G. and Donolo, C. (1988). Familismi Morali. In C. Donolo and F. Fichera (eds) *Le vie dell'innovazione.* Milan: Feltrinelli.

Ventimiglia, C. (1987). *La differenza negata.* Milan: Franco Angeli.

Ventimiglia, C. (1991). *Donna delle mie brame.* Milan: Franco Angeli.

Virgilio, M. (1987). La donna nel Codice Rocco. In T. Pitch (ed.) *Diritto e Rovescio.* Naples: ESI.

Zuffa, G. (1993). L'insidia della moralità sessuale 'per legge'. *Democrazia e diritto,* 2–3. 225–30.

6

The place and status of feminist criminology in Germany, Denmark, Norway and Finland

MARIE-ANDRÉE BERTRAND

Introduction

One part of this chapter is a personal account of what I have seen and heard concerning the place of feminist criminology in four countries of Northern Europe from March 1993 to September 1994. That is the outsider's view. Another part comes from indigenous sources: women teaching in universities in these four countries have kindly responded to my request for inside information on the status of feminist theory in criminology and related fields in their own country. That is the insiders' view.

The outsider's account has its limitations. It is based on *ex post* notes: my reason for staying in Northern European universities was not to study the state of feminist criminology in Europe; it was to enhance my grasp of epistemologies and sociologies of law and social control and to allow me to gather data for a comparative study on women's prisons in Northern Europe.[1] In that last task, however, I needed the help of local colleagues known for their work on women and penal control, feminists and pro-feminists who were kind enough to bring me into their circle. Hence, part of my work abroad was connected with the question of feminism and feminist theory. Another limitation comes from the fact that my account is a picture taken at a particular point in time in the life of university centres of criminology and lacks historical and contextual perspective. Finally, my report is limited to four of the Northern European countries; it does not cover Sweden, where, I am told, there is a good number of students interested in criminology, or the Netherlands or Belgium, which has four departments of criminology. In that case, however, the long history of very close links between the Montreal and Belgian schools of criminology allows me to say that feminist criminology is absent from Belgium's criminology curriculum and research programmes.

The insiders' reports interspersed with mine will more than make up for the limitations of my account. In fact, not only did my respondents (see Acknowledgements) in Germany, Denmark, Norway and Finland answer my questions in writing but they later exchanged views with me, reviewed the first draft of my report, reacted to it and enlarged their own account for the purpose of this chapter.

The state of criminology in Germany, Denmark, Norway and Finland

The outsider's view

For feminist criminology to exist in any one country, one would think it useful, facilitating or opportune[2] if within the academic structure there were a designated place where criminology was taught and/or criminological issues researched.[3] Before my last stay in Europe, I knew intellectually that criminology centres are relatively few, small and generally non-autonomous academic units in Northern European universities compared to the ones in which I have taught and done research in Canada, the United States and Australia. But knowing something intellectually and experiencing it is different. Experiencing the difference meant that, except in Norway at the Institute of Criminology of the University of Oslo, the 'criminologists' to whom I was introduced were generally professors of criminal law; the institutes of criminology, small research units in law faculties. But more disorienting for me was the absence of a student population that identified itself with criminology, again with the exception of Norway and the Oslo Institute of Criminology.

The issue of criminology as an autonomous field has been the object of many debates in Europe, North America and Australia; I have attended more than one meeting where representatives of criminology centres in Belgium, France, Norway, Germany, the United Kingdom, Canada, the United States, Australia, Italy, Poland, Hungary etc. debated the question. The appropriate academic status of criminology had been the object of the international conference at Hamburg University in 1986. The project of an institute of criminology in Hamburg had been hotly discussed; many opponents of the idea of establishing criminology as an academic discipline would commend it as a field of research, while others would see it as a professional sub-speciality of social work or 'social pedagogy'. But there were some who saw it as a field that should be taught and researched in autonomous departments (see Löschper *et al.* 1986).

Again, knowing all that theoretically is different from experiencing it. There were occasions when I thought that the advantage was on the side of smallness, if not on that of contingency. Nowhere did I feel envious of a criminology ensconced in a two-room research unit in a section of criminal law; but I loved sitting with ten undergraduate students or six graduate ones quietly exchanging views with an assistant professor at the Aufbau-und Kontakstudium Kriminologie at Hamburg University, comparing their fate to what takes place in the 150 to 250 student classrooms for undergraduates at the School of Criminology in Montreal. However, not all the centres in question were small. Observing the 300 students coming and going in the beautiful outside yard of the Oslo Institute of Criminology in June 1993, I had to review my generalization about the small number of the student body in European centres of criminology.

On the issue of the academic status of criminology in Northern Europe, I needed inside and contextualized information, as much as I did on the place of feminist theory, the existence and number of researchers who use that perspective, the presence of courses and seminars that deal with social control issues in a feminist perspective and the relative importance and influence of the works of feminists in the field. And those were the questions that I put to my correspondents and informers.

The insiders' view

The first question that I asked my European informers had to do with the relative importance of feminist teaching and research in the programme of their respective institute of criminology or in their country as a whole. The question read as follows: How many feminists teach and do research at your institute or elsewhere in your country? How many courses and seminars have to do with women and are taught from a feminist perspective? It escaped none of my respondents that the answer called for some assessment of the status of criminology as a discipline in their country.

The Danish and Finnish colleagues have similar terms to describe their national situation:

> In a way your questions are easy to answer due to the fact that criminology as an academic discipline is a very minor enterprise. At the Law Faculty of the University of Copenhagen to which the combined Institute of Criminology and Criminal Law belongs, criminology is only offered as elective courses for fourth and fifth year law students.
>
> (Annika Snare, Institute of Criminology and Criminal Law,
> Copenhagen)

> From the Finnish point of view, the situation is very shortly described as there is an obvious lack of teaching of criminology in the universities. It is mainly at Helsinki University that courses of criminology are taught; and that is done at the very basic level. You cannot get a degree in criminology in Finland.
>
> (Tarja Pösö, Department of Social Policy,
> University of Tampere, Finland)

The picture is different in Germany and Norway:

> In Hamburg, the institute of criminology is a nearly autonomous academic unit with two Professors and three tenured Assistants. It has some forty registered students. It grants diplomas in criminology.
>
> (Gabi Löschper, Aufbau- und Kontakstudium Kriminologie,
> Hamburg University)

> The Department of Criminology at Oslo University is a well-established one with a relatively important number of tenured professors (six); it has many assistants (fifteen) and a respectable body of students.
>
> (Cecilie Høigård and Rachel Paul, Institute of Criminology,
> University of Oslo)

The place of feminist theory in criminology teaching and research

The outsider's view

Although I knew, again theoretically, the differences between continental Europe and North America with regard to the academic hierarchy and the place that women occupy in the ranks, I was surprised by the minute number of women among the 'chairs', 'professors' and tenured teachers and researchers, and the absence of feminists among the authority figures in academia in general and in criminology in particular. All of that, of course, has a direct impact on the place that feminist theory occupies in the disciplines.

I observed in many departments the *pro temp*, contingent status of the non-tenured assistants, very often women. I witnessed the practical consequences of that status: the size of many of the assistants' offices (when they have one), their subservient duties, the lack of autonomy that goes with being the assistant of a professor and teaching his course or replacing him during his absences. And right on target with what this book is about, one of my observations had to do with the near total absence of feminists among the chairs and professors except in Oslo, and more generally among the academic staff with permanent status in general and in criminology in particular, certainly more so than in sociology.

I experienced intellectual and moral climates that were not only very male but also sexist in the universities where I stayed: men professors and male assistants dominate the scene; they negate the intellectual validity of non-male pronouncements and avoid any feminist issue that has not become a politically correct preoccupation. That climate is well supported (or 'engendered') by the university gender structure, at the faculty level if not at the students'.

The male atmosphere was certainly there at the Aufbau- und Kontakstudium Kriminologie at the University of Hamburg, where the faculty consists of two 'professors', both men, and three assistants, none being feminist. Feminist candidates did compete for the permanent teaching job recently advertised but none was hired. The position is now filled by a woman who is not a feminist, although, as I discovered through my role as tutor during my stay, there is a real interest in feminist theory among students. In the course of the academic year 1993–4, there was one course on 'female crime'; it was given by a male visiting teacher who, far from being pro-feminist, had difficulty formulating any critique of traditional criminology. On the occasion of one of my presentations at the Aufbau, a feminist exposé (Bertrand 1995) comparing the theories of Catherine MacKinnon (1989) and Drucilla Cornell (1991), there was an obvious malaise among the male assistants and professors and a good deal of resistance. To get across to my audience, I had to work harder than I ever had in thirty years of university teaching and public presentations to establish the validity of feminist critique of law and social control; I doubt that I succeeded. I made my reactions known to my hosts afterwards. Elsewhere in Germany, at Humboldt University in what was East Berlin, what I experienced was not resistance as much as a relative absence of anyone directly involved in criminology. On the occasion of my stay, the woman president of the university, whom some of us consider a feminist, had called upon professors in the criminal law section to organize a small seminar where I was to speak on criminology and feminist theory. I met three male criminal law teachers, all from the former West Germany, who had chosen to teach at Humboldt because they saw the need for and were interested in exposing a critical view of criminal law at this time in an important institution of the former East Germany. One of them was a pro-feminist attempting to stir some debate in his criminal law classes on issues relevant to women, such as abortion, domestic victimization and rape. But that was it and that is as far as criminology and feminist criminology go at Humboldt.

At Bremen, things were different. At the invitation of a pro-feminist male colleague, a professor of sociology, law and criminology in the faculty of law, I presented our study on women's prisons, and discussed such topics as abolitionism and the feminist critique of penology in a lively group of thirty students and professors in law and sociology, men and women, one of whom was a woman inmate working on prison reform. Some of the students had just returned from study visits to prisons in other European countries in the cadre of the Erasmus Programme; many voiced well-thought and sometimes feminist critiques of the carceral system. During the supper that followed my presentation I gathered that law students receive little if any feminist theory at the faculty of law proper, but there is a relatively important group of feminists in sociology among students and faculty and some women teachers dispense courses with a definite feminist orientation that law students may attend.

My experience of Denmark was confusing. My contacts with the feminists involved in doing teaching and research in criminology and sociology of deviance, their strength and conviction and the quality of their works had lulled me into imagining something more than what the academic structure allows – which is very little. Yet in the Institute of Criminology and Criminal Law at the Institute of Copenhagen and around it there are a few feminists who manage to do solid research and publish. How do they do that? Where do they find the stimulation, the support?[4]

In Norway, there are women and feminists among the staff at the Institute of Criminology and Criminal Law of the Faculty of Law at the University of Oslo. Their presence cannot be missed. They are present among the professors and among the assistants. There are also many students interested in feminist issues. The work of Norwegian feminists is known in other universities, as I could see while in Hamburg, Bremen, Berlin, Copenhagen and Hameenlinna (Finland). That situation, especially the presence of a number of feminists among the professors and the assistants, stands in sharp contrast with that I have seen elsewhere in Northern Europe. Feminist production is impressive; yet I do not see it quoted in the works of the non-feminist colleagues in Norway.

The unintended findings about feminist theory and social control in Finland were something else again. I had been looking for a mentor to help me with the study of the central prison for women in that country and felt very fortunate to have met at a seminar on women in detention organized by the Ministry of Justice of the Netherlands in 1991 a woman trained in social policy, an assistant professor at the University of Tampere School of Social Work, whose contribution at the seminar showed her grasp of the very difficult question of mothers and children in detention. The other delegates from the Scandinavian countries made no secret of the fact that she was 'the' person in Finland whom I should consult. She agreed to become my informer on the issue of feminist criminology in Finland as she had guided me in the prison research. She uses political science theory to analyse the treatment of young delinquent girls in the social control system of Finland. Her network has nothing to do with criminology; here again the question is 'How can she do that alone?'

The insiders' view

On the place and academic status of women and feminists teaching and doing research in criminology and in related fields, my correspondents have many things to say:

> In Germany, at the Hamburg Aufbau- und Kontakstudium Kriminologie, the assistant professors have tenure, and among them there are two women and one man; none is a feminist.
>
> (Gabi Löschper)

> In Denmark, a tenured assistant feminist teacher has a well-established position; there are some researchers including a woman feminist who have the status of assistants with tenure at the Copenhagen Institute of Criminology.
>
> (Annika Snare)

In Finland, even the non-tenured assistant teachers have relatively good academic conditions: the young assistants normally have a five-year contract, they have their own offices, their own teaching and formally they are entitled to take part in the democratic decision-making of the departments and universities. In principle they should have independent positions. What happens in everyday life might be different. Yet it is true that there are not so many permanent posts and that the proportion of women who hold professorships is much smaller than among assistants or lecturers. I cannot give you the exact numbers of professors in law or in sociology at this time but both subjects are male dominated.

(Tarja Pösö)

In Norway, four of the six tenured teachers at the Institute of Criminology of Oslo are women; of the two professors with chairs, one is a woman and a feminist (Cecilie Høigård). Three of the six tenured ones have a clear feminist orientation. Among the fifteen assistant teachers and researchers revolving around the department on contracts and grants, eight have a feminist perspective.

(Høigård and Paul)

As one can readily see, the situation in Norway is unique: half the tenured faculty are feminist, as are more than half the contract assistants.

With regard to the existence of courses and seminars in the criminology centres of these countries that are clearly feminist in orientation, the answers of the Danish, Finnish and German respondents converge in the direction of the negative:

The elective courses in criminology in the Faculty of Law at the University of Copenhagen have so far been taught by the three tenured criminologists and it is my understanding that an explicit feminist perspective hardly saturates the teaching. However, at Äarhus University, Beth Grothe Nielsen, with a tenured position in criminal law, teaches elective courses on sexual abuse/incest and related topics for law students. She can be noted as 'the criminologist' in Denmark holding a permanent academic slate and being directly involved in feminist teaching and research.

(Snare)

Because one cannot get a degree in criminology in Finland it means that the status of feminist criminology is very vague. I do not know anyone who calls herself a feminist criminologist.

(Pösö)

The place of feminist criminology in the curriculum? Zero. We do not have a feminist professor (not even a female one!) in the Institute, or a feminist (tenured) 'assistant'. I would not consider myself a 'real' feminist although I teach on women and criminal law and have had students who write their thesis with an explicit feminist perspective. There may be some teaching having to do with women and the criminal justice system but these may not be feminist in orientation; the woman question and feminist criminology are not part of the curriculum. In the last three terms, approximately 10 to 20 per cent of the formal teachings concerned women and the criminal justice system or feminism. But this is/was exceptional. In the years/terms before we didn't have a single course in this area. It's improving! But there are two feminists working on a research project on a feminist theme. They have a contract for two years and work part-time.

(Löschper)

The picture is very different at the Institute of Oslo:

Concerning the curriculum, the programme of study at the undergraduate level is built around issues and required readings rather than in topical courses and seminars. Hence there is no teaching devoted completely to feminist theory or the woman question in criminology; but a good indicator of the place and importance of feminist theory and issues in the curriculum is to be found in the amount of compulsory reading that has to do with feminist issues. At the undergraduate level, among the approximately 4500 pages of required readings, 780 are specific to feminist issues. At the master's level, there are presently two series of lectures on feminism and the list of required readings include some works by feminist authors.

(Høigård and Paul)

On the visibility and influence of feminist criminologists in Norway:

The feminists, like the other faculty members at the Institute, are very visible; they are often in the media. They are involved in very sensitive issues like prostitution, drugs, family violence and police work, themes that are very well covered by the media. The feminists at the Institute are also generally known as political activists and as active participants in the broader social debate in Norwegian society.

(Høigård and Paul)

My Finnish correspondent rightly points out that criminology is not the only discipline where the gendered aspects of social control are examined and interpreted. Such courses may take place in faculties of law and in 'general social sciences':

In Finland there are research groups in women's law at the University of Helsinki which do serious work in women's law, studying, in particular, family law. This group is small but has achieved a lot. A larger project has just been subsidized. [Elsewhere] the topics of gender and social control are on the margins, even if one could say that the interest is growing. As an example of the latter, a new chair in social sciences was established at Kupio University which involves a specialization in deviance. This chair is held by Martti Gronfors, who is actively studying the male nature of violence from a comparative perspective.

(Pösö)

The Norwegian correspondents elaborate on feminist studies in general:

With respect to feminist research in Norway, one can mention that there exist independent interdisciplinary centres of women's studies at the universities of Oslo and Trondheim. They have invited reputed feminists like Dorothy Smith, Helene Cixous, Sandra Harding, Evelyn Fox Keller and Luce Irigaray. There are also women's studies centres and research groups within various disciplines, like medicine and law. There are also two feminist journals, one of them published in English and called *Nora* (after the heroine in Ibsen's *A Doll's House*).

(Høigård and Paul)

Back with criminology but still in line with the interdisciplinary nature of the works done from a feminist perspective, Høigård and Paul note that feminist criminologists are not bound to limit themselves to criminological issues:

Female criminologists in Norway have taken an interest in more general analyses of gender, in the gender system of society, apart from criminology. Kjersti Ericsson, for example, has written two books that directly address the power relation issue in the gender system of society. The first, *Sisters, Comrades*, pictures the oppression of women as 'enmeshed in the economic and political system of capitalism'. The book discusses the relationship between class and gender, and treats issues like the value of female labour power, the function of housework in the capitalist economy, the family as an economic and political institution. The second book, titled *The Multi-voiced Revolution*, addresses the question of strategies for social change and how to found such strategies on a woman's perspective.

(Høigård and Paul)

My Danish correspondent mentions the transdisciplinary character of issues that relate to women and deviance; these can well be tackled in departments of sociology, for instance. Sadly enough, though, that discipline has been silent for some time in the country:

Let me add that in Denmark sociology as a separate academic discipline has been nearly phased out since 1986. This autumn (1994), the Institute of Sociology at the University of Copenhagen will reopen, and the future will show us how feminist issues in deviancy and social control are taken care of. One of the new faculty members is Margaretha Järvinen, formerly affiliated with the Institute of Criminology and Criminal Law as an independent researcher. Her work on prostitution in Helsinki (Järvinen 1993), and more recently on homeless women, incorporates a definite feminist understanding.

(Snare)

The importance of feminist production

The third question that I addressed to my correspondents had to do with the relative importance of feminist production in the publications on criminology in their countries. During my contacts with feminist colleagues in these countries and following my work in the documentation centres and university libraries, I had gained the impression that the feminist work produced was good but recent and sparse. That is confirmed by insiders who point to relatively isolated studies from Denmark, Germany and Finland. But they make interesting distinctions:

> The works by a few researchers connected to our Institute in one way or another cannot be classified as 'feminist' in orientation. Though, again, the gender demarcation is another matter. Way back, in the later 1970s, feminist issues in criminology seem to have been more topical. At that time research on rape and on women in prison were carried out by a group of women, who all but one have found jobs outside the university.
>
> (Snare)

> The work of feminists is on the whole only of minor influence or importance in our criminology department. But in my eyes it is slowly becoming better. It does not mean that feminists have too much of a problem getting their works published. The *Kriminologisches Journal* publishes feminists' works. There are of course fewer possibilities in other more conservative prominent journals. But they too had articles on feminist topics or by feminist authors or on feminism.
>
> (Löschper)

In Norway there are, obviously, works by feminists and a collective reflection on feminist theory, ethics and methods:

> Not only is the production by feminists important but all the important segments are covered: the offender, the victim, the control system and the interplay between them. *Women as victims*: there are a number of studies dealing with sexual violence, the guiding theory here being that of power relationships. *Women in the control system*: there have been studies on women's encounters with the police and the prison system. One central question here is about the two following issues. Yes, feminists should accept the criminal justice system apparatus when it comes to putting the responsibility on the shoulders of the actor. No, if it means putting the guilty man in prison. The methods of inquiry borrow from social anthropology (going out into the field)

in both areas. *Female offenders*: the challenge here is to explain the small but stable increase in the number of women caught by the control system in nearly every Western society in the last decades. According to Norwegian criminology, that increase is owing to the changing relations between social class and gender and the marginalization processes that affect women in particular in society.

(Høigård and Paul)

In Finland, we have seen that it is mostly in law, social policy and sociology that gender studies flourish. My correspondent signals a number of interesting publications in these areas (Feranen 1990; Simonen 1990; Nikander 1992; Varsa 1993). In the analysis of the family structure, I found the Finnish publications, including the government's ones, remarkably interesting.

The influence of feminists in their academic milieu

The outsider's view

Experiences in Europe lead me to surmise that leading European criminologists can appear unaware of, and uninterested in, feminist criticism. Repeated attempts to achieve a fair place for feminist perspectives in the plenary on theory and methodology at the International Congress of Criminology in Budapest in 1993 met with no response. Finally, and only with the support of colleagues from Denmark and Germany, I was able to give such a presentation (Bertrand 1994).

There was another experience during the Twenty-first Congress of the European Group for the Study of Deviance and Social Control in Prague in 1993. These meetings are attended by criminologists who have worked for twenty years at critically confronting traditional criminology. One would therefore expect to find a less inimical reception for feminist theory, but this was not the case. In short, it appears that feminism and the feminist critique of criminology have as yet had relatively little impact on senior criminologists. Can this situation be changed, or must feminists await the next generation?

The insiders' view

Do my European correspondents feel that their feminist production is better received than I describe? The question that I put to them in this regard was: Are the works done by feminists referred to in the works of non-feminist colleagues?

Even in Norway, where the feminists are productive and visible, their influence on their own colleagues may not be demonstrable. Elsewhere, the work of feminists has little impact.

Male colleagues who are not feminist do read the production of their feminist colleagues. There is an interesting and oppressive division of labour among the non-feminists and feminists at the department. The male colleagues feel that their responsibility is to cover general criminology, which in their view does not include feminist issues. The female colleagues are expected to cover this general criminology and any feminist critique would have to be in addition.

(Høigård and Paul)

In Germany, my correspondent had already answered the question about the influence of feminist criminologists on their colleagues when she wrote that 'the work of feminists is on the whole only of minor influence or importance in our criminology department', adding that she felt that 'it is slowly becoming better' and that feminists manage nevertheless to have their works published (Löschper). In Denmark, Annika Snare answered: 'In sum, there are hardly any Danish feminist works in criminology that could be quoted by other non-feminist people in the field. The field is very small in numbers.' In Finland: 'Sadly enough their [the feminists'] work has got more status as a part of women's studies only and it is not widely referred to by other scholars of law. That is also very much the case with other criminological feminist writing' (Pösö).

Criminology students' interest in feminist theory

Are the students in criminology interested in feminist theory and perspective? To this question I received the following answers.

Annika Snare in Denmark noted that there are no students in criminology proper and that the field itself does not attract many people. Her remark concerning the ethnic origin of two PhD students showing interest in women's issues speaks of the transferability of the 'difference' reality and concept from the gendered world to the cultural one:

Newcomers into criminological research – feminist or non-feminist – are more or less lacking, which is not surprising in light of the general academic situation. Perhaps it is indicative that two current PhD theses (of which one is under way) dealing with women's issues are written by female researchers temporarily at our Institute who come from Pakistan and Uganda.

Löschper from Germany noted:

There are students who write their thesis with an explicit feminist perspective. Students are very much interested in feminist perspectives. Over the last years about one or two out of fifteen to twenty-five students each year write their thesis with a feminist perspective or on a topic concerning women and the criminal law, or at least dedicate a part of their thesis to feminist subjects, e.g. deviance, crime and gender; the work of MacKinnon, women as victims and perpetrators, new realism and the image of women.

The answer from Norway was:

> Women constitute the majority of the student body, which consists of some 230 undergraduates and some fifty graduates. Many are interested in doing their theses on women's issues and in feminist theory at the department. The presence of influential feminist teachers and feminist assistants of research is conducive to that, as is the composition of the student body. In the last year, seven students completed their masters degree in criminology; three of the theses dealt with feminist issues.
>
> (Høigård and Paul)

Conclusion

A good title for this chapter would have been 'Lessons to be learned from a transnational comparison of the state of feminist criminology in four Northern European countries on how to counter conditions that are adverse to the emergence and development of feminist theory in criminology and related fields.' What we have seen are adverse conditions. In view of the severity of the adversity, it is astonishing that there is a feminist production in criminology in Germany, Denmark and Finland. It is even astonishing that the Norwegian feminists manage to hold the fort and grow against the challenge to the feminist perspective voiced by some very influential male colleagues. How can one survive, think and be intellectually productive when one is alone with one's views or working in an environment that belittle one's perspective and one's works? To that last question, the Norwegian colleagues answer in part in their critique of my very academic perspective on the development of feminism (see below).

There are at least four lessons that can be learned from this transnational study of the place and status of feminist criminology in Northern Europe, lessons that were reiterated by my respondents:

1 Studies done from a feminist perspective on social control issues do not have to take place in criminology centres.
2 Studies done by feminist criminologists do not always have a bearing on social control issues.
3 Studies done by feminist criminologists may not always use the critical perspectives derived from feminism because the object of the study does not call for that kind of interpretation.
4 For feminist criminology to exist and flourish, there must be a critical number of feminists in one place, some of them in solid positions of intellectual authority.

That is also true of criminology: it is useful and opportune to have at least one and perhaps two or three well-connected places in the academy, where sociology of law, social control, the criminalization process and its selectiveness are critically examined, for the same reasons that play in favour of a critical number of feminists in academia. For the critique of social control to succeed, that 'place' or these 'places' must be open to a re-evaluation of their epistemological, theoretical and methodological assumptions, including the re-evaluation that comes from the feminists.

I saw some of these conditions realized at the Bremen faculty of law, but mostly because of the presence of feminists in the sociology department and the connections between the two departments that the *students* manage to keep alive. Had my field trips brought me more often to departments of sociology and social policy in Germany, Norway and Finland I most probably would have encountered more of that transdisciplinary fertilization of the critical perspectives offered by feminist theory on the question of social control. But as we have seen, in criminology proper it is only at the Oslo Institute of Criminology that feminism and feminist theory are alive and growing. Elsewhere either criminology is relatively non-existent or feminism is kept at a clear distance, as in Hamburg, whatever the interest of the students in that perspective.

In their concluding note my Norwegian correspondents express a critique that is well placed here. It has to do with the general orientation of my questions, which imply that feminist theory is constructed in the university. The search for support for the feminist perspective is ill-directed, they say, when it looks to the university. Not only is there little help to be gained in many cases from the scientific community but it is an error to work at developing feminist theories in the ivory tower.

> [We] look critically at the questions posed in this chapter and think that the problems as set are too inner oriented, turned too much towards the inside hierarchy of the university, and focus too little on the content and impact outside the university. Feminists and feminist theory get nourished by the constant interrelations between women's groups and the feminists in the universities; in fact the latter have to be themselves very much in the community, never divorced from the reality of women.
>
> (Høigård and Paul)

I agree with that critique. But to me there is an imperious need to do solid work at the highest conceptual level in feminist epistemology and methodology. I recognize the importance of never losing touch with women's groups and the material conditions of women's lives, but I also believe that many more feminists must be part of the academy and research centres; that is what inspired my questions to my informants. No theoretical progress will take place in feminism without a *critical number* of us being in the place where that is normally done, where theories are developed and validated. There must be many more of us allowed to do just that and to get the means to do it, then to be read and discussed by intellectuals and social actors of both genders, feminists and pro-feminists.

The German correspondent pointed to an important issue, that of the publications opened to feminists' writings. That also deserves more attention – in a future book? The Finnish correspondent touched on another issue of interest when she mentioned the flowering in her country of feminist studies coming from the examination of family and work conditions. What she did not mention in her modesty was her own work and critique of the family and the representation of motherhood in Northern Europe, which, in my view, is of capital interest and very closely connected to social control issues.

Law and sociology students and teachers

In Germany and Norway, I met groups of law students, feminists, who act as legal advisors in prison; in faculties of law in Germany I met many women and men professors who seem to have come more readily (than colleagues from criminology, for instance) to the realization that feminist critique is important for the renaissance of the discipline. That realization is not at all uncommon in faculties of law in Canada and the United States (quite the opposite). Lately, it is from feminists teaching in law faculties in the United States that some of the most powerful feminist theses on women and social control have come.

The limits of criminology

There is nothing sacred about criminology and, I hope, nothing eternal. For one thing, in the universities where it has been institutionalized as an autonomous discipline, its existence and importance has often served as an excuse for sociology to stop teaching social control and deviance courses; in some cases, it has even served as an excuse to give up sociology of law altogether. In other places or in the same, the presence of large departments of criminology has served as an excuse for law faculties to do away with their responsibility to offer a serious, credible and critical teaching in criminal law, on issues like the limits of criminal sanction. My Danish correspondent had a good concluding remark on that topic:

> Finally, perhaps I have employed a too-narrow definition of what constitutes 'criminology' and for that matter what 'feminism' entails. There do exist several feminist-oriented academic networks of an interdisciplinary nature. Today, however, this research is more often referred to as 'gendered' than explicitly feminist and the 'criminological input' is largely missing. There is plenty of room for a more marked focus on deviancy and social control.
>
> (Snare)

Perhaps this book on feminist criminology will show that the two categories that we were asked to analyse – criminology and feminism – are in a state of revolution. At the empirical level, we can see that criminology seems more inhospitable than law and sociology to feminist theory. It is my strong conviction that if feminist critique were to succeed in occupying a real space in criminology, its deconstructive power (of gender relations, of nature, of the notion of crime) would bring about paradigmatic changes and epistemological ruptures of such magnitude that the whole discipline would become unrecognizable or implode. That may be one of the reasons why criminology entrepreneurs keep it at bay.

Acknowledgements

I wish to express my gratitude to the editors of this book, Frances Heidensohn and Nicole Hahn Rafter, for having taken the initiative to bring our contributions together. Their collection not only will keep alive the exchanges among those of us who took part in the 1991 Mont Gabriel International Feminist Conference on Women, Law and Social Control, but, I am sure, will increase the solidarity among feminist criminologists in the world. In addition, I would like to thank them for their helpful suggestions on the structure, form and content of earlier versions of this chapter. My thanks also go to the colleagues from Germany, Denmark, Norway and Finland who have contributed to this chapter: Gabi Löschper, from the Aufbau- und Kontakstudium Kriminologie, University of Hamburg, Germany; Annika Snare, Institute of Criminology and Criminal Law, University of Copenhagen, Denmark; Cecilie Høigård and Rachel Paul, Institute of Criminology, University of Oslo, Norway; Tarja Pösö, Department of Social University of Tampere, Finland. The section on the University of Bremen was reviewed by Johannes Feest, Faculty of Law, University of Bremen, Germany. The conversations, correspondence and revisions took place between June 1993 and September 1994.

Notes

1 The study is now at the pre-publication stage. It is called 'A comparative study of women's prisons in Canada, the United States, the United Kingdom, Germany, Denmark, Norway and Finland'. The research team is Marie-Andrée Bertrand, Louise L. Biron, Concetta di Pisa, Andrée B. Fagnan and Julia McLean. The team has studied twenty-four prisons for women, eighteen closed and six open.

2 Depending on one's conviction on the capital issue of monodisciplinarity, or multi- or pluri- or transdisciplinarity, as the best vector for the production and transmission of knowledge in general and criminology in particular, and depending on one's experience with feminist studies.

3 Works of great importance in the field have been written by academics working in departments of sociology, social policy, anthropology and law. But the recognition of criminology as a discipline has had enormous effects on the development of the field.

4 Perhaps in some subgroup of women and feminists within the Scandinavian association of criminology.

References

Bertrand, M-A. (1994). From *la donna delinquente* to a postmodern deconstruction of the 'woman question' in social control theory. *Journal of Human Justice*, 5(2), 43–57.

Bertrand, M-A. (1995). The power of the male gaze. *Kriminologisches Journal*, in press.

Cornell, D. (1991). *Ethical Feminism, Deconstruction and the Law*. Cambridge, MA: Harvard University Press.

Feranen, M. (ed.) (1990). *Gender and Politics in Finland*. Ashgate Publishing.

Järvinen, M. (translated by K. Leander) (1993). *Of Vice and Women: Shades of Prostitution*, Scandinavian Studies in Criminology, Vol. 13. Oslo: Scandinavian University Press.

Löschper, G., Manke, G. and Sack, F. (eds) (1986). *Kriminologie als selbständiges, interdisziplinäres Hochschulstudium*. Proceedings of an international symposium, University of Hamburg, 8–10 May. Pfaffenweiler: Centaurus-Verlagsgesellschaft.

MacKinnon, C. (1989). *Deconstruction and the Law*. New York: Routledge.

Nikander, T. (1992). *The Woman's Life Course and the Family Formation*. Helsinki: Statistics in Finland.

Simonen, L. (ed.) (1990). *Finnish Debates on Women's Studies*. Tampere: University of Tampere Research Institute for Social Sciences, Centre for Women's Studies and Gender Relations.

Varsa, H. (ed.) (1993). *Shaping Structural Change in Finland: the Role of Women*. Helsinki: Equality Publications.

7

What it's like for women: criminology in Poland and Eastern Europe

MONIKA PLATEK

To write about feminist perspectives in criminology may seem natural for a Western social scientist, but it is very unusual, almost weird, for the East European. For us it is strange even to write about teaching criminology. Years ago when I lectured on this topic at Hamburg University, I was surprised at the interest and the lengthy discussion that followed my presentation (Platek 1986). After all, I did not find myself very original. I was merely describing the reality behind teaching a rather specific subject under rather specific conditions that often made my life difficult, and I had a hard time finding that fascinating.

It had not yet occurred to me to ask whether I could approach the subject from a feminist perspective. But to ask the question is to create the reality. To ask the question is to make people conscious of a reality they were not aware of. To ask the question is to get out of the foggy tunnel of meaningless slogans, to excavate forgotten words and name the nameless.

This is what it means to write on feminist perspectives in Polish criminology. But to do this well I will have to begin by separating the female from criminology, just as they were separated for years, and to explain the social context in which this science developed in Poland. Next, to show why criminology was so divorced from feminist issues, I will have to talk about the social situation of Polish women. Then I will turn to victimology as a way of examining contemporary Polish efforts to engender the study of crime.

The development of Polish criminology

The forbidden science

Like astronomy during the Middle Ages, criminology in Eastern European countries after the Second World War threatened authorities and therefore was forbidden. Between 1944 and 1989 Poland was only formally a sovereign nation. The communist system imposed upon Poland and other Eastern European countries at the Yalta Conference gave Russia, with the Western powers' connivance, authority to control many aspects of our political, economic and social life.

Important positions in criminal justice were occupied by Soviet 'advisors' who often influenced not only the substance of law but also court decisions. They considered criminology a bourgeois, groundless pseudo-science. Lombroso with his notion of a born-criminal; Durkheim with his thesis of the inevitability of crime; Sutherland's revelations about white-collar crime – all were wrong, according to the communist regime. Crime might characterize a feudal society or the 'rotten West', but not a socialist or communist nation. Because the new society was supposed to be crimeless, there was no need for a science for finding the causes of crime. Because crime was so obviously rooted in the socio-economic conditions of capitalism, everything was clear and research was unnecessary. These were the official explanations for shutting down academic and government departments that had dealt with criminology before the Second World War.

Communist ideology only partially explains why criminology was forbidden – and forbidden with such fierce animosity. Criminology means research. Criminology means statistics. Criminology means data! And what is even worse, criminology tries to deal objectively with certain realities. It establishes an environment for creative thinking. An authority intent on controlling people's minds and actions has to curb access to such information.

Officially, then, criminology was useless. In truth, criminology was too dangerous to tolerate.

The revival of criminology

When Stalin died in 1953, political upheavals convulsed Eastern European governments, including those of Hungary, East Germany, Czechoslovakia and Poland. People can bear only so much injustice, and only for a period of time. Political 'thawing' becomes possible when the authority in power is weakened. Because the Soviets were unable to improve Eastern bloc economies and supply people with money and goods, they had to make political concessions and give people back some of their freedom. Thousands were released from prison. Thousands more, already killed, had their good names restored. And criminology returned to the universities and the Academy of Science.

Communism is cynical, hopeless, boring, hypocritical and deceptive. It is certainly not eager for modification or compromise. Communists allowed criminology to reappear in name but harnessed it to support and justify state policy directed, as earlier, towards restraint and restriction.

Socialism and communism, despite their ideology, leave little room for respecting the individual. They have no real interest in what people have to bear. They treat law as an ornament rather than a tool to regulate relations among citizens and between citizens and the state. Sociologists and criminologists whose research showed otherwise were very highly estimated by intellectuals but harassed by officials.

The authorities needed a scapegoat to explain why the happiness they promised could be guaranteed for our grandchildren (perhaps) but not us. Criminals and the growing number of crimes provided a perfect way to account for hell in the promised land. But how could the presence of criminals be explained? They were supposed to have vanished. Marx said so, Lenin said so, and no one would dare to contradict these leaders' words even if they were obviously wrong.

If necessity is the mother of invention, it can also lead to reinvention. The regime reinvented criminology to strengthen bonds with our 'Big Brother' Russia.[1] The Soviet Union faced the same problems as the Eastern bloc: criminality created an acute dilemma there, too. The Russians decided that criminality comes from the remainders of previous, capitalistic systems that stayed with people unwilling or unable to get the proper socialization. This 'theory of the relict' dominated Russian criminology in the late 1950s and was brought to Poland by advisors sent to propagate the science. Good apparatus members were sent from prosecutors' offices and the courts to teach criminology at the universities – and control the environment.

They included not one woman, and they did no research. The purpose, as Lernell (1973) points out, was to write criminology textbooks that spread the official ideology. Some criminological research was being done, however, within the Ministry of Justice and the Polish Academy of Science. The Ministry of Justice researchers, like the university ideologues, aimed at justifying official policies and had almost nothing to do with science. But the Academy of Science research was a different matter. The Academy's criminology department was chaired by Professor Stanisław Batawia, who had begun his criminological work after the First World War. Polish criminology established itself and extended its range in the period between the two world wars. The founding of the Polish Criminological Society in 1921 and of the Department of Criminology at the Free Polish University in 1922 (transformed in 1932 into the Criminological Institute) contributed to this situation. In the inter-war years Polish criminology faced the task of identifying the basic individual and social causes of crime. It also tried to relate these factors to the preparation of a Penal Code and the shaping of criminal justice policies (Nelken 1986). Professor Batawia played a key role in developing the science of the offender's personality, or 'criminal biology' (Batawia 1931). However, he stressed that criminal-biological research must be conducted from the sociological as well as the psychological and medical viewpoints. Batawia attached particular importance to environmental research in the case of juvenile delinquents. He could not resume his research immediately after the Second World War, but once he restarted after 1956, Batawia refused to take the relict theory seriously and simply returned to his earlier work (Batawia 1958).

Thus, by the end of 1950s there were three movements within Polish criminology. We had ideological, non-scientific 'criminology' at the universities; flunky, trashy ministerial 'criminology'; and genuine, open research being conducted at the Academy of Science. Then a strange thing happened: during the 1960s those sent to dish out official criminology rewrote their textbooks, admitting they had been wrong. They acknowledged the authority of 'old' criminology professors like Batawia, Pawel Horoszowski, Ludwik Krzywicki, E. Krzymuski, A.S. Ettinger, Leon Rabinowicz (later Radzinowicz) and others who had never confused Russian ideology with science (Rabinowicz 1933; Horoszowski 1965; Lernell 1973: 15).

Under communism we enjoyed neither freedom nor democracy, but within this generally grey reality there were islands of freedom. Universities, after 1968, proved to be one of them.

Chicago on the Vistula[2]

I became a law student at Warsaw University just after the workers' uprising of 1971, when many were killed in the mines and shipyards. The university was one of the very few places where problems could be openly discussed. Of course our main problem was communism and how to get rid of it. Criminology seemed likely to be helpful in unmasking the communist state. Women? Female perspectives? No, there was no place for that. More than 50 per cent of the students were female, and in most cases we did better than the men. We did not feel unequal, and the American women's liberation movement seemed a whim of people with too much free time. We were busy fighting communism and had no time for 'frivolous' goals. We could not get into prisons to do our research; we could not obtain basic data. Each step was strenuous. It did not occur to us that actually our problems might have a lot to do with the very male order of the reality. Within the university we felt we could be open. Were we also open to talk about relations between men and women? I do not know. We did not really try.

I had a teacher who had been sent in the 1950s to impose the Soviet line within the university. By that time he had written many books, all based on Western sources rarely available in Poland. He never ceased being a communist, and we never – not even once – agreed on anything we discussed. He insisted that I give him elaborate arguments about why I thought him wrong and never – not even once – lowered my grade because I differed so strongly. He used to place the responsibility for crime within the person, while I, of course, blamed the state and social conditions. But he encouraged academic freedom and in effect promoted the Americanization of Polish criminology.

To us, American criminology had a scent of freedom. It was real science, contrary to anything that could possibly come from Russia. The only Russian works I can recall from my criminology syllabus are Dostoevsky's *Crime and Punishment* and *Notes from the House of the Dead*, Tolstoy's *Resurrection* and Paszukhanis's *Theory of Crime*. Everything else came from the United States. 'Our' principles of criminology were Edwin H. Sutherland and Donald R. Cressey's *Principles of Criminology*. When I started to teach, I used Don Gibbons's *The Criminological Enterprise*.

The criminology I learned was Chicago School criminology, and that is the point at which I have started many of my own courses. I wanted to be as close to the truth as possible – and as far as possible from Russia. It took me some time to realize that American realities are not much more relevant than Russian realities to Polish conditions. Not until I visited the United States from 1992 to 1994 and taught in Chicago did I understand that while the Chicago School's teachings might apply to Chicago and possibly New York, Los Angeles and Miami, they had little to do with Bloomington, Indiana, Charlotte, North Carolina or Columbus, Ohio. They had even less to do with Warsaw, Prague or Budapest. Theory must be based on local circumstances. But I didn't know that then.

The awakening

A long time passed before we questioned revered texts. Criminal law formed the framework for most criminological studies. At some point we started doubting whether that was the best way to frame issues, but I never suspected that criminal law might have something to do with gender. Nor did I think of my questions as part of a gendered process. Rather, I considered mine to be a 'radical perspective' in criminology (Platek 1985). Women were rarely mentioned in criminology textbooks. They were on the margin of interest, and therefore even women in the field were not interested in them. After all, there were so few women among criminals, and victimology was not yet in fashion.

We were not much different from our teachers. We were not used to questioning authority we respected. It was easy to oppose the communist system but much harder to think differently from those whom we perceived as 'real' scientists.

The development of feminist perspectives

Women: perfect and unimportant

In Poland the awakening of women coincided with the Solidarity movement for political independence. The first feminist organization was established at Warsaw University in 1981. Our aim was to create better conditions for women, a goal we thought we could achieve by endowing women with more dignity and satisfaction. We didn't realize that achieving the goal would require major legal and social changes. Politically we were fighting for freedom of speech, democracy and minority rights. It did not occur to us that we lived in a land run by and for men, one in which we in fact had little influence on legislation or legal practice. We also did not understand that the political changes we had been fighting for so long, side by side with men, were not meant to affect traditional attitudes towards gender. Our efforts to call attention to such issues as rape, family violence and crimes committed out of desperation by battered women made small progress. Once again other issues were deemed more important. Political rights, unions and freedom from communism – these issues had to be addressed first. Women's issues were left for the future, for a better time, should it come.

Equality of the sexes is written into the constitutions of all Eastern European countries. None of us believed in most of what our Constitution said. Most of it was not observed in practice. Only the notion of equality between men and women was taken seriously, and taken seriously by men and women alike. Women did, after all, have access to education, and we were working.

Men alone could not support their families so women had to work, whether they wanted to or not. It was not a right but a necessity. Having a job is a great thing, but equality is not an automatic or spontaneous process. We worked just as hard as men in the workplace. We also worked at home, where men shared none of the family and housekeeping chores. Our work outside the home was said to be an achievement of socialism. Our work within the home was said to be a tradition with noble history. Women were said to be 'better' – better at cleaning, shopping, bringing children into the world and then bringing them up, washing, laundering, sewing, repairing, cooking and then washing up. Everything that is tedious, women had to do because they were 'better'.

Many women had professional lives, were married with children, received poor wages, went home to alcoholic, abusive husbands and lived in a constant state of exhaustion. But few understood until recently that they were in many cases facing social injustice. There were no words to express this and no groups to represent us. The social atmosphere and economic realities worked against women's empowerment. In addition, there was no clear vision of social transformation. Yet more and more women realized that change, if it were to come, would come only through efforts by women themselves. This was not easy knowledge, and it was won only through strenuous and time-consuming efforts.

First stirrings

Let me again cite my own experience, for I have been teaching criminology, criminal law and corrections for almost twenty years. I often instinctively rejected the official perspective, groping in the dark towards a new understanding of crime. But I had no idea that I was striving towards feminist legal theory. Nor did I always understand that teaching about women and crime is less important than the way we do it. It seemed wonderful to be able to talk about women at all, but it wasn't clear that we might get different stories depending on who was talking. How could we know that? Women had been silent, and we had only the story told and constantly repeated by men.

Even under communism I was free to choose the courses I wanted to teach, the materials I wanted to use and the way I planned my syllabus. I am a lawyer as well as a criminologist, and lawyers are treated leniently by every regime; after all, we are needed. Moreover, the communists never really took university professors seriously. Then too, we were (and are) paid so little – less than an unskilled labourer – that losing my job wasn't a threat.

Even though I was probably freer under the communist regime than many untenured American academics are, I almost deliberately concentrated my research and teaching on everything but women. Women's issues, like those of children and the mentally handicapped, weren't 'scientific enough', weren't 'intellectually sophisticated' – and after all criminal women were so few in number. I was very ambitious and wanted to deal with serious matters; nothing concerning women was perceived as such. Frankly, it wasn't even easy to think about women.

A turning point came in 1986 when, during a university meeting with American feminist Jill Bystydzienski, I heard an angry Polish woman student attacking the American women's movement. She said that if American women have *time* to fight for their rights they in fact have nothing to fight for. The angry woman made an important point: Polish women have no time. We are always in a hurry, always tired, always without time to read or reflect on our condition. Women didn't want any 'rights' that might deplete them further. It was then that I decided to teach about the specific situation of Polish women, differentiating it and our goals from those of feminists elsewhere.

My attitudes began to change and polarize during a seminar on women and law that I organized for the first time in 1987. We tried to discover why, if women are so equal, we have so many more obligations and so few privileges. That question led to others, many of them related to criminology and law. Why were women not represented in governmental bodies? Why is the law constructed so as to impose disadvantages in the guise of privileges? (For example, only women can take a leave of absence if a child is ill, women cannot work during the night shift and women cannot work in ninety occupations.) Why are contraceptives rarely available and abortions becoming difficult to obtain?[3] Why is so much done to punish us but so little to bring about the changes that would prevent crime? Why do we discuss the problems of alcoholic men but never the problems of their wives? Why do we study only crimes involving men, erasing females from our field of interest? Why is it so obvious that rape within marriage is legally impossible?[4] Why is it such a great crime to commit shoplifting but nothing more than a political mistake to build a factory without a refinery for poisonous sewage? Our long list of 'whys' showed that the feminist perspective is concerned with more than women's problems. It questions the very definition of crime. It redistributes the emphasis on topics within criminology and introduces topics never studied before.

Most of my colleagues (men and women) reacted to my first seminar on women and the law with tolerance and general disregard. But I got a nickname, 'feminist', meant to be offensive and used when rational arguments failed.

Ironically, further suppression of women led us to deeper understandings of social realities and to a new strength to act on women's behalf. The debate on abortion and waves of unemployment that cruelly affected women radicalized women's attitudes. Suddenly there were hundreds of different women's organizations representing different women's interests. At the universities there are now more lectures and seminars on women's issues, and more work is being done by women, for women and about women. Slowly we are rejecting the hostile definition of 'feminist' imposed on us and giving this word our own meaning.

The process of transformation, having started, cannot be stopped. But Poland is still in its infancy with respect to feminist criminology. Male-oriented studies framed by the criminal law still dominate the field.[5] There are almost no statistics and very few studies including women's issues (but see Blachut 1981, 1988; Kolarczyk et al. 1984; Niedworok 1988). Even victimology, which elsewhere has included excellent studies of female victimization, rarely includes women in Poland. What relates to men is considered public and important; what relates to women is considered merely cultural and insignificant.

Victimology

To engender criminology is not only to study women who commit crimes; it is also to challenge traditional attitudes towards crime victims. In Western countries, victimology has served as one of the most powerful tools for injecting feminist perspectives into criminal law and criminal justice. In what follows I review our current work on victimization to show both how far we have to go and how victimology might transform the criminological enterprise.

Victimology began in Poland about twenty years ago, when radical and liberal researchers were building their careers. But contrary to what one might have predicted, they have paid no attention to women's victimization (e.g. Falandysz 1979, 1980). Although we do have some studies of rape victims (Leszczynski 1973; Bieniek 1974), these often attribute to the victim a role in initiating the crime (e.g. Bienkowska 1984). Over and over one reads that the victim is to blame, that well-behaved ladies are not raped, that rape is a 'normal' part of male nature and that women can prevent rape if they want to. Court decisions reinforce these attitudes, thus promoting violence against women, as do victimologists' studies.

In fact, some victimological research makes matters even worse by dividing rape victims into the categories of 'guilty' and 'innocent'. Bieniek (1974), for instance, found that of 287 rape victims, nearly 13 per cent were 'careless' or 'provocative' and only 46.4 per cent completely innocent. Similarly, Bienkowska (1984) found that of 655 victims, fewer than one-quarter were raped 'involuntarily'. It would of course be much more constructive to study how rape affects victims and what the state can do to meet victims' needs.

Other crimes against women are simply ignored. One is the offence of evading alimony obligations. Here the immediate victims are the children (as those entitled to receive alimony); but the indirect victims are the single mothers who must raise the children (Kolakowska-Przelomiec 1989). We have no proper terms for sexual harassment, stalking or incest. We lack statistics on women who are battered or must fight for survival. Researchers (e.g. Kuczynski 1980) lump battered women in the general category of 'family members', reinforcing the view that women are important only as part of a family and not as individuals.

Today, as during the Cold War, the Polish government hides its head in the sand, denying that crimes against women occur. These are said to be the problems of Western countries, even though if anything they are more acute here. Moreover, we have no crisis centres, no shelters, not even help lines for battered women. Women who manage to divorce abusive partners have to continue sharing an apartment with them. (The average waiting period for an apartment is twenty to thirty years, and renting is much too expensive for most people.) In addition, the general opinion is that one should not 'publicly launder family dirt'. In other words, women should put up with everything. Priests reinforce this view, discouraging separation even from abusive husbands. In the case of crime against women, the communist government and Catholic Church both counsel victim passivity.

Conclusion

In 1994 the Polish Parliament had no more women than it had in 1949. If you listen to political debates on abortion and other social issues, you will hear few women's voices. With Poland facing major economic and social changes, women are still last hired and first fired. We are still responsible for maintaining the household. There are plenty of goods, but this time around we cannot afford them. To feed one's family has become an acute problem. Whereas Polish women used to listen with amazement to accounts of prostitution in Russia, wondering how young girls could choose this career, today many openly engage in prostitution.

During my year in Chicago I studied the impact of women's movements on not only criminology but also many aspects of American society. Two things struck me. One was that what many women described as problems actually derived from luxury, especially the luxury of free time. Only recently have I started to share the perspective that free time and quality of life are not necessarily the same, and to realize that US women are talking about the quality of life. The other thing that struck me was how much American feminists have accomplished in a very short time. They have changed not only thinking about crime but also social manners, morals, attitudes and policies.

Poles today are in the grip of a brutal, primitive and very cynical capitalism. Newspapers are filled with advertisements for 'man only' or 'young, very attractive women' who are natives of the United States, Sweden or Holland. Business representatives would not dare to advertise that way in their home countries, but here anything goes, even though it is against the law. No one cares when money is at stake. But if this debasing capitalism comes to us from the West, from the West we are also getting new patterns of social relations.[6] American women in particular – no matter how much they complain of discrimination – give us a great example of how to recognize and name problems and how to harness science to change social reality.

What we learn from abroad would be useless if we were barred from political involvement. Today, however, Polish women have a right to organize. We *are* organizing, and there is much for us to do in criminology. Introducing the feminist perspective means starting to talk and write about violence in the family, rights for single mothers and lesbians, sexual harassment in the workplace and the victimization of women by the courts. The problem of rape has to be entirely redefined. We also need to create a new discourse that will use some familiar words in new ways and bring into common usage other terms (like 'self-esteem' and 'assertiveness') that we rarely use today.

With a group of friends, I have established a Polish Association of Citizen Education in the Law. One of our first aspirations is to undertake a joint study with Western specialists on the legal situation of women under current conditions of political, social and moral change. We hope to organize and consolidate women to force legal changes, and we aim at educating society about more than just relations between women and men. This is just one feminist organization among many. We have a long way to go, but believe that success is possible.

Acknowledgements

Special and very sincere thanks go to Nicky Hahn Rafter, who helped me extensively not only with my English but also with the context of this chapter. She found time in her busy schedule to discuss many issues that helped to clarify the context and encourage me in my work.

Notes

1 Poles were always careful to call Russia 'Big Brother' – and not, for example, 'Big Friend'. Friends you choose, but siblings you've got, and even if they are pains in the neck it is hard to get rid of them.
2 The Vistula (Wisla) River rolls from the south to the north of Poland, flowing through the length of the country and entering the Baltic sea.
3 The old Penal Law allowed abortion during the first three months of pregnancy. The new law of January 1993 abolished the right to abortion except in cases of rape, severe fetal brain damage and immediate danger of pregnancy-induced death. The new Parliament elected later in 1993 and dominated by ex-communists proposed an amendment to the abortion law that would permit abortion for women facing difficult social conditions. The new law was passed in the Parliament but the President refused to sign it. Therefore the law came up for a vote again at the end of August 1994. It could pass only with a majority of two-thirds. The attempt to abolish the President's veto failed by forty votes. Abortion has for years been hotly debated in Poland. The debate effectively divides people but seldom addresses the rights and status of women.
4 The present interpretation of the law includes rape within marriage, but discussions are for the most part theoretical rather than based on actual court decisions.
5 In the Polish *Criminality and Criminogenic Conditions* bibliography (Lazarski and Niedzialek 1977), there is no index entry for 'women' or 'women's criminality' (not to mention 'women's perspective'). Several articles discuss rape but most examine the law rather than the problem. They concentrate more on the punishment than on victims of rape or on prevention. It is also characteristic that most of them are written by men.
6 Poland is a strange place where only two sides of the world exist, 'West' and 'East'. Even Japan is in the 'West', and Cuba is in the 'East'.

References

Batawia, S. (1931). *Wstep Do Nauki O Prezestepcy (Introduction to the Science of Offenders)*. Bydgoszcz: Bibljoteka Polska.
Batawia, S. (1958). *Proces Spolecznego Wykolejania Sie Nieletnich Prezetsepcow (The Process of Being Led Astray among Young Offenders)*. Warsaw: Państwowe Wydawnictwo Naukowe.
Bieniek, M. (1974). Rola Ofiary w Genezie Przestępstwa Zgwałcenia (The role of the victim in rape). *Służba MO*, 4–5, 669–77.
Bienkowska, E. 1984 *Wpływ Zachowania Ofiary na Rozstrzygniecie Sprawy o Zgwałcenie (The Impact of the Victim's Behaviour on Court Decisions in Rape Cases)*. Wroclaw: Ossolineum.
Blachut, J. (1981). *Kobiety Recydywistki w Swietle Badan Kryminologicznych (Women Recidivists in Criminological Studies)*. Wroclaw: Ossolineum.
Blachut, J. (1988). *Sadowy Wymiar Kary Wobec Kobiet (Judicial Orders with Regard to Punishments for Women)*. Krakow: Wydawnictwo Uniwersytetu Jagiellonskiego.
Falandysz, L. (1979). *Wiktymologia (Victimology)*. Warsaw: Wiedza Powszechna.
Falandysz, L. (1980). *Pokrzywdzony w Prawie Karnym i Wiktymologii (The Position of the Victim in Criminal Law and Victimology)*. Warsaw: Wydawnictwo Prawnicze.

Horoszowski, P. (1965). *Kryminologia (Criminology)*. Warsaw: Panstwowe Wydawnictwo Naukowe.

Kolarczyk, T., Kubiak, J.R. and Wierzbicki, P. (1984). *Przestepczosc Kobiet Aspekty Kryminologiczne i Pentencjarne (Women's Criminality: Criminological and Penal Aspects)*. Warsaw: Wydawnictwo Prawnicze.

Kolakowska-Przelomiec, H. (1989). *Przestepstwa Niealimentacji (The Offence of Evading the Obligation of Alimony)*. Wroclaw: Ossolineum.

Kuczynski, M. (1980). Przestępstwo Znęcania Się (Kilka uwag) (The crime of ill-treatment: some remarks). *Patologia Społeczna-Zapobieganie*, 8, 181–6.

Lazarski, A. and Niedzialek, M. (1977). *Przestepczosc i Zjawiska Kryminogenne. Bibliografia. (Criminality and Criminogenic Conditions. Bibliography)*. Warsaw: Departament Szkolenia i Doskonalenia Zawodowego MSW.

Lernell, L. (1973). *Zarys Kryminologii Ogolnej (Outline of Genderal Criminology)*. Warsaw: Państwowe Wydawnictwo Naukowe.

Leszczynski, J. (1973). Z Problematyki Etiologii Przestępstwo Seksualnych (Problems of the aetiology of sexual crimes). *Przeglad Penitencjarny*, 1, 18–35.

Nelken, J. (1986). Polska Mysl Kryminologiczna Od Schylku XIX W. Do 1939 (Polish criminology from the end of the nineteenth century to the year 1939). *Archiwum Kryminologii*, 13, 223–60.

Niedworok, J. (1988). *Matki Wiezniarki i ich dzieci w zakladach penitencjarnych. Zagadnienia Podstawowe (Imprisoned Mothers and Their Children: Basic Issues)*. Wroclaw: Wydawnictwo Uniwersytetu Wroclawskiego.

Platek, M. (1985). The law as a crime-inducing factor. *Archiwum Kryminologii*, 7, 189–98.

Platek, M. (1986). Kriminologie als eine selbständige wissenschaftliche Disziplin (Criminology as an autonomous scientific discipline). In G. Löschper, G. Manke and F. Sack (eds) *Kriminologie als selbständiges, interdisziplinäres Hochschulstudium*. Pfaffenweiler: Centaurus-Verlagsgesellschaft.

Rabinowicz, L. (1933). *Podstawy Nauki O Wieziennictwie (Principles of Corrections)*. Warsaw: Gebethner i Wolff.

Part III
North America

8

Canadian criminology and the woman question

DOROTHY E. CHUNN AND ROBERT MENZIES

Historically, all academic disciplines, including criminology,[1] have been premised on a 'regime of rationality' that structures the activities of and relations among their human practitioners (Smith 1992a: 208). Established by the Enlightenment, this regime of rationality is deeply contradictory. Ostensibly grounded in principles of universality and the equality of reasoning subjects, it is in practice fundamentally hierarchical and exclusionary. The universal, 'objective' standards which underpin the traditional model of university education actually reflect the specific life experience of the (usually) young, white, middle-class man who is unencumbered by any responsibilities outside academia (e.g. financial, domestic) and can devote all his time to his studies.

Within the university, the inherent masculinity of these relations of rationality translates into the 'stag' effect, whereby men identify as scholars only with other men (Bernard 1964, cited in Smith 1992a: 218). A historical abundance of male faculty members to act as role models and mentors has guaranteed generations of men graduate students a smooth career path in terms of access to employment, research funding, publication in mainstream journals and so on. Anyone who deviates from the male 'norm' will have more difficulty entering and moving through a graduate programme and pursuing an academic career. Formal equality is undercut by substantive inequalities among individuals related to gender, race and class.

Criminology has been one of the most androcentric disciplines – an entrenched male preserve resistant to change and deaf to voices from the margins. With few exceptions (Heidensohn 1968; Bertrand 1969; Klein 1973; Klein and Kress 1976; Smart 1976), the 'criminological enterprise' remained impervious to feminism until the 1980s, when feminist academics began to demonstrate and challenge the historical gender-blindness of the discipline. Their analyses are heterogeneous, ranging from straightforward exposés of how women are rendered invisible or marginalized in mainstream criminology to the attempted development of new inclusive paradigms, and focusing on diverse issues related to theory and method (Rafter and Natalizia 1981; Gavigan 1982; Heidensohn 1985; Naffine 1985; Daly and Chesney-Lind 1988; Gelsthorpe and Morris 1988, 1990; Simpson 1989; Cain 1990), research and publication (Bertrand et al. 1990a,b; Eigenberg and Baro 1992), curriculum and pedagogy (Menzies and Chunn 1991; Wilson 1991; Lynch et al. 1992; Baro and Eigenberg 1993; Daly 1993a,b; Renzetti 1993) and law and policy (Rafter and Stanko 1982; Boyle et al. 1985; Adelberg and Currie 1987; Carlen and Worrall 1987; Klein et al. 1992).

Like their counterparts elsewhere, Canadian criminologists have been extremely slow to confront feminism. Moreover, academic criminology in Canada is a relatively young discipline that has been shaped by two unique factors: the linguistic division between Anglophone and Francophone criminologists, and the decisive impact of British, Western European and US criminologies (Arnold 1984). The feminist presence in Canadian criminology has been heavily constrained by these historical developments. Indigenous, disciplinary retrospectives are only now beginning to accumulate (Bertrand et al. 1990a,b; Chunn and Menzies 1993; Menzies et al. 1993).

Notwithstanding the traditional conservatism of academic criminology, a feminization of the criminological enterprise has occurred in the United States and other Western countries since the 1960s; women are being rendered visible as students, teachers, authors and researchers. Yet much of the existing literature suggests that, despite the emergence of feminist enclaves in the discipline, a fundamental engendering of the discipline has yet to be effected. Women remain either absent from or 'add-ons' to most criminological teaching, research and publication. In short, feminism has been ghettoized and contained rather than legitimated as an alternative perspective for criminologists (Baro and Eigenberg 1993: 28). Consequently, feminists quite often find themselves at the 'prove it' stage with respect to gender bias, since there is no disciplinary consensus that sexism even exists, much less that it pervades the field (Martin 1993).

These observations have important implications for feminists who want to develop strategies for transgressing and transforming criminology (Cain 1990; Morris and Gelsthorpe 1991). In organizing for change, feminists always confront a tension between mainstreaming and disengagement: if they focus too much on integration they are co-opted, and if they distance themselves from the institutional structures they are isolated and marginalized. Arguably, this also creates possibilities for resistance and transformation (Adamson et al. 1988: 176–90), but it remains an open question whether feminist criminologists will be able to exploit the contradictions within the discipline that will lead to fundamental change.

Clearly, the questions raised above have no definitive answers at the present time, given the dearth of empirical research on the organizational structure and professional character of academic criminology, especially in relation to the participation and status of women (and other marginalized groups). This chapter is an attempt to begin filling the empirical void. Using documentary materials and survey data on current and former graduate students, we develop an exploratory and provisional assessment of the woman question in Canadian criminology from 1963 to 1993 as part of a larger research project intended to track systematically the origins, institutionalization and structure of the discipline in our country (Chunn and Menzies 1993; Menzies *et al.* 1993).

The chapter is divided into three sections. First, we provide some historical background on the development of academic criminology in Canada, review the findings from the few Canadian studies that speak of the impact of gender on the discipline, and outline our own research objectives and design. Second, we examine our survey results and assess the engendering of Canadian criminology with respect to three main issues: structures and hierarchies in the profession and the professionalization process; knowledge production, distribution and consumption; and ideologies and understandings of crime, justice work and socio-legal control practices. Third, we discuss the contradictory implications of our research findings and assess the possibilities for the development of a 'transgressive criminology' (Cain 1990) in Canada and in Western societies more generally.

Disciplinary context and research design

Despite its status as a relative late-comer in the history of Canadian social sciences, academic criminology has experienced immense growth in Canada since the 1960s. Over the course of little more than two decades, criminology centres were established at seven universities across the country: Alberta, Dalhousie, Montreal, Ottawa, Regina, Simon Fraser and Toronto. Moreover, criminology programmes and individual scholars with research interests in crime, law, justice, social control and related concerns have emerged in other disciplines, notably history, sociology, psychology, law and political science. By the late 1980s, academic criminology was a 'growth industry' in Canada. Most universities and many colleges included at least some criminological offerings among their undergraduate and/or postgraduate curricula; several university-based research institutes specializing in crime and justice had been created; volumes of work had appeared in both national and international publications; and many academics were active outside the universities and colleges as participants in and consultants to various criminal justice and correctional agencies, policy institutes, law reform commissions, media organs and diverse political, economic, cultural and community organizations.

It was in this context of expansion that a few criminologists began to examine the extent to which critical and/or feminist perspectives have influenced the organizational structure and professional character of the discipline (Taylor 1983; Arnold 1984; Ratner 1984, 1989; Brickey 1989). However, the first major study of the woman question in Canadian criminology was not conducted until the late 1980s, when a research team at the Université de Montréal decided to analyse the production of criminological work on girls and women from 1964 to 1989 (Bertrand et al. 1990a,b). To determine the quantity of academic output, the proportion of feminist content and the authorship of writings on this topic, the research team surveyed 125 professors and researchers attached to the above-noted Canadian criminology centres and conducted interviews with twenty-one respondents who were identified as the primary producers of texts on the 'question of women' during the period studied (Bertrand et al. 1990a: 2–4).

The findings from the Montreal study are contradictory. On the one hand, they indicate that an apparent[2] feminization of academic criminological knowledge production has taken place in Canada over time. Whereas only forty-four studies on women had been produced from 1964 to 1978, there were sixty-one completed between 1986 and 1988 alone (Bertrand et al. 1990a: 9, 18). In over half of the 206 documents analysed the author(s) also adopted a feminist perspective (Bertrand et al. 1990a: 26–9).

On the other hand, this study lends support to the conclusion of researchers elsewhere (Baro and Eigenberg 1993) that feminism's impact on criminology is contained rather than diffused. For example, more than 60 per cent of the 206 works examined were produced by adherents of 'critical' as opposed to mainstream criminologies (Baro and Eigenberg 1993: 22–3; see also Arnold 1984: 29), and a large majority of the writings informed by a feminist orientation were authored by 'critical' criminologists. Moreover, whereas 68 per cent of the writings authored by women had a feminist orientation, the opposite was true of works by male authors (Bertrand et al. 1990a: 28). In other words, mainstream men, who have traditionally dominated Canadian criminology, remain largely untouched by feminist perspectives.

While it speaks to gender issues, our research was not designed to focus exclusively on the woman question in the criminological enterprise, but rather to begin piecing together a history and sociology of Canadian academic criminology. A central objective of such an endeavour is simply to chart the characteristics of the players – administrators, faculty members and students who embody the constituency of academic criminology in Canada. What is the class, gender, racial, ethnic and age structure of the profession? What are the motivations and expectations of the people who pursue an interest in criminology? How can their 'careers' be characterized and how do they develop over time? Overall, are there any discernible differences between the people who teach, study and research criminological questions and those in the social sciences and law who focus on other substantive areas?

We initiated the search for answers to these questions by focusing primarily on the consumers of academic criminology in Canada – specifically, the population of graduate students formerly and currently enrolled in masters and doctoral programmes[3] – assuming that a look at the activities and experiences of criminologists-in-training over the past three decades would yield valuable information about the developmental trajectory of the discipline in our country. During 1992 and 1993, a semi-structured survey instrument was developed, pre-tested and then mailed to a sample of individuals who had previously undertaken or were then pursuing postgraduate degrees in criminology at four Canadian universities. The questionnaire was devised to assemble the socio-demographic, pedagogical and professional profiles of the target group. Survey items elicited participant reflections on the relevance and impact of their graduate instruction, ideas about criminological theory, research and practice, opinions on current controversies in conventional, critical and feminist criminologies, and perspectives on wider issues related to law, politics and social justice.

Because virtually no one affiliated with the Université de Montréal completed the questionnaire,[4] we have based our analysis on survey responses from current and former criminology graduate students at three universities: Ottawa, Simon Fraser and Toronto. Thus, the data speak primarily to the development of Anglophone, academic criminology in Canada. The survey sample comprised 413 individuals out of a total population of 649 who had been or were enrolled in graduate programmes at the three institutions.[5] Of the 413 mail outs, thirty-eight were returned as undeliverable, and 175 were completed, for an overall return rate of 46.7 per cent. Table 8.1 reveals that sixty-six respondents were current and 103 former graduate students at the three institutions (six persons did not specify); ninety-two respondents were women and eighty-three were men; and the vast majority of respondents (78 per cent) were or had been enrolled in MA programmes, 13 per cent in the Master of Criminal Justice Administration (MCA) programme at Ottawa and just under 10 per cent in doctoral studies.[6] The following section presents a preliminary overview of genderized patterns in Canadian academic criminology based on survey findings as well as documentary data.

Engendering academic criminology in Canada

Women's exclusion from the regime of rationality in academia has been achieved largely through their sexual objectification by men, and has been experienced as a 'chilly climate' characterized by insensitivity, confrontation and/or sexual harassment (Smith 1992a). None the less, women have demanded and struggled to become full participants in the regime of rationality and their partial success is evidenced by a clear but uneven feminization of the academy. To assess the historical impact of gender on Canadian academic criminology since the 1960s, we centred our data analysis on three broad questions. To what extent have the structure of the discipline and professionalization process been feminized over time? Are

Table 8.1   General attributes of graduate student respondents

	N^a	%		N^a	%
Gender			*Age in 1993*[d]		
Women	92	52.6	22–29	52	30.8
Men	83	47.4	30–39	77	45.6
			40–49	36	21.3
Former–current			50–59	3	1.8
Former students	103	58.5	60+	1	0.6
Current students	66	37.7			
Degree type[b]			*Citizenship status*		
Former MA	96	54.9	Canadian	142	81.1
Former MCA	15	8.6	Visa student	19	10.9
Former PhD	1	0.6	Landed immigrant	7	4.0
Current MA	41	23.4	Foreign citizen	6	3.4
Current MCA	8	4.6	Other	1	0.6
Current PhD	16	9.1	*Prior to enrolment*[b]		
Affiliation[b]			Undergraduate	88	50.2
Former U of O	32	18.3	Full-time work	63	36.0
Former SFU	38	21.7	Part-time work	40	22.9
Former U of T	42	24.0	Unpaid volunteer	17	9.7
Current U of O	15	8.6	Qualifying student	15	8.6
Current SFU	36	20.6	Graduate student	13	7.4
Current U of T	17	9.7	Unemployed	5	2.9
			Unpaid home worker	1	0.6
Student living status[b]			Other	6	3.4
Single	107	61.1			
Married	51	29.7	*Following graduation*[b, c]		
With partner	37	21.1	MA, other discipline	5	4.9
Separated	4	2.3	PhD, other discipline	16	15.5
Divorced	6	3.4	PhD, criminology	6	5.8
Widowed	1	0.6	Law school	7	6.8
			Post-doctoral	1	1.0
When graduated[c]			Full-time academic	7	6.8
1973–5	5	4.7	Full-time research	20	19.4
1976–80	11	10.3	Full-time CJS	41	39.8
1981–5	28	26.2	Full-time other	20	19.4
1986–90	40	37.4	Part-time academic	11	10.7
1991–3	23	21.5	Part-time research	8	7.8
			Part-time CJS	7	6.8
			Part-time other	6	5.8
			Unpaid volunteer	9	8.7
			Unemployed	9	8.7
			Other	10	9.7

Notes
[a] $N < 175$ where one or more participants did not respond.
[b] Overlapping categories (percentage > 100).
[c] Former students only.
[d] Mean = 34.2.

women more central to the production and dissemination of criminological knowledge now than they were in 1963? Are women's perspectives on crime and justice significantly different from those of men and, therefore, potentially transformative of the discipline?

Structure of the discipline and professionalization process

The first question focuses attention on the existence and, more specifically, the reduction of gender hierarchies at the departmental level. In analysing our data, we looked for evidence of changes over time in: the proportion of women faculty and students; the acceptance of feminist perspectives as rational and legitimate; the status of women as reflected by sexual harassment and other 'chill' factors; and the amelioration of substantive differences among students. While the survey did not generate information on all these issues, our data revealed some clear feminizing trends. For example, women faculty and graduate students have established an increasingly visible presence over time. By 1992 each department had at least two tenured or tenure-track women faculty who potentially could serve as role models, supervisors and mentors for women students: seven of twenty-three at Simon Fraser; two of fifteen at Toronto; and three of nineteen at Ottawa. Women also comprised four of nineteen faculty at Montreal.

Ultimately, this feminizing process may help to alleviate the problems experienced by some women graduate students during the early and mid-1980s. As one of our survey respondents declared:

> Overall I was satisfied with my programme but I did find some troubling areas . . . Although I perceived it, at the time, to be fair, I wonder if the paucity of women faculty could not be construed as being unfair treatment of the women graduate students . . . After four months of research my [female] thesis supervisor left [the] university and I had to choose another supervisor. This left me choosing from a slate of faculty with little knowledge of my topic, indeed of the entire area of feminist research in criminology. I do not think this is 'Fair treatment of women graduate students'.
>
> (Respondent 128, F, MA, 1984–8)

However, the impact of increased numbers of women faculty is not yet clear. For example, Table 8.2 reveals that, while the majority of respondents did not select a graduate criminology programme because of a particular faculty member's reputation, women (both former and current) were even less likely than men to do so. This may suggest either that most women who pursue criminology graduate studies simply are not woman-identified, or that some recently hired women faculty at Simon Fraser, Ottawa and Toronto have had insufficient time to establish themselves in the discipline as teachers, supervisors and researchers.[7]

What does seem clear from the data is that increases in the number of women faculty have not been proportionate to increases in the number of

Table 8.2 Significant gender differences in experiences, attributes and perspectives (both MA and PhD students)

	Women		Men		χ^2	d.f.	P
	N	%	N	%			
Why was criminology chosen?							
Prior experience teaching criminology					3.88	1	0.05
No	86	94	69	84			
Yes	6	7	13	16			
Wanted to be academic criminologist					6.97	1	0.008
No	71	77	48	59			
Yes	21	23	34	42			
Why this institution?							
General reputation of programme					6.08	1	0.01
No	40	44	21	26			
Yes	52	57	61	74			
Particular faculty member reputation					3.95	1	0.05
No	70	76	51	62			
Yes	22	24	31	38			
Income source							
Off-campus employment					6.28	1	0.01
No	60	65	38	46			
Yes	32	35	44	54			
Family/partner assistance					10.49	1	0.001
No	53	58	66	81			
Yes	39	42	16	20			
Subsequent to degree (former students)							
Enrolled in PhD other than criminology					6.49	1	0.01
No	51	94	45	78			
Yes	3	6	13	22			

	N	Mean	N	Mean	t	d.f.	P
Part-time work as an academic						1	0.04
No	52	96	49	85	4.41		
Yes	2	4	9	16			
Demographics							
Age	90	32	82	36	−3.53	170	0.001
Level of satisfaction							
From 1 (extremely dissatisfied) to 7 (extremely satisfied)							
Computer resources	88	5.25	82	4.57	2.51	135	0.01
Variety of courses	91	3.85	80	4.34	−2.01	169	0.05
Perspectives on crime and social justice							
From 1 (strongly disagree) to 5 (strongly agree)							
Crime is a meaningful concept	88	3.44	79	3.92	−2.85	165	0.005
Too much emphasis on crimes of powerful	89	1.84	80	2.21	−2.92	167	0.004
Criminologist central role social change	88	4.11	82	3.85	2.00	170	0.05
Criminal justice system is gender biased	88	4.24	79	3.51	4.89	165	<0.001
Criminal justice system is class biased	88	4.15	82	3.78	2.51	168	0.01
Too many people in Canadian prisons	89	4.24	82	3.72	3.23	169	0.001
Treatment of criminals is too harsh	89	2.80	80	2.40	2.33	167	0.02

women graduate students entering criminology programmes. The enrolment and completion patterns of students at the three universities do exhibit an accelerated feminization over time. Of the eighty-two women survey respondents who indicated their year of enrolment, only five had begun the programmes between 1970 and 1979, as opposed to twenty-four between 1980 and 1985, and fifty-three between 1986 and 1993. The comparable figures for the eighty-three men enrollees are fifteen, twenty-four and forty-four respectively. Similarly, of the fifty women who had graduated in criminology, nine did so between 1973 and 1981, eleven between 1982 and 1987, and thirty between 1988 and 1993. Equivalent figures for the sixty-three men graduates are sixteen, twenty-five and twenty-two respectively.

In short, the substantial majority of women criminology graduate students in Canada have enrolled or obtained their degrees since 1986. Moreover, women who were barely visible during the 1970s are fast achieving numerical parity with men. This latter development is consistent with a general trend towards women's increased participation in graduate education, especially at the masters level (Yeatman 1992: 56). However, it is noteworthy and encouraging that women also comprised 38 per cent of survey respondents enrolled in or graduated from criminology doctoral programmes.

Perceptible changes in the status of women as evidenced by a reduction in 'chill' factors are another indication of an academic engendering process. Evidence of change would be reflected in shifting perspectives over time on such issues as fairness to women students, freedom from academic exploitation and sexual harassment, and quality of any given department as a learning and social environment. Our survey generated mixed findings on these questions. On the one hand, the data indicate that graduate education in criminology has been and continues to be a 'chilly' experience for some women. With regard to fairness, for example, some women respondents clearly found their departments less supportive of them than of their male counterparts. Some women felt that they were not taken seriously as students, not encouraged to pursue academic studies and/or not assisted in their search for postgraduate employment:

> I was surprised to find myself regarded as 'ideological' because I was a socialist feminist. I was disappointed that no one [in the department] encouraged me to 'stay' to do further graduate work there. (I have recovered(!) from both experiences).
>
> (Respondent 082, F, MA, 1980–1)

> My [male] thesis supervisor gave a good job lead to a male colleague and never mentioned it to me. My thesis was well received by the review committee and I was a good student.
>
> (Respondent 143, F, MCA, 1987)

Moreover, as Table 8.2 shows, women with a criminology masters degree were significantly less likely than were men to enrol subsequently in a doctoral programme other than criminology[8] or to find part-time work as an academic.

Similarly, our data support the findings of researchers in other jurisdictions (e.g. Stanko 1992)[9] that sexual harassment in the form of unwanted comments, remarks and behaviour has been and continues to be problematic for some women criminology graduate students:

> Overall the experience has been quite positive although [there have been] serious problems re sexual harassment.
>
> (Respondent 072, F, MA, 1988–)

> I would like to clarify that I myself was not the victim of sexual harassment . . . However, for the sake of this study, and at least that someone should hear, there is general consensus amongst women in the department regarding which professors we know to avoid in personal settings.
>
> (Respondent 106, F, MA, 1992–)

Moreover, as noted in Table 8.3, among doctoral students in criminology, women respondents were significantly less satisfied than men with respect to freedom from academic exploitation.

On the other hand, our survey data do not reveal any significant aggregate gender differences in responses to these 'chill' factors. Moreover, when criminology doctoral students were analysed separately from masters students, some of the significant gender differences were the reverse of what might have been anticipated (for example, women PhD respondents, contradictorily, actually expressed significantly *more* satisfaction than did men about freedom from sexual and non-sexual harassment).

When it came to climate issues, differences *among* women graduate students were clearly far more important than gender differences themselves. Furthermore, when we looked exclusively at women, levels of satisfaction with fairness to women and freedom from sexual harassment were significantly correlated with perceptions of other experiences related to climate. Specifically, the more dissatisfied women were about the former, the more unhappy they were about the treatment of other student groups such as visible minorities, the learning and social environments in their departments, the quality and commitment to graduate students of faculty and other related 'chill' factors.

Finally, we consider whether and to what extent there may have been an amelioration in the gendered substantive differences which historically led women entering graduate studies to hold lower academic aspirations, less money and more domestic responsibilities than their male counterparts. On these questions, our survey findings are once again mixed. Some data indicate that the gender differences among criminology graduate students have not been reduced radically over time. With regard to aspirations, for example, Table 8.2 tells us that women respondents were and remain less likely than men to enter graduate criminology programmes because they want to become academics.

Table 8.3 Significant gender differences in experiences and perspectives on crime and social justice (PhD students only)[a]

	Women		Men				
	N	Mean	N	Mean	t	d.f.	P
Experiences in PhD programme (1 = extremely dissatisfied to 7 = extremely satisfied)							
Freedom from academic exploitation	7	2.71	7	4.57	-2.16	12	0.05
Fairness to international students	3	5.00	7	3.14	2.56	8	0.03
Freedom from sexual harassment	7	5.57	4	4.00	2.20	9	0.05
Freedom from non-sexual harassment	5	5.40	5	3.60	1.88	8	0.10
Perspectives on crime and social justice (1 = strongly disagree to 5 = strongly agree)							
Crime is a meaningful concept	6	2.67	10	3.90	-1.82	14	0.09
Too much emphasis on crimes of powerful	6	1.67	10	2.80	-1.79	14	0.09
Criminologist central role crime prevention	6	1.83	10	3.20	-2.31	14	0.04
Criminal justice system is gender biased	6	4.67	10	3.60	1.95	14	0.07
Criminal justice system is class biased	6	4.67	10	3.70	1.91	14	0.08
Too many in Canadian prisons	7	4.43	10	3.50	1.71	15	0.10
Treatment of criminals is too harsh	7	3.57	10	1.90	4.03	15	0.001
Self-assigned political identity (1 = far left to 9 = far right)	7	2.71	7	4.57	-2.16	12	0.05

Note
[a] Only those responses attaining significance levels ≤ 0.10 are displayed.

Similarly, the following comment from one of our survey respondents buttresses the conclusion from Yeatman's (1992: 107) cross-disciplinary interview study of MA leavers at Simon Fraser University that lack of money is a more important factor in the attrition of women than of men graduate students:[10] 'I would not have dropped out of the program if I had been able to provide for my family financially. It . . . was very difficult to attend because of finances' (Respondent 009, F, MA, 1989–90).

Whereas both women and men graduate respondents complained about the lack of sufficient departmental and institutional funding, women were significantly more apt to have obtained income from partners and/or other family members, while men were more likely to support themselves through off-campus employment (see Table 8.2). The implications of this apparent gender difference in financial status, however, are uncertain. Are more women than men criminology students able to fit the male model of graduate education, or are they simply less economically viable? Do more men than women enrollees have good jobs and therefore choose to continue working while they are at school, or do they reluctantly endure double and triple work days?

Our survey contained no explicit questions about domestic responsibilities. While men respondents were totally silent on this issue, some women did stress the difficulties they faced in trying to complete a graduate degree while caring for children and/or other family members without any recognition or accommodation of their 'private' circumstances at the departmental or institutional level:

> [The graduate programme] is not supportive of part-time students or women with children.
>
> (Respondent 104, F, PhD, 1989–)

> One of the biggest impacts on my education . . . has been my children – and the political, emotional, etc., factors which come into conflict with trying to parent small children while doing a doctorate.
>
> (Respondent 115, F, PhD, 1987–)

According to Yeatman (1992: 67), as with financial precariousness, the stress and exhaustion experienced by women graduate students who have a 'dual' or 'triple' work day are major determinants of attrition among them. We were also interested in the attrition issue, and whereas our survey population included people who had withdrawn from criminology graduate programmes, very few of them completed and returned questionnaires.[11] One who did respond clearly confirmed Yeatman's findings about the human toll exacted on women graduate students who struggle to do it all:

> Had a dream but unrealistic demands of senior supervisor and selfish family members exhausted me . . . Husband is a special needs adult . . . It was a tremendous hardship to travel . . . to [the university] on days off or between shifts . . . It was one hell of a struggle to never be able to

satisfy my supervisor or my family ... At forty-seven years of age it
really is painful to fail to achieve my dream.

(Respondent 121, F, MA, withdrew 1992)

At the same time, the available evidence suggests that attrition rates
among masters students fluctuate across and within universities but are not
markedly different across gender. From 1985 to 1990, for example, Simon
Fraser University reported an overall graduate student attrition of 30 per
cent, with women actually experiencing slightly lower rates than men
(Yeatman 1992: 60–1). The figures for criminology MA students, however, were much higher at 41 per cent of women, 58 per cent of men and
49 per cent overall. What these relatively equal or lower attrition rates
may indicate is that women graduate students are working harder to achieve
the same level of success as men (Yeatman 1992: 68), therein adapting
themselves to the male model of graduate education rather than resisting
it.

In sum, although there has been a clear feminization of Canadian academic criminology over time among both faculty and graduate students at
the three universities surveyed, our findings do not provide evidence of any
fundamental transformation to date in the internal structure and socialization process of the discipline. The traditional (male) model of academic
education persists despite radical changes since the 1960s, particularly in
the humanities and social 'sciences', in the demographic profiles of both men
and women. It appears that women have been added on to existing criminological structures and that a considerable number of them are competing
successfully within the parameters of the male model.

Knowledge production, distribution and consumption

The following discussion is based on documentary evidence, supplement-
ing the work of Bertrand et al. (1990a,b), about the structure and process
of knowledge production in Canadian criminology.[12] While the latter research concentrated on the authors and content of work about women, we
were instead concerned with the gender of criminological knowledge producers in Canada over time, and whether or not their work focused on
women. Our questions included the following. Have women criminologists
become proportionately more central to knowledge production over the
past thirty years as the authors of dissertations and theses, articles and
books? Do women publish increasingly in mainstream criminological and
socio-legal journals or are they still effectively excluded from these forums? Are more women sole or first authors of criminological publications
now than in the past? Has the work of women criminologists become
more feminist in orientation over time?

To find answers to these questions, we calculated the percentage of MA
theses authored by women at the Universities of Montreal, Simon Fraser
and Toronto from the inception of their respective masters programmes to

1991; the proportion of doctoral dissertations produced by women at the Université de Montréal between 1968 and 1991; and the percentage of articles by women appearing annually in three refereed Canadian journals that publish criminological work. In addition, we attempted to identify the number of feminist graduate theses and published articles that were written between 1970 and 1992.

These documentary analyses reveal generally that women criminologists in Canada have become more prominent over time as producers and disseminators of criminological knowledge. This visibility is quite obvious with respect to MA theses authored by women. Reflecting the general historical trend towards the feminization of graduate studies at the masters level, the proportion of women-generated MA theses, with fluctuations, has risen overall since graduate criminology programmes were first established. At the Université de Montréal, the annual proportion of woman-authored Mémoires de Maîtrise was generally well under 40 per cent between 1963 and 1978, but by the 1980s had jumped to 60 per cent or more of the total (Chunn and Menzies 1993). Similarly, women at Simon Fraser University produced fewer than 20 per cent of masters theses yearly between 1981 and 1985, and 60 per cent or more from 1986 to 1991 (Chunn and Menzies 1993). Interestingly, a somewhat different production pattern emerged at the University of Toronto Centre of Criminology, where, with two or three exceptions, women graduate students authored at least half of the MA theses every year from the inauguration of the masters programme in 1972 to 1990, with an annual average of close to 60 per cent for the entire period (Chunn and Menzies 1993).

Predictably, when we looked at the production of doctoral dissertations, the picture changed. The Université de Montréal, which has the only long-standing criminology PhD programme in Canada, began graduating students in 1968. By the end of 1991, forty-two people had completed doctoral degrees, but only eight of them were women (Chunn and Menzies 1993). Moreover, the number of woman-authored doctoral dissertations has not shown the marked increase over time that is so evident in the production patterns for criminology theses at the masters level; three of the eight were written between 1968 and 1979 and five from 1980 to 1991 (Chunn and Menzies 1993). None the less, women did generate a higher proportion of the doctoral theses at Montreal during the latter period (26 per cent) than the former (13 per cent), given that relatively fewer men completed PhDs between 1980 and 1991.

Next, we calculated the percentage of women authors who have published each year in three Canadian journals that are representative of mainstream criminological, socio-legal and critical/feminist criminological approaches respectively: the *Canadian Journal of Criminology* (*CJC*), the *Canadian Journal of Law and Society* (*CJLS*) and the *Journal of Human Justice* (*JHJ*). Established in 1970, the *CJC* was the only criminology journal in Canada accessible to unilingual Anglophones until the formation of the *JHJ* in 1989. Our longitudinal analysis of women's authorship in the

CJC between 1970 and 1992 revealed a fluctuating pattern of publication throughout the entire period. On the one hand, it was clear that women have been consistently under-represented in that journal, comprising no more than 20 per cent of authors annually for fifteen of the twenty-two years. On the other hand, there was at least some indication that women's contributions to the *CJC* might be increasing; women made up more than 20 per cent of authors (with a high of 47 per cent) in five of the six years from 1987 to 1992 (Chunn and Menzies 1993).

The gender patterns of authorship in the two other Canadian journals were also revealing. Between 1986 and 1992, women comprised about one-quarter of all authors in the *CJLS*. But the number of works by women, which ranged from zero to two per year up to 1991 and never made up more than 29 per cent of items published, increased dramatically to eleven (44 per cent) during 1992. Finally, as might be expected, among these three periodicals it is the *JHJ* that has consistently contained the highest concentration of woman-authored work: never dropping below 25 per cent of the total from 1989 to 1992, and rising as high as 65 per cent in 1991 when a special issue on feminist justice studies was published.

While women's increased participation in the promulgation and distribution of criminological knowledge is important, we also wanted to determine the extent to which feminism has been a presence in this development. Clearly, not all women are feminists (nor are all feminists women). Therefore, if disciplinary transformation is the goal, it is essential to have a critical mass of feminists who can contribute to that process through, among other things, their research and publications. We carried out a very rudimentary categorization, based on titles, of the graduate theses completed at the three universities along with articles in the above-discussed three journals, to separate the feminist from the non-feminist criminological work produced between 1970 and 1992. We discovered a small but apparently expanding body of feminist theses and journal articles. The number of dissertations with feminist content completed by criminology students at Montreal, Simon Fraser and Toronto showed a marked increase over time: five during the 1970s, twenty during the 1980s and six during the first three years of the 1990s (Chunn and Menzies 1993). The growth in the number of feminist journal articles was even more striking: two from 1970 to 1979, three from 1980 to 1989 and twenty-eight from 1990 to 1992.

Overall, our documentary data indicate that women have indeed expanded their contributions to criminological knowledge in Canada since the 1960s and that a growing number of theses and journal articles now have an explicit feminist orientation. What we cannot say for certain is who might be the main consumers of this woman-generated body of work on criminality, justice and related socio-legal issues. It seems probable, though, that feminist work is still more ghettoized than diffused, being confined primarily to explicitly critical/feminist forums such as the *JHJ* and/or concentrated in special issues.

Moreover, given the limited scope of our documentary data, we are unable to assess with any accuracy whether or how much the proportion of criminological knowledge produced by women has increased in relation to that generated by men, i.e. to determine if women are more *central* to knowledge production now than they were in the past. To do so, it would be necessary to look more broadly at the authorship and content of criminological work published in other Canadian journals and texts as well as in periodicals and books emanating from outside the country.

Perspectives on crime and justice and politics

What mindset do graduate students in criminology have about crime, justice and politics? Are they more conservative than other students in the social sciences, students in general or the population at large? Whereas Canadian studies on undergraduate students yield contradictory conclusions about the radicalizing impact of social science education (Guimond and Palmer 1994), none of this work expressly examines inter- or intra-gender differences within a specific discipline. Hence our own gendered analysis of criminological students' perspectives on academic, social and political issues offers some revealing insights into the ideological and attitudinal contrasts between women and men, and among women themselves, that may well offer a transformative potential for the discipline as a whole.

To determine the perspectives of graduate students about the structure and politics of the criminological enterprise, we asked respondents for opinions on a number of controversial issues in the field. Using a five-point scale, we elicited reactions to twenty-one statements about: the nature and role of criminology; the role of the criminologist; the administration of criminal justice; and the social and carceral functions of punishment.

Among statements addressing the nature and role of criminology, two items elicited markedly divergent responses between women and men: 'crime is a meaningful concept' and 'criminology focuses too much on crimes of the powerful'. Across all survey respondents, women were less likely than men to agree with either of these statements over time (see Table 8.2). The same gender differences held for doctoral students (see Table 8.3), although women PhD candidates exhibited even less agreement with the items while concurrence by men remained the same or increased. And when women alone are included (see Table 8.4), a significant difference emerged between present and former students on whether crime is a meaningful concept, with currently enrolled women being much less likely to agree.

Three statements about the role of the criminologist also prompted diverse responses. Across all respondents, women were significantly more likely to concur than were men that 'a central role of the criminologist should be to effect social change' (see Table 8.2). Among doctoral students specifically, women agreed less often than did male counterparts that 'a central

Table 8.4 Differences in criminological–social justice perspectives among women respondents

From 1 = strongly disagree to 5 = strongly agree	F	d.f.	P	R	Main effects (d.f. = 6)	Age (d.f. = 1)	Now v. then (d.f. = 1)	Which campus (d.f. = 2)	Canada/ other (d.f. = 1)	Which degree (d.f. = 2)
1 Criminology is a scientific discipline	0.40	7,73	0.90	0.19						
2 Criminology is autonomous from other academic disciplines	1.23	7,77	0.30	0.32						
3 Crime is a meaningful concept	2.13	7,76	0.05	0.41	2.49*		6.90**			
4 Criminology is of little relevance to Canadian society	0.85	7,75	0.55	0.27						
5 Criminology in Canada is distinct from criminology elsewhere	0.64	7,79	0.72	0.34						
6 Criminology in Canada is predominantly identified with criminal justice studies	1.16	7,73	0.34	0.32						
7 Criminology focuses too much on crimes of the powerless	0.44	7,78	0.88	0.19						
8 Criminology focuses too much on crimes of the powerful	0.66	7,76	0.70	0.24						
9 A central role of the criminologist should be to prevent crime	3.48	7,75	0.003	0.50	3.92**			10.47***		
10 A central role of the criminologist should be to facilitate legal reform	1.24	7,76	0.29	0.32						2.38*

11 A central role of the criminologist should be to promote social justice	1.51	7,76	0.18	0.35						2.78*
12 A central role of the criminologist should be to effect social change	0.93	7,77	0.49	0.28						
13 The Canadian criminal justice system is gender biased	2.24	7,77	0.04	0.42	2.36*		4.02*		4.64*	
14 The Canadian criminal justice system is class biased	1.60	7,75	0.15	0.36						
15 The Canadian criminal justice system is racially biased	2.60	7,77	0.02	0.44	3.03*		3.81*			
16 The Charter of Rights has had a positive impact on the quality of Canadian life	1.37	7,75	0.23	0.34			4.58*			
17 By and large, Canadian police are doing a good job	0.64	7,74	0.72	0.24						
18 Prisons should foremost be places of punishment	1.37	7,74	0.23	0.34				3.97*		
19 There are too many people in Canadian prisons	0.59	7,76	0.77	0.23						
20 The primary goal of criminal justice should be the rehabilitation of offenders	2.94	7,76	0.009	0.46	2.47*	5.74*				
21 The treatment of criminals is too harsh	0.70	7,76	0.67	0.24						2.51*

Note
*$P < 0.05$; **$P < 0.01$; ***$P < 0.005$.

role of the criminologist should be to prevent crime' (see Table 8.3). Looking solely at women's perspectives, we find marked inter-university differences of opinion on the crime prevention item (with Ottawa enrollees more likely to concur), and higher levels of endorsement for MA than for other students on whether 'a central role of the criminologist should be to promote social justice' (see Table 8.4).

Two statements on the administration of criminal justice ('the Canadian criminal justice system is gender biased' and 'the Canadian criminal justice system is class biased') revealed highly significant differences in respondents' perspectives, with the former item yielding the greatest divergence of opinion of any statement in the survey, and with women being far more likely to agree than were men (see Table 8.2). These same patterns were evident among PhD candidates, although there the gender differences were not so pronounced (see Table 8.3). Interestingly, the intensity of feeling about gender bias was observed to elicit 'backlash' from one male respondent:

[The] Canadian criminal justice system is gender biased . . . (in favour of women) – this response applies to sentencing disparity (i.e. women seem to receive more lenient sentences than men in my experience). It also applies to hiring and promotion in the field . . . This question- naire appears to be gender biased.

(Respondent 006, M, MA, 1981–5)

Among women alone, it was Canadians rather than others, and current as opposed to former students, who were more likely to agree that the Canadian justice system is biased (see Table 8.4). Moreover, women's perceptions of sexism were strongly correlated with their views on other issues. Those who saw gender bias were apt to believe that the system is class and racially biased, that Canadian police are not doing a good job, that there are too many people in Canadian prisons, that the treatment of criminals in Canada is too harsh, that crime is not a meaningful concept and that prisons should not primarily be places of punishment.

The statement on class bias in the criminal justice system also evoked strongly divergent opinions. Again, women were significantly more likely, overall and among doctoral students, to agree that the administration of justice is class biased (see Tables 8.2 and 8.3). Interestingly, however, while there were no marked differences among women respondents on the class bias item, Table 8.4 tells us that women currently enrolled in gradu- ate programmes were more apt than former students to agree that 'the Canadian criminal justice system is racially biased' and less likely to con- cur that 'the Charter of Rights has had a positive impact on the quality of Canadian life'.

Among statements on the social and carceral functions of punishment, two items evoked highly divergent perspectives. Across all respondents, women were far more apt than men to agree that 'there are too many people in Canadian prisons' and that 'the treatment of criminals in Canada is too harsh' (see Table 8.2). These patterns were also apparent for PhD students (see Table 8.3), although at a rather lower level of significance. Interestingly, Table 8.4 reveals no noteworthy differences in women's opinions on either item.

To establish some sense of the politics embraced by Canadian criminology graduate students in Canada over time, we also asked respondents to locate themselves on a nine-point 'political identity' scale ranging from 'far left' to 'far right'. No marked differences emerged, either between women and men overall or among women respondents. However, Table 8.3 shows that, within the PhD cohort specifically, women students were significantly more left-wing than were men. Moreover, women who identified themselves as on the political left registered significantly lower mean levels of satisfaction on the issues of fairness to women and freedom from sexual harassment than did their more right-wing counterparts.

Overall, we see some interesting patterns emanating from our survey of participants' views on crime, justice and politics. Across all respondents, the data reveal significant gender differences in opinions expressed about seven of the twenty-one statements about key issues in criminology and, in every instance, women were more critical and less punitive than were men. The former were more likely than the latter to question the very meaning of crime, to empathize with the powerless, to identify discriminatory criminal justice practices and to reject the extensive use of penal sanctions. Among doctoral students, we discern the same gender division in stated views on these same seven issues, although the differences are for the most part less pronounced than with the entire cohort.

If we look exclusively at women, there are signs that those undertaking graduate criminology programmes at the time of our survey were more critical, and more oriented towards feminism, than were former students. Current enrollees were less likely, for example, to believe that crime is a meaningful concept, and more apt to feel that the criminal justice system is gender and racially biased. From a feminist perspective, we think these findings bode well for the future development of academic criminology in Canada. If women faculty and graduate students continue to grow in number, they could become a transformative force both within and beyond the discipline.

Feminism and a transgressive criminology in Canada

Although we make no definitive claims about feminist impact, we can say with confidence that there has been a gendering of Canadian academic criminology since the 1960s. But several questions remain unanswered. What is the extent of that engendering? Is feminism becoming a significant force in the discipline? In Smith's (1992b) terms, how likely is it that women (and other excluded groups) will be able to transform the hegemonic 'regime of rationality'? And can women criminologists ultimately transcend the male model of graduate education so that the white, middle-class, unencumbered man is no longer the 'norm' against which everyone else must be assessed?

In addressing these questions, feminist criminologists might learn and take solace from the experience of academic sociology in Canada, which is deviant relative to other social 'sciences' (for example, anthropology and political science) in having been forced, albeit reluctantly, to deal with the 'feminist fact' at a relatively early stage of disciplinary development (Eichler 1992; Maticka-Tyndale and Drakich 1992; Smith 1992b). But feminists in criminology have faced three major problems which are not necessarily shared by their sociological counterparts, and which create resistance to change. First, the subject matter of the discipline is masculine to the core: focused squarely on the criminal law and criminal justice, and therefore on men, who dominate every facet of the field as both authorities and subjects. Second, there is no national professional academic organization analogous to the Canadian Sociology and Anthropology Association through which feminists can organize. Moreover, academic criminology historically did not have feminists inside the universities who could work with the women's movement outside the academy to effect change (Maticka-Tyndale and Drakich 1992).

What are the odds of reversing this historical legacy? Regrettably, it seems unlikely that a transgressive Canadian criminology (Cain 1990) will emerge in the near future. A gradualist model of change, based on mainstreaming strategies aimed at granting women access to existing positions and resources within established institutional structures, continues to dominate criminology as it does other disciplines. Such an approach is limited because women are simply grafted on to the status quo and still must fit within the parameters of male-defined graduate education and academic life more generally. Moreover, co-optation is always a danger. Thus to concentrate solely on steady, incremental movement towards a glorious feminist future in criminology will not lead to transformation (Adamson et al. 1988: 176–90).

At the same time, we do not share Smart's (1990) pessimism about the criminological enterprise, at least as the discipline has been unfolding within the Canadian context. Because power is never monolithic, openings are continuously being presented for feminists to develop synthesized strategies for change that integrate mainstreaming with disengaged activism outside established institutional structures. Overall, then, we prefer to voice a tempered, and perhaps somewhat diffident, optimism about the possibilities for disciplinary transformation, based in no small part on the history and experience of feminism as it has evolved in our own department at Simon Fraser University.

Until very recently here, the critical mass necessary for the establishment and preservation of feminist interests and activities was lacking. In the seven years following the department's 1975 formation, only two permanent women faculty were hired and neither was a feminist. Since 1982, though, a growing emphasis on mainstreaming by some faculty has arguably produced a critical mass of women/feminists and resulted in a partial feminization of the department. This engendering process took a number of forms: the hiring of four feminist women since 1989; the conversion of two other women faculty to feminism; the introduction of several men faculty to feminism (within the limitations and contradictions of what that may mean); the mounting of three undergraduate courses, and frequent special topics seminars and graduate courses, explicitly focusing on women; the election of a feminist woman as director in the early 1990s; the admission to our graduate programme of increasing numbers of women (and men) doing critical feminist work; and the 1990 establishment by six women of the Feminist Institute for Studies on Law and Society, which aims to forge links between academics studying socio-legal issues, and between academics and feminists outside the academy who are concerned with socio-legal issues.

These changes will be difficult to erase, given the hard-won knowledge that reform is always a political and perverse process. By its very constitution, context and subject matter, feminist criminology, or feminism in criminology, is deeply immersed within and reproductive of a litany of contradictions, which can assert themselves at three different but interrelated levels – the departmental, the institutional and the societal – and in the process can both facilitate and impede the development of a transformative politic.

At the *departmental* level, contradictions arise because in criminology (as elsewhere) feminism was introduced into prevailing academic power structures, and more specifically into existing gender hierarchies, with two main consequences. First, as Eichler and Tite (1990) discovered in their retrospective of women's studies, those with more power (primarily men) can and do profit from feminism. For example, men who introduce feminist content into courses (which is what we want) get more 'credit' for their efforts than do feminist women. Similarly, men who develop research proposals on 'women's' issues, such as spousal/partner violence and sexual assault (which is also what we want), often receive huge research grants and hire women research assistants. Sometimes, feminist women are used to provide credibility for men as co-researchers and co-authors; they are likely to be junior, untenured assistants or graduate students who are powerless to protest against their academic exploitation.

Second, many women do not embrace feminism. Consequently, the hiring of non-feminist women faculty who are then deployed against feminism remains a distinct possibility. Similarly, self-professed feminists, both faculty and students, may not translate their language into practice; they may play the system, and work only or primarily with men who are more senior and useful to career advancement in a shrinking academic job market. Moreover, gender is not the only basis of structured inequalities in the academy; there are differences among women and among men generated by class, race, ethnicity, sexuality, (dis)ability and so on. Focusing solely on eradicating gender divisions will not in and of itself democratize and transform existing power relations.

At the *institutional* level, contradictions are generated by the fact that feminism has been introduced into settings that are integrally linked to wider university hierarchies, and to state structures and private enterprises located beyond the university altogether. Academic feminism, in criminology as elsewhere, does not reside in a vacuum. It is subject to the impact of these broader arrangements on teaching, research, publication records, career contingencies and so on. These influences are two-fold, emanating from both without and within the university environment. Externally, we can pinpoint the emergence of neo-conservative governments during the 1980s, which emphasized privatization, slashed educational spending and entrenched the 'corporate' university by downplaying the humanities and social studies and upgrading business and the sciences. In Canada, this trend continues into the 1990s, notwithstanding the election of social democratic governments in three different provinces.

Internally, we see how the entrenchment of the 'corporate' university and the corresponding emphasis on the private sector make so-called 'marginal' areas of study and research vulnerable because they are generally less attractive to corporate/private funding agencies, because they are more susceptible than longer-standing programmes/courses to cuts and eliminations, and because they draw fewer students. In criminology, the result has been an intensifying pressure to focus narrowly on criminal law and criminal justice and to transform gender into sex (a variable) or to erase it altogether in teaching, research and publication – because that is where the rewards are. All of these developments affect 'junior' faculty (disproportionately women) who are more at the mercy of cutbacks, and more likely to be denied tenure, since funding sources and publication outlets are less accessible to feminists who rely mainly on non-corporate funding.

At the *societal* level, we need recurrently to remind ourselves that feminism is, after all, primarily about praxis and transformation, and that its impact on criminology must be assessed in that light. And here, too, feminist criminologists are facing a wall of internal and external contradictions. Within the institution, it is apparent that what is good for feminist strategic practice is not always politically feasible. Without, the prevailing relationship between (institutional) academic feminism and the women's movement beyond the university walls has become increasingly fractious, with a welter of attendant complications and constraints that we cannot even begin to explore in a chapter of this kind.

What these various twists and turns seem to be leading to, at this juncture in the engendering of Canadian criminology, is an array of diverse formations and forces that are cutting across both feminism and criminology in complex ways, and creating a kaleidoscope of alliances and conflicts that will work themselves out in unpredictable patterns over the coming years. But however unresolved may be the current picture, some recently observed trends are, we must confess, less than reassuring. We note, for example, the emergence in some sites of a focus on 'gender studies' and/

or the expectation that courses on 'women' will not 'just' be by and about feminists. Such developments can potentially translate into a receding feminist presence in a genderized criminology, or alternatively a feminist criminology without women, or a women's criminology without feminism. Further, we can witness elsewhere the transformation of gender into a variable (that old criminological standby) and the creation of a 'wheel of oppression' whereby women compete with other marginal 'interest groups' for a share of ever-diminishing resources (Daly 1993a). In areas such as harassment and employment equity policy, there has also been a mounting (and in many places highly toxic) backlash, in the alleged name of academic freedom, against reforms that have been only recently secured after many years of struggle.

Whether these resistances can be met and overcome – and whether the engendering of criminology will ultimately have meaning beyond the university walls – depends in the final instance on the capacity of feminist women (and their allies in other progressive domains) to come to terms with these contradictions; both to work within and to explode the limitations imposed by a masculinist academic environment; to push forward the beachheads in the likely face of ever-mounting resistance from the traditional core of an enterprise that is still fundamentally about controlling dissent and securing order; and to recognize that the engendering of Canadian criminology is, in the final analysis, about the transgression and transformation of the discipline itself.

Acknowledgements

We are grateful for project funding received from Simon Fraser University through its President's Research Grant and Social Sciences and Humanities Research Council Small Grant programmes. Thanks are due to Lenore Aspell for her research assistance, to Diane Croteau, Lucie Major, Monica Bristol and Aileen Sams for facilitating our survey research, to the current and former criminology graduate students who participated in the survey, and to Nicole Hahn Rafter and Frances Heidensohn for their helpful comments. An earlier version of this chapter was presented at the British Criminology Conference, Cardiff, Wales, 28–31 July 1993. Our reference to the woman question in criminology was inspired by Bertrand *et al.* (1990a: 1–2).

Notes

1 While the debate over the status of criminology as a discrete discipline is, of course, long-standing and ongoing, in this chapter we are working from the premise that it is a distinctive, interdisciplinary social science.

2 We say 'apparent' because the researchers were not able to compile exhaustive data on the scholarly productivity of women and men at these seven centres during the entire timespan (1964–89) of the investigation (Bertrand *et al.* 1990a: 24).

3 Another project that entails a survey of and follow-up interviews with former and current part-time instructors in criminology at one Canadian university is now in progress.

4 We sent forty-two questionnaires to current and former students at Montreal in the first mail out and received four responses. The low response rate is doubtless attributable both to our inability, for financial reasons, to translate the questionnaire into French, and to the saturation of potential Université de Montréal respondents from earlier surveys conducted by researchers at their own institution.

5 The sample included all current graduate students at the three universities in 1992–3 (68, 34 and 47 at Simon Fraser, Toronto and Ottawa respectively); all former students at Simon Fraser (74); and a 50 per cent sample of all former students at Toronto and Ottawa (total populations of 203 and 223 each).

6 This preponderance of masters level respondents reflects the fact that the Université de Montréal has the only long-standing Canadian doctoral programme in criminology. The University of Ottawa has offered MCA and MA curricula in criminology since 1967; the University of Toronto began offering MA degrees in 1971–2 and PhDs in 1990; and Simon Fraser University inaugurated its MA and PhD programmes in 1978 and 1985 respectively.

7 At Simon Fraser, for example, four of seven tenure-track women faculty have been hired since 1989.

8 We found no significant gender difference among respondents who subsequently enrolled in criminology doctoral programmes, but the small number (six) may account for this result.

9 A 1991 survey of members in the Division on Women and Crime, American Society of Criminology revealed that 59 per cent of sixty-five respondents (220 distributed) had received unwanted comments or remarks about their sexuality during professional and graduate training; about one in three had been sexually harassed while undertaking fieldwork and research; and 53 per cent had received unwelcome sexual comments during their professional employment, with half of these working in a harassing situation at the time of survey (Stanko 1992: 3–5).

10 However, all visa students without substantial scholarships or independent financial resources lead a financially precarious existence because they cannot engage in full-time employment.

11 Yeatman (1992: 11) had the same experience; she had to abandon the quantitative component in her study of leavers at Simon Fraser because of the low response to her questionnaire. For obvious reasons, many people who fail to complete their graduate degrees do not wish to revisit their experience.

12 The original version of our survey questionnaire contained questions about knowledge production in relation to theses or dissertations. However, respondents found the instrument excessively time-consuming and, to increase the return rate, we shortened the follow-up questionnaire by eliminating those items.

References

Adamson, N., Briskin, L. and McPhail, M. (1988). *Feminist Organizing for Change: the Contemporary Women's Movement in Canada*. Toronto: Oxford University Press.

Adelberg, E. and Currie, C. (eds) (1987). *Too Few to Count: Canadian Women in Conflict with the Law*. Vancouver: Press Gang.

Arnold, B. (1984). Criminal justice education in British Columbia: a political perspective. *Canadian Criminology Forum*, 7(1), 21–40.

Baro, A. and Eigenberg, H. (1993). Images of gender: a content analysis of photographs in introductory criminology and criminal justice textbooks. *Women and Criminal Justice*, 5(1), 3–36.

Bertrand, M.A. (1969). Self image and delinquency: a contribution to the study of female criminality and woman's image. *Acta Criminologica*, 2, 71–144.

Bertrand, M.A. *et al.* (1990a). *Analysis of Studies on the Question of Women Produced in University Centres of Criminology in Canada from 1964 to 1989.* Montreal: International Centre for Comparative Criminology, University of Montreal.

Bertrand, M.A. *et al.* (1990b). *Major Sources of Studies on the Question of Women in Canadian University Centres of Criminology.* Montreal: International Centre for Comparative Criminology, University of Montreal.

Boyle, C. *et al.* (eds) (1985). *A Feminist Review of Criminal Law.* Ottawa: Status of Women Canada and Ministry of Supply and Services.

Brickey, S. (1989). Research funding for critical criminology and progressive justice studies. Unpublished paper, Canadian Law and Society Association Meeting, Quebec, June.

Cain, M. (1990). Towards transgression: new directions in feminist criminology. *International Journal of the Sociology of Law*, 18(1), 1–18.

Carlen, P. and Worrall, A. (eds) (1987). *Gender, Crime and Justice.* Milton Keynes: Open University Press.

Chunn, D.E. and Menzies, R. (1993) Discipline in dissent: the gendering of Canadian criminology. Unpublished paper, British Criminology Conference, Cardiff, 28–31 July.

Daly, K. (1993a). Class-race-gender: sloganeering in search of meaning. *Social Justice*, 20(1–2), 56–71.

Daly, K. (1993b). Teaching criminology with a feminist flourish. *Focus on Law Studies*, 8(2), 5, 8.

Daly, K. and Chesney-Lind, M. (1988). Feminism and criminology. *Justice Quarterly*, 5(4), 497–538.

Eichler, M. (1992). The unfinished transformation: women and feminist approaches in sociology and anthropology. In W.K. Carroll *et al.* (eds) *Fragile Truths: 25 Years of Sociology and Anthropology in Canada.* Ottawa: Carleton University Press.

Eichler, M. and Tite, R. (1990). Women's studies professors in Canada: Collective self-portrait. *Atlantis*, 16(1), 6–24.

Eigenberg, H. and Baro, A. (1992). Women and publication patterns in criminal justice journals: a content analysis. *Journal of Criminal Justice Education*, 3(2), 293–314.

Gavigan, S.A.M. (1982). Women's crime and feminist critiques: a review of the literature. *Canadian Criminology Forum*, 5(1), 40–53.

Gelsthorpe, L. and Morris, A. (1988). Feminism and criminology in Britain. In P. Rock (ed.) *A History of British Criminology.* Oxford: Clarendon Press.

Gelsthorpe, L. and Morris, A. (eds) (1990). *Feminist Perspectives in Criminology.* Milton Keynes: Open University Press.

Guimond, S. and Palmer, D.L. (1994). The politics of Canadian social scientists: a comment on Baer and Lambert. *Canadian Review of Sociology and Anthropology*, 31(2), 184–95.

Heidensohn, F. (1968). The deviance of women: a critique and an enquiry. *British Journal of Sociology*, 19, 160–75.

Heidensohn, F. (1985). *Women and Crime.* London: Macmillan.

Klein, D. (1973). The etiology of female crime: a review of the literature. *Issues in Criminology*, 8(2), 3–30.

Klein, D. and Kress, J. (1976). Any woman's blues: a critical overview of women, crime and the criminal justice system. *Crime and Social Justice*, 5, 34–49.

Klein, D., Daly, K. and Bertrand, M.A. (eds) (1992). *Proceedings of the International Feminist Conference on Women, Law and Social Control*, Mont Gabriel, Quebec, 1991.

Lynch, M.J. *et al.* (1992). Cultural literacy, criminology, and female-gender issues: the power to exclude. *Journal of Criminal Justice Education*, 3(2), 183–202.

Martin, S. (1993). Proving gender bias in the law and the legal system. In J. Brockman and D.E. Chunn (eds) *Investigating Gender Bias: Law, Courts and the Legal Profession*. Toronto: Thompson Educational Publishing.

Maticka-Tyndale, E. and Drakich, J. (1992). Striking a balance: women organizing for change in the CSAA. In W.K. Carroll *et al.* (eds) *Fragile Truths: 25 Years of Sociology and Anthropology in Canada*. Ottawa: Carleton University Press.

Menzies, R. and Chunn, D.E. (1991). Kicking against the pricks: the dilemmas of feminist teaching in criminology. *The Critical Criminologist*, 3(1), 2–3.

Menzies, R., Chunn, D.E. and Aspell, L. (1993). The getting of wisdom: ideological perspectives among Canadian graduate students in criminology. Unpublished paper, Canadian Law and Society Association Meeting, Ottawa, 7–9 June.

Morris, A. and Gelsthorpe, L. (1991). Feminist perspectives in criminology: transforming and transgressing. *Women and Criminal Justice*, 2(2), 3–26.

Naffine, N. (1987). *Female Crime: the Construction of Women in Criminology*. Sydney: Allen & Unwin.

Rafter, N.H. and Natalizia, E.M. (1981). Marxist feminism: implications for criminal justice. *Crime and Delinquency*, 27, 81–98.

Rafter, N.H. and Stanko, E.A. (eds) (1982). *Judge, Lawyer, Victim, Thief*. Boston: Northeastern University Press.

Ratner, R.S. (1984). Inside the liberal boot: the criminological enterprise in Canada. *Studies in Political Economy*, 13, 145–64.

Renzetti, C.M. (1993). On the margins of the malestream (or, they *still* don't get it, do they?): feminist analyses in criminal justice education. *Journal of Criminal Justice Education*, 4(2), 219–34.

Simpson, S. (1989). Feminist theory, crime, and justice. *Criminology*, 27(4), 605–31.

Smart, C. (1976). *Women, Crime and Criminology: a Feminist Critique*. London: Routledge & Kegan Paul.

Smart, C. (1990). Feminist approaches to criminology or postmodern woman meets atavistic man. In L. Gelsthorpe and A. Morris (eds) *Feminist Perspectives in Criminology*. Milton Keynes: Open University Press.

Smith, D.E. (1992a). Whistling women: reflections on rage and rationality. In W.K. Carroll *et al.* (eds) *Fragile Truths: 25 Years of Sociology and Anthropology in Canada*. Ottawa: Carleton University Press.

Smith, D.E. (1992b). Remaking a life, remaking sociology: reflections of a feminist. In W.K. Carroll *et al.* (eds) *Fragile Truths: 25 Years of Sociology and Anthropology in Canada*. Ottawa: Carleton University Press.

Stanko, B. (1992). Sexual harassment and the criminological profession. *The Criminologist*, 17(5), 1–5.

Taylor, I. (1983). *Crime, Capitalism and Community: Three Essays in Socialist Criminology*. Toronto: Butterworths.

Wilson, N.K. (1991). Feminist pedagogy in criminology. *Journal of Criminal Justice Education*, 2(1), 81–93.

Yeatman, M. (1992). *Master's student attrition at Simon Fraser University: a portrait*. Unpublished MA thesis, Simon Fraser University.

9

From patriarchy to gender: feminist theory, criminology and the challenge of diversity

JAMES W. MESSERSCHMIDT

The second wave of the US feminist movement illuminated the patterns of gendered power that social theory to that point had all but ignored.[1] In particular, radical feminism actually put second-wave feminism on the map, secured for sexual politics a permanent role in popular culture and moved analysis of normative heterosexuality and gendered power to the forefront of feminist thought. Moreover, radical feminist research – both within and without criminology – spotlighted the nature and pervasiveness of violence against women.

Specifically within criminology, feminist scholars have documented the repeated omission and misrepresentation of females ('girls and women') in criminological inquiry, and subsequently examined crime by females in order to correct traditional masculine mythologies. Moreover, several scholars in the late 1970s and early 1980s 'tested theories derived from all-male samples to see if they apply to girls or women' (Daly and Chesney-Lind 1988: 514). Not surprisingly, feminist criminologists rejected these well-known and purportedly general and comprehensive theories. As Leonard (1982: 1–2) concluded after a careful review, theoretical criminology

> is simply not up to the analytical task of explaining female patterns of crime. Although some theories work better than others, they all illustrate what social scientists are slowly recognizing within criminology and outside the field: that our theories are not the general explanations of human behavior they claim to be, but rather particular understandings of male behavior.

Because criminology failed miserably to explain crime committed by females, it seemed logical to turn to feminist theory. As Frances Heidensohn

(1985: 162) put it in the mid-1980s, 'we have to step outside the confines of criminological theories altogether and seek models from other sources in order to achieve a better understanding of women and crime.' Heidensohn went on to argue for a perspective that made use of the 'interesting and challenging analysis . . . which feminist theory and studies have to offer' (p. 200).

In what follows I briefly review two of the most visible second-wave feminist perspectives that attracted the attention of feminist criminologists. After outlining the positive and the problematic natures of these perspectives, I discuss new feminist efforts at theory construction – in particular the shift in theoretical focus from patriarchal sexual difference to the situational construction of gender itself. I then apply this latter approach to one specific area of crime by females – girls in street gangs – to demonstrate how this new development, which illuminates both gender difference and gender similarity in crime, provides a more fruitful and promising approach to the study of gender and crime.

On patriarchy and difference

It was Kate Millett (1970: 25), writing in *Sexual Politics*, who first theorized gender power as 'patriarchy', a form of societal organization whereby 'that half of the populace which is female is controlled by that half which is male.' For Millett, patriarchy is universal and reproduced through the socialization of 'core gender identities', which are

> based on the needs and values of the dominant group and dictated by what its members cherish in themselves and find convenient in subordinates: aggression, intelligence, force, and efficacy in the male; passivity, ignorance, docility 'virtue', and ineffectuality in the female.
>
> (Millett 1970: 26)

Millett emphasized that men and women are trained under patriarchy to accept a social system that is grounded in unequal power relations and divided into 'male' and 'female' spheres – 'domestic service and attendance upon infants to the female, the rest of human achievement, interest, and ambition to the male' (Millett 1970: 26). However, Millett's concentration on men's *social* power quickly became the biological essentialism of subsequent radical feminist scholars. The theoretical emphasis within radical feminism over the past twenty years shifted away from the socialization of 'core gender identities' to a concentration on essential sex differences between men and women as the foundation of patriarchy. In particular, what became known in the USA as 'cultural feminism' assigned strictly dichotomous and intrinsic natures to men and women as the ultimate 'root cause' of patriarchy. Eventually, this essentialism nurtured both a celebration of 'femaleness' as the ultimate virtue and a condemnation of 'maleness'. I have criticized this perspective elsewhere (Messerschmidt 1993: 45–50), and there is no point in repeating that critique here. What is important, however, is the continued impact of cultural feminism on certain segments of feminist criminology in the USA. For example, in a recent attempt to develop a framework for explaining gendered crime, Steffensmeier and Allan (1991: 73) argue that

> men and women differ significantly in their moral development, and that women's moral choices are more likely to constrain them from criminal behavior that could be injurious to others. Because women are bound more intimately into a network of interpersonal ties, their moral decisions are more influenced by empathy and compassion . . . This 'ethic of care' presupposes nonviolence, and suggests that serious predatory crime is outside women's moral boundaries.

Steffensmeier and Allan ignore the fact that there exists no 'scholarship which demonstrates that the greater conformity of women is a function of their special virtues' (Naffine 1987: 133). But beyond this, are females always empathetic and compassionate? In such an analysis, we are hard put to explain why, for example, white 'mistresses' (normally the wives of plantation owners or 'masters') in the antebellum south engaged in some of the most barbaric forms of punishment, resulting in permanent scarring of African-American female slaves (Fishman 1993: 7). Indeed, as a group, white mistresses were notorious for the 'veritable terror' they perpetrated upon African-American women. Consider the following examples (Fox-Genovese 1988: 309):

> Ida Henry's unpredictable mistress could be either tolerant or mean. One day the cook was passing potatoes at the table and 'old Mistress . . . exclaimed to de cook, "what you bring these raw potatoes out here for?" and grabbed a fork and stuck it in her eye and put it out.' Once Anna Dorsey, failing to hear her mistress call her, continued with her work until the mistress 'burst out in a frenzy of anger over the woman not answering.' Despite Anna Dorsey's protestations, her mistress 'seized a large butcher knife and struck at Anna,' who, 'attempting to ward off the blow . . . received a long gash on the arm that laid her out for some time.' Hannah Plummer's mother's mistress 'whipped her most every day, and about anything. Mother said she could not please her in anything, no matter what she done and how hard she tried.' Once, the mistress returned from town especially angry and 'made mother strip down to her waist, and then took a carriage whip an' beat her until the blood was runnin' down her back.'

Moreover, an exclusively focused 'sex difference' perspective does not account for what Laura Fishman (1993: 21) recently labelled African-American female slave 'criminal resistance' to their oppression – such as 'Sally, who hit her master over the head with a poker and put his head in the fireplace,' or another female slave who, after being whipped, knocked the overseer from his horse and proceeded to pounce upon him, eventually chopping off his head, mutilating his body and killing his horse.

What are we to make of contemporary forms of female violence, such as the following by a member of the Turban Queens, a 'girl' gang in New York City (Campbell 1991: 262):

> But once you're in a fight, you just think – you've got to fuck that girl up before she does it to you. You've got to really blow off on her. You just play it crazy. That's when they get scared of you. It's true – you feel proud when you see a girl you fucked up. Her face is all scratched or she got a black eye, you say, 'Damn, I beat the shit out of that girl, you know.'

In short, such violence becomes incomprehensible in an analysis that concentrates on sex differences. Departures from what is considered 'appropriate female crime' are either ignored – indeed, there is a dearth of theorizing about female violence in feminist theory – or are treated as inappropriate at best, 'masculine' at worst (such as in the work of Freda Adler 1975).

Other feminists of the second wave, however, did not follow the essentialist path. Initially working within the Marxist tradition, such theorists developed an alternative feminist perspective that eventually became known as socialist feminism. Appropriating the concept of patriarchy from radical feminism to explain masculine dominance under capitalism, socialist feminism attempts to understand how capitalist production (of food, shelter and clothing) and patriarchal reproduction (through sexuality, socialization and daily maintenance) interact to frame the social organization of a society. Moreover, in this perspective individual life experiences are shaped by both class and gender and, just as class experiences differ, the social experiences of women and men differ. This *differing* social experience inevitably shapes and limits the lives of both women and men. Accordingly, since there are gender- and class-appropriate forms of conforming behaviour, there also are gender- and class-appropriate forms of nonconforming behaviour. Again, this perspective concentrates on 'appropriate-male' and 'appropriate-female' crime. Indeed, in *Capitalism, Patriarchy, and Crime* (a socialist feminist text), when crimes by women are examined *only* 'female-appropriate' crimes are discussed: such non-violent forms of theft as shoplifting, fraud and embezzlement, as well as prostitution (Messerschmidt 1986). As with radical and cultural feminism, socialist feminist criminology focuses on differences between females and males, obscuring not only the differences among women (and among men) but the similarities between men and women as well.

A major result of this feminist concentration on male–female difference has been to direct theory away from issues that seriously complicate difference, such as race, age and female engagement in 'male crime'. Feminists of colour have, of course, berated much of second-wave feminism for assuming that all female experiences are similar. Scholars such as bell hooks (1984) have criticized the race bias that occurs when specific experiences of privileged white women are universalized as the experiences of all women. In the same way, theory must not universalize female crime. Although second-wave feminism has disrupted assumptions about men and women and offered new ways to speak of 'female crime', when girls and women engage in 'male crime' it is as theoretically significant as when they engage in 'female crime'. Accordingly, such feminist approaches obscure a full and complete situational understanding of gender and crime: where gender differences in crime are the exclusive focus, similarities in crime are often ignored. Abstracting gender from its social context and insensitive to issues of agency, such perspectives mask the possibility that gender patterns of crime may vary situationally, and that occasionally females and males engage in similar types and amounts of crime. As Karlene Faith (1993: 57) recently declared, to concentrate solely on crimes consistent with traditional femininity 'is to deny women's diversity and to promote gender-based objectification and stereotyping.'

By understanding the limits of existing frameworks we are better positioned to construct theory that builds on feminist insights. Rather than simply contrasting females and males, several feminist women and pro-feminist men have been developing more sophisticated ways of thinking about gender inequality. One important analytical approach involves a shift in theoretical object from patriarchal sex difference to an emphasis on situational construction of gender itself (Connell 1987; West and Zimmerman 1987; Messerschmidt 1993; Thorne 1993; West and Fenstermaker 1993). Conceptualizing gender in terms of social situation and structured action permits a deeper formulation of not only what has been visible, but what previously has been hidden, such as masculinities (Messerschmidt 1993; Connell 1995) and, for our purposes here, what usually is considered atypical gendered behaviour, such as female violence. This newly emerging feminist perspective focuses on what people in specific social settings do to construct gendered social relations and social structures, and how these structures in turn constrain and channel behaviour in specific ways.

Gender as structured action

Candace West and Don Zimmerman (1987) argue that in Western industrialized societies there exist but two 'sex categories', and individuals are assigned at birth to one or the other. In addition, in all social situations we attempt to adorn ourselves with culturally appropriate 'female' or 'male' fashion and in every interaction we consistently engage in gender attribution – identifying and categorizing people by appropriate sex category while simultaneously categorizing ourselves to others (see also Kessler and McKenna 1978).

Nevertheless, as West and Zimmerman (1987) argue, *gender* entails much more than the social signs of a sex category. Rather, gender involves a situated accomplishment: 'the activity of managing situated conduct in light of normative conceptions, attitudes, and activities appropriate to one's sex category' (p. 127). Because gender is the outcome of social practices in specific settings it serves to inform such practices in reciprocal relation. Thus, while sex category defines social identification as woman or man, gender systematically corroborates that identification through social interaction: we coordinate our activities to 'do' gender in situational ways.

Crucial to conceptualization of gender as situated accomplishment is the notion of 'accountability'. Because individuals realize their behaviour is accountable to others, they configure and orchestrate their actions in relation to how they might be interpreted by others in the particular social context in which they occur. In other words, in their daily activities individuals attempt to become socially identified as female or male. Accountability thus 'allows individuals to conduct their activities in relation to their circumstances' (West and Fenstermaker 1993: 156) and thereby highlights the possibility that gender varies by social situation and circumstance. Within every interaction, then, we expect others to attribute a particular sex category to us, and we facilitate the ongoing task of accountability by demonstrating that we are a 'male' or a 'female' by means of concocted behaviours that may be interpreted accordingly. We construct our behaviours so that we are seen unquestionably by others in particular social situations as expressing our 'essential nature'. In this way we do masculinity or femininity differently, depending upon the social situation and the social circumstances we encounter. Thus 'doing gender' renders social action accountable in terms of normative conceptions, attitudes and activities appropriate to one's sex category in the specific social situation in which one acts (West and Fenstermaker 1993: 157).

In this view, femininity is systematically accomplished and is not something done to women or settled beforehand. Although early in life we develop relatively firm individual identities as a member of one sex category, femininity (as with masculinity) is never a static or a finished product. Women and girls construct femininities in specific social situations. In other words, females involve themselves in a self-regulating process whereby they monitor their own and other's gendered conduct. Although femininity is 'made', so to speak, through the unification of self-regulated practices, these practices do not occur in a vacuum. Rather, they are influenced by the social structural constraints we experience. Following Connell (1987), I outline elsewhere (Messerschmidt 1993) that three specific social structures – gender division of labour, gender relations of power and sexuality – underlie relations between women and men. These social structures are not external to social actors or simply and solely constraining; structure is realized only through social action and social action requires structure as its condition. Moreover, women and men do gender in specific social situations; in so doing, they reproduce and sometimes change social structures. Because women reproduce feminine ideals in socially structured specific practices, there are a variety of ways to do femininity. Although femininity is always individual and personal, specific forms of femininity are available, encouraged and permitted, depending upon one's social situation, class, race and sexual orientation. Accordingly, femininity must be viewed as *structured action* – what women do under specific social structural constraints.

In this way, social relations (such as class, race and gender) join each of us in a common relationship to others: we share structural space. Consequently, common or shared blocks of knowledge evolve through interaction in which particular feminine ideals and activities play a part. Through such interaction femininity is institutionalized, permitting women to draw on such existing, but previously formed, feminine ways of thinking and acting to construct a feminine identity in any particular situation. The particular criteria of feminine identities are embedded in the social situations and recurrent practices whereby social relations are structured (Giddens 1989: 285).

We must thus recognize, first, that women are positioned differently throughout society and, therefore, that they share with other women the construction of femininities peculiar to their position in society. We must also admit that socially organized power relations among women are constructed historically on the basis of class, race and sexual preference, and in specific social situations; that is, in specific contexts particular forms of femininity are privileged, granting those constructing the favoured type greater power than 'subordinated' femininities. Nevertheless, because femininities are constructed in the context of gender relations of power, femininities are polarized around accommodation or resistance to masculine dominance (Connell 1987: 187). Although power relations among women do exist – as viewed earlier in the relationships between white mistresses and African-American slave women – forms of femininity sustain themselves in contrast to one another and to situationally specific types of masculinity under which they are subordinated. In this sense, femininity can be understood only as a relational construct.

Connell's (1987: 187) notion of 'hegemonic masculinity' and 'emphasized femininity' are relevant here. Hegemonic masculinity and emphasized femininity are the culturally idealized forms of gender in a given historical setting. They are culturally honoured, glorified and extolled at the symbolic level in the mass media. In Western industrialized societies hegemonic masculinity is characterized by work in the paid labour market, the subordination of women and girls, heterosexism and the driven and uncontrollable sexuality of men, and underscores practices toward authority, control and aggressiveness.

Emphasized femininity is a form that complements hegemonic masculinity and is defined through

the display of sociability rather than technical competence, fragility in mating scenes, compliance with men's desire for titillation and

> ego-stroking [and] acceptance of marriage and childcare . . . At the
> mass level these are organized around themes of sexual receptivity in
> relation to younger women and motherhood in relation to older women.
>
> (Connell 1987: 187)

Emphasized femininity, as the culturally dominant ideal, influences but does not determine gendered behaviour. As Barrie Thorne (1993: 106) notes, 'individuals and groups develop varied forms of accommodation, reinterpretation, and resistance to ideologically hegemonic patterns.' Although women attempt to express emphasized femininity through speech, dress, physical appearance, activities and relations with others, these social signs of femininity are associated with the specific context of one's actions and are self-regulated within that context. Thus, femininity is based on a social construct that reflects unique circumstances and relationships, a social construction that is renegotiated in each particular context. In other words, social actors self-regulate their behaviour and make specific choices in specific contexts. As Connell (1987: 186) points out, everyday gendered practices draw on the cultural ideals of emphasized femininity but do not 'necessarily correspond to actual femininities as they are lived. What most women support is not necessarily what they are.' In this way, women construct varieties of femininities through specific practices. Although gender is frequently constructed in terms of difference, 'the presence, significance, and meanings of differences are refocused when one asks about the social relations that construct differences – and diminish or undermine them' (Thorne 1993: 106). By emphasis on diversity in gender constructions, a more fluid and situated approach to gender is realized.

Taking this approach permits us to conceptualize gender and crime more realistically and completely, enabling us to explore how and in what ways femininity is constituted in certain settings at certain times, and how that construct relates to various types of crime. The focus of the remaining sections, then, is an exploration of what sustains the privileging of a highly specific version of femininity – the 'bad girl' – through observation of the work of its construction in specific settings and through certain practices. Arguably, this particular form of femininity is sustained, reproduced and privileged in the youth gangs of primarily lower working-class racial minority girls. A review of the empirical evidence on 'girls in the gang', with an eye to the social context in which both gender and crime are accomplished, reveals that gender is a critical organizing tool in these gangs and that the result is the construction of gender differences, as well as gender similarities, in the commission of crime.

Girls in the gang

For both boys and girls, joining a youth gang represents an idealized collective solution to the lived experience of class and race powerlessness.

For girls in particular, Karen Joe and Meda Chesney-Lind (1993: 10) point out that

> they exist in an environment that has little to offer young women of color. The possibility of a decent career, outside of 'domestic servant', is practically non-existent. Many come from distressed families held together by their mothers who are subsisting on welfare. Most have dropped out of school and have no marketable skills. Future aspirations are both gendered and unrealistic with the girls often expressing the desire to be rock stars or professional models when they are older.

Additionally, alarmingly high rates of physical and sexual abuse have been reported for delinquent girls, ranging from a low of 40 per cent to a high of 73 per cent (Chesney-Lind and Shelden 1992: 90; see also Moore 1991; Campbell 1993). In the social context of a bleak future and the overall violence that surrounds them in the street as well as at home, the youth gang becomes *family* to these girls. One Chicana ex-gang member reflects on how, for her, the gang

> was very important. Because that's all I had to look forward to, was my neighborhood, you know. That's all. It was my people – my neighborhood, my homies, my homeboys, my homegirls – that was everything to me. That was everything, you know. It wasn't all about my *familia*; it was all about my homeboys and homegirls.
>
> (Moore 1991: 77)

Similarly, Harris (1988: 101) reported in her study of Latino gang girls that they exhibited a strong need for safety, belongingness and companionship. One gang girl stated the importance of the gang in the following way: 'It was family. We protected each other. We took care of each other. We stole for each other' (p. 119). And in a recent exploration into why girls join gangs in Hawaii, Joe and Chesney-Lind (1993: 20) argue that the gang 'offers "friendship" and a social support system for coping and managing their everyday life problems.' As one Samoan girl expressed it, 'We all like sistas, all taking care of each other' (p. 21).

In short, the gang is where many lower-class, racial minority girls and boys develop strong 'family' ties with members of their neighbourhood – persons with whom they are acquainted and whom they perceive to be 'like themselves'. In the gang, they find companionship, safety and a sense of belongingness (Fishman 1988; Lauderback *et al.* 1992).

Doing difference

Coming together on the street, girl-and-boy gang members interact to construct gender-separate groups; this appears to occur regardless of class and race position. Indeed, from the early works of Ashbury (1927) and Thrasher (1927), to the more recent research of Quicker (1983), Schwendinger and Schwendinger (1985), Fishman (1988), Hagedorn (1988), Harris

(1988), Vigil (1988) and Moore (1991), young females have been found to construct 'auxiliary' gangs to the male gangs. Notably, these auxiliary gangs are not simply composed of separate, identifiable groups but, rather, reflect gendered boundaries based on *power*. For example, Campbell's (1984) important ethnographic study of lower working-class racial minority gangs in New York City reported that both females and males assume positions within the group that might be available to them in society at large. As Campbell (1984: 266) points out, the 'true gang' is composed of young males, and specific female groups 'exist as an annex to the male gang, [where] the range of possibilities open to them is dictated and controlled by the boys.' Similarly, Harris (1988: 128) reports that 'while the girls purport to be independent of their male counterparts, belief in male superiority and the corresponding deference to male gang members became clear.'

Other relevant research reports analogous gendered power relations in youth gangs and the construction of 'girl gangs' as secondary to 'male gangs' (Fishman 1988; Moore 1991). Thus, although girl gangs have limited autonomy – over their own rules and type of organization – they are usually connected yet subordinate to male gangs (Campbell 1993: 132). Youth gangs, then, reflect the gender relations of power in society and the related practices by which they are reproduced. Consequently, gender difference here is in part related to the social construction of gendered dominance and subordination in gang arrangements.[2]

The realm of sexuality is also an important arena in gang life for doing difference. Normative heterosexuality is a decisive 'measuring rod' for group participation and a means by which gang members construct gendered difference. In the context of the gang, some sexual exploitation seems undeniable. For example, the Schwendingers (1985: 167) found that sexist exploitation of girls is common to both middle- and working-class youth groups. Similarly, a 'homeboy' in Moore's (1991: 54) study stated: 'I would say 90 per cent was treated like a piece of ass . . . Usually we just used them as sexual need things, and companions. We needed companions in sex.' Another male gang member from the same study echoed this position:

> Ah, it's just there, you know what I mean. The – you know, when you want a *chapete* (fuck) it was there, you know what I mean. The guys treat them like shit, you know what I mean. And then when they want something you know, get it – wham bam. Sex. Just to have a partner for the time, you know. They were just there, you know, we used to get them in, throw a *linea* (lining up to have sex with a girl), you know what I mean.
>
> (Moore 1991: 55)

Thus relationships of power and sexuality merge within the context of exploitation. Girl gang members are constructed as sexual objects, which concomitantly accentuates difference by emphasizing their 'femaleness', and ultimately is an exercise of power over some girls' existence in the gang. Indeed, a female auxiliary gang that is defined primarily through its sexuality becomes a source of prestige and power among males in the gang.

Nevertheless, diversity exists in the way gangs construct heterosexual meanings. For example, Anne Campbell (1990: 179) found in New York girl gangs that 'serial monogamy' was the norm and once a girl became involved with a boy she usually remained 'faithful' until the relationship ended. These girls, then, construct a femininity that complies with emphasized femininity. However, other research indicates that doing difference through sexuality requires neither monogamy nor exploitation and, consequently, girls in gangs construct different types of femininity. For example, many girls effectively avert boys' claim to their bodies and actively negotiate the gang as a site for securing sexual pleasure (Carrington 1993). As one gang girl stated to Joan Moore (1991: 55): 'Not *me*, they didn't treat *me* like that. They think we're possessions, but we're not . . . No way. I pick my own boyfriends. I'll be with anybody I want to be with. You don't tell *me* who to be with.' This girl has constructed an 'opposition femininity' through sexuality; she has challenged culturally emphasized patterns. Alternatively, the Vice Queens 'unabashedly placed themselves at the boys' disposal and openly encouraged them to fondle and have sexual relations with them' (Fishman 1988: 17). Granting sexual favours to the Vice Kings was a means of gaining status among female peers in the gang, and thus seen as a reinterpretation of emphasized femininity resulting in the construction of a unique type. Indeed, this type of femininity has its oppositional qualities as well; although the boys thought the girls were simply sexual objects of exploitation, status among the girls partially depended upon 'being able to keep four or five boys "on the string" without any boys knowing of the others, but at the same time, avoiding sexual relationships with too many boys at one time' (Fishman 1988: 21).

For both boys and girls, then, the street gang is ideal for 'doing gender' in terms of difference. Through maintenance of and emphasis on the 'femaleness' of girl gang members – for example, through specific heterosexual meanings and practices – gender difference is preserved and specific types of masculinities and femininities are both validated and strengthened. Consequently, girl gang members are not simply passive recipients of 'patriarchy', but actively participate in the construction of gender relations and orchestrate the various forms of heterosexuality that result in varieties of femininity. Indeed, these girls do difference differently.

The gang can be a site for sexual restriction and exploitation as well as for sexual exploration and pleasure and, thus, we find variety in terms of accommodation, reinterpretation and opposition to emphasized femininity. Nevertheless, for the vast majority of girls, their significance in the gang is acquired through affiliation with boys. That is, gang girls accomplish gender in relation to the specific masculinities of the boys. This is so even for girls who develop the type of opposition femininity identified earlier.

Further, members of youth gangs engage in 'male' and 'female' crimes as a resource for doing difference. For example, in *Masculinities and Crime* I describe how, for male gang members, robbery is the most available criminal resource for obtaining money and constructing a specific type of masculinity: 'Within the social setting of the street group, robbery is an acceptable practice for accomplishing gender' (Messerschmidt 1993: 108), and, therefore, doing difference. For girls, however, prostitution seems to be the principal criminal resource for obtaining money and doing difference.[3] A study of youth growing up poor in six different cities across the USA reported that in all the cities 'prostitution is the main occupation for girls' (Williams and Kornblum 1985: 61). Moreover, Fishman (1988: 16) notes that all members of the Vice Queens participated in prostitution as their chief source of income:

> Customers were procured in taverns and on the street or at other locations not connected with organized houses of prostitution. The girls were aware of the prostituting activities of their peers and prostitution was accepted as standard behavior for the group.

Clearly, gender is a situated accomplishment in which individuals produce forms of behaviour that are seen by others in the same immediate situation as either masculine or feminine. Within the confines and social settings of the street, economically marginal boys and girls form youth gangs partly for economic survival and partly for doing gender in terms of difference. Although the examples of robbery and prostitution show how some members of youth gangs produce material survival as well as gender, it is through prostitution that these gang girls construct a femininity that both confirms and disaffirms emphasized femininity – yet simultaneously does difference. Prostitution confirms emphasized femininity in the sense that these girls construct themselves as sexually seductive to men and receptive to the sexual 'drives' and special 'needs' of men. In addition to these conventional aspects of femininity, however, involvement in prostitution ridicules emphasized femininity by advocating extramarital sex, sex for pleasure, anonymous sex and sex not limited to reproduction and the domesticated couple. This construction of a specific type of femininity challenges and reinterprets emphasized femininity. The result is a gendered gang in which boys and girls do masculinity and femininity in specific ways – crime often utilized as a resource for facilitating the accomplishment of gender – and thus construct difference.

Uniting for the 'hood'

In the daily life of the youth gang, girls not only participate in the social construction of difference but also engage in practices common to boys. Although there is a whole variety of common practices, most time is spent in such non-delinquent activities as simply 'hanging out' at a favourite spot or attending sporting and social events. In addition, boy and girl gang members partake in such delinquent activities as drinking, taking and selling drugs, committing theft and fighting (Chesney-Lind and Shelden 1992: 45; Lauderback *et al.* 1992).

The last activity, fighting – usually considered atypical gendered behaviour by females – affords considerable insight into the diversity of gender construction. In fact, one recent feminist text identifies female violence as so rare that it is labelled as an 'anomaly' and not in need of much further investigation (Faith 1993: 100). From the point of view of privileged white women, female violence may indeed be infrequent and unusual, but for lower-class racial minority girls in the USA violence is far from an anomaly. Young lower working-class racial minority girls – in particular, African-American girls – commit interpersonal crimes of violence at a much higher rate than do other girls. In a review of the literature, Sally Simpson (1991: 117–18) reported that African-American girls have higher rates of homicide and aggravated assault than white girls, and that racial minority girls participate in Uniform Crime Reports violent offences 5.5 times as often as white girls (see also Sommers and Baskin, 1992). Moreover, violent crime rates are highest in lower working-class communities, urban communities that are disproportionately racial minority in composition (Simpson 1991: 119).

It is well established that the leading cause of death among African-American male teenagers is homicide. Less well known is the fact that homicide is the leading cause of death for African-American women between the ages of fifteen and twenty-four (US Department of Health and Human Services 1993: 76–7). Additionally, males are not always more likely than females to die by homicide. At every age until the late forties, an African-American female faces a higher risk of death by homicide than a white male.[4] Although the perpetrators of this homicide are overwhelmingly men,[5] a recent study of 'sister against sister' homicide in six US cities (with homicide rates equal to or higher than the national rate) found that

> women who kill other women basically resemble the portrait depicted over the past two decades by previous researchers: they are young, black, undereducated, and unemployed. Thus, they reflect the current American portrait of an expanding group of women of color who are marginal to the larger society.
>
> (Mann 1993: 219)

This intra-gender violence by lower working-class racial minority girls generally occurs within the context of the youth gang. Youth gangs confer a dubious prestige on *both* boys and girls with a proven ability to fight – boys and girls to whom street fighting is an essential source of meaning, reputation and status. The development of this reputation begins during the initiation ceremony, for the gang will not accept just anyone. A female gang member describes one such initiation:

> We used to take a new girl to the park. Now that girl had to pick one of our girls. And whoever she wanted, she had to fight that girl to see

that she could take the punches. Without crying . . . Like if I'm walking down the street with you, you have to be able to count that I'm
going to throw my life for you. Just like I expect you to do it for me.
I have to be able to say, 'I'm going to stay here and fight because I
know you're going to stay here and fight too.'

(Campbell 1993: 136)

In East Los Angeles, girls become gang members by being 'jumped in'. One
gang member explained the process to Quicker (1983: 15–16):

Q: What happens when you get jumped in? What do they do?
R: When you get jumped in, what they do is they get around you and
then there'll be a girl counting. Like there will be a girl out there
and she'll go okay and then they'll start jumping you. She'll count
to 10 and when she finishes counting, they'll stop.

Demonstration of toughness not only gains entrance to the gang but also
proclaims oneself a 'bad girl'. Indeed, in girl gangs 'the ability and willingness to fight, facing the enemy, not running from confrontation, to be "bad",
to be "crazy", to be tough . . . are all prized behaviors' (Harris 1988: 106).
'Bad girl' femininity serves to rank girls in terms of capacity to display
physical violence and power; girls who do not 'measure up' are ignored
and 'jumped out' of the gang. Indeed, 'bad girls' take pride in their fighting
ability and their consequent acquired reputation and status. These girls
accomplish gender by specific relational means that violently oppose other
girls. Such social practice gains currency in relation to girls who fail to
'qualify' and, predictably, constructs power relations among girls, as the
following comment indicates:

Girls around here see a girl that's quiet, they think that she's a dud.
Yeah – let's put it that way. They think they don't know how to
fight . . . Round here you have to know how to fight. I'm glad I got
a reputation. That way nobody will start with me – they *know*, you
know. They're going to come out losing. Like all of us, we got a
reputation. We're crazy. Nobody wants to fight us for that reason –
you know. They say 'No, man. That girl might stab me or cut my face
or something like that.'

(Campbell 1987: 462–3)

Differences among girls hinge on how they construct femininity. Thus,
'bad girl' femininity is sustained through its relation to situationally defined 'dud' femininity.

Similarly, in gangs that emphasize heterosexual monogamy for girls but
not for boys (because it is considered 'unnatural' for boys to refuse offers
of sex), girl violators are controlled fiercely, as the following example
shows:

'Hey, I hear you made it with my old man.' This and that. And blat,
and that's it. The whole thing is over 'cus they don't even raise their

hands. They put their head down and they cut out fast. 'Cus they know – like if I was hitting a girl and they hit me back and all *these* girls see it, they're all gonna get in, you know? And she's going to get a worse beating. So she takes a slap or two and goes home and cries.

(Campbell 1991: 258)

In this situation, not only is a specific type of heterosexuality reproduced, but power relations between girls and femininities are constructed: mono-gamy is privileged and enhanced through violent attack (and group support for that attack) on situationally constituted promiscuity.

Probably the most positively sanctioned site for displaying one's 'bad-ness' is participation in *group* violence. Bonding with peers of common residence, marginalized and racial-minority youths tend to develop a col-lective loyalty to their neighbourhood and to form territorial control over their turf or 'hood' (Messerschmidt 1993). A street gang's specific terri-tory, carefully branded and defended at levels of conspicuous absurdity, defines the group and its perimeters of activity. In fact, turf serves as a boundary between groups and as an arena of status and potential conflict. Obviously, street gangs are intolerant of invasions of their space by out-siders. When outsiders do invade their local 'hood', this is viewed as inherently offensive. One gang member explains how easily a fight erupts when entering another girl gang's turf:

Like if you go somewhere. Let's suppose we go to San Fernando. And like we don't get along with San Fernando. And like we go to the park and a bunch of girls from SanFer are over there, and us Blythe Street Girls. And they're going to give us hard looks, and we're going to give them hard looks, and that's where it's going to start. And they'll say, 'Where are you from?'

'Blythe Street. Where are you from?'

'Well, fuck you.' And then we go. Just for the street. Uno Blythe. Blythe Street's number one. That's all it is.

(Harris 1988: 104)

As the quoted scenario indicates, it is not the territory *per se* that is sig-nificant, but the local group's identification with that particular territory. Indeed, support for the group (as representative of the neighbourhood) is held in highest esteem and fighting exhibits loyalty to the 'hood' and, therefore, to the gang (Fishman 1988: 14). If a gang girl cannot or will not fight, she is summarily rejected. As one gang girl explained to Harris (1988: 109),

You can belong as long as you can back up your shit and don't rat on your homegirls or back away. If you don't back them up and you run we'll jump that girl out because she ain't going to take care of nothing. All she wants is our backup and our support but she ain't going to give us none of hers, so what's the use of her being around! She has to be able to hold up the hood.

Clearly one shores up the hood through violence. As Harris (1988: 174) states, girls in gangs 'will fight instead of flee, assault instead of articulate, and kill rather than control their aggression.' Indeed, for 'girls in the gang', status is not achieved from excellence in school or at work but from 'the perfection of fighting techniques' and 'the number of times the girls willingly fought and with whom they fought' (Fishman 1988: 23).

In the world of the street, different gangs are allocated different turfs and those who venture out of their socially defined neighbourhood are chastised and punished. In this social situation, boys and girls unite on the basis of neighbourhood. Because gender is not static but dynamic, in a social context where 'hood' is elevated to pre-eminence (that is, neighbourhood differences become highly salient) the path for similarity in behaviour is much less obstructed. In the context of the street fight, interaction involves at once *caring* (for the 'hood' and other gang members) and *physically aggressive* practices (against another gang) by *both* boys and girls. Moreover, the criteria of femininity are embedded in specific social situations and recurrent practices within them. In the particular context of the youth gang, the criteria of 'bad girl' femininity involve physical strength and power as resources for publicly demonstrating individual proficiency at defending the 'hood' by conquering adversary gang girls. Indeed, girls (as representatives of a rival 'hood') are the subject of competition in the struggle to secure a situationally specific feminine identity. In other words, what is usually considered atypical feminine behaviour outside this situation is, in fact, *normalized* within the social context of inter-neighbourhood conflict; girl gang violence in this situation is encouraged, permitted and privileged by *both* boys and girls as appropriate feminine behaviour. Thus, 'bad girl' femininity is situationally accomplished and context bound within the domain of the street.

However, girl gang violence is sometimes subordinated to boy gang violence. For example, in some gangs girls serve merely as weapon carriers for the boys and, if needed, as 'back-ups' (Chesney-Lind and Shelden 1992: 45–6). As one gang girl expressed to Harris (1988: 127):

Yah, we back up the homeboys . . . And if they were into a fight, somehow it will get to us and we will go and back them up, even though we're girls and we're from the Tiny Locas, we'll still back up our homeboys.

Girl gang violence in this setting occurs within the context of gender relations of power: these girls are doing femininity in a specific way through their affiliation and, therefore, relation to boys. In other words, they are accommodating to masculine dominance.

However, girl gang violence is not always marginal and secondary to boy gang violence. For example, with regard to her gang's involvement in violence, one gang girl stated: 'We would do our thing and they would do their thing' (Harris 1988: 127). In other words, girls are involved routinely in violence without the boys being present. Even when boys are nearby, the boys may actually play a secondary role as 'back-ups':

> The guys would back us up sometimes. They'll be there. And they'll watch out like two girls on one or something and they'll get one girl off. Whenever they seen that one of us was getting more hurt. But it usually didn't happen that way. We usually didn't need backup that much . . . But they'll be there because sometimes guys came from other gangs and they want to get on the girls too, so like they'll be there in case the other guys came.
>
> (Harris 1988: 127–8)

For girls in the gang, doing femininity means occasionally, and in appropriate circumstances, doing violence. However, because participation in violence varies depending upon the setting, girls are assessed and held accountable as 'bad girls' differently. Given that gang girls realize that their behaviour is accountable to other girls and boys in the gang, they construct their actions in relation to how those actions will be interpreted by others in the same social context. These girls are doing femininity in terms of activities appropriate to their sex category and in specific social situations.

Accordingly, violence by young women in youth gangs should not be interpreted as an attempt to be 'male' and 'pass' as the other gender. Yet, in the past as well as today, some women do pass successfully as men, in part to acquire male privileges.[6] For example, a study of 'gender-bending females' – young women who pass as men in public settings – found that these women were better treated and were generally afforded more respect in public as 'men' than they were in public as women. As Devor (1987: 34) concludes, these women passed as men to obtain greater privileges and freedom of movement while simultaneously avoiding some of 'the odious aspects of being female in a society predicated on male dominance'.

Arguably, girls in youth gangs are not attempting to pass as boys or as 'gender-bending females' in the above sense. Indeed, these girls value emphasized femininity, for the most part display themselves as feminine in culturally 'appropriate' ways and do not construct an ambiguous gender outside the gang milieu. As Campbell (1993: 133) points out, gang girl concern

> with their appearance, their pride in their ability to attract men, their sense of responsibility as mothers left me in no doubt that they enjoyed being women. They didn't want to be like men and, indeed, would have been outraged at such a suggestion.

Girl gang violence is but one practice in the overall process of constructing a specific type of femininity. Accordingly, femininity is assessed in terms of willingness to defend the 'hood' and on doing difference. Thus, within the gang, girl members do most of, if not all, the cooking and childcare, prepare the food and drink for 'partying' and are 'very fussy' over gender display (clothes, hair, make-up) (Campbell 1984; Vigil 1988: 111–12). By engaging in such practices girl gang members are not simply preparing, for example, the necessities for adequate 'partying' – they are also producing gender difference. As West and Zimmerman (1987: 144) point out, for women to engage in this type of labour and men not to engage in it represents for both an opportunity for doing difference. In addition to carrying out the practices of doing difference identified earlier – separate but connected gendered gangs, specific forms of heterosexuality and 'gender-appropriate' crimes – by engaging in activities identified with emphasized femininity, girl gang members are assessed successfully as women, even when participating actively in street violence. Accordingly, their 'bad girl' femininity consists of a combination of conventional gender practices (such as cooking and childcare) and atypical gender practices (such as violence), each practice justified by appropriate circumstances. Thus, the case of gang girls exhibits a unique fluidity of gender in which different gender identities are emphasized or avoided depending upon the social setting. Indeed, within the social context of the gang, 'bad girls' construct a femininity that secures approval as members of the gang and as women.

This fluctuating femininity bears a striking resemblance to the femininity constructed by women in the US Marines. As the following quote indicates, certain events demand 'hard' femininity while others justify emphasized femininity, paralleling the flexibility of gender accomplishment seen among girls in youth gangs.

> Like when we're marching, the woman part drops out. It's just recruits out marching, slamming our heels down on the deck. When we're not in our cammies or out marching, it's put on your makeup and say yes or no, and don't bend down with your knees apart.
> (Williams 1989: 76)

Similarly to 'bad-girls', these women are constructing a femininity that wins acceptance as 'marines' and as women.

Moreover, Barrie Thorne (1993) reported in her important work on gender in elementary schools that when classroom events are organized around an absorbing task – such as a group art project – the cooperation encouraged between boys and girls helps to clear a path towards gender similarity. Likewise, for both boys and girls in the gang, one of the most absorbing tasks is common defence of the 'hood'. Indeed, the symbolic essence of the gang is triggered and becomes meaningful only through inter-neighbourhood conflict. In this social situation, gang boys and girls unite and work together to protect 'their' neighbourhood from the threat of adjacent neighbourhood gangs. As Campbell (1987: 459) points out, girl gang members see themselves as part of 'a vigilante force on behalf not only of themselves but of friends and neighbors too'. Under such conditions *gender* difference becomes secondary to *group* difference and the result is a social site for the construction of 'bad girl' femininity.

Conclusion

Owing to their position in class, race, and gender divisions of labour and power, many young, marginalized, racial minority girls form or join violent street gangs. They adapt to economic and racial powerlessness by competing with rivals of their own class, gender and race to protect their 'hood'. For girls in the gang, the struggle with other young women of their class (and usually race) is a means for constructing a specific type of femininity: 'bad girl' femininity. Because girls in the gang collectively experience their everyday world from a specific position in society, they construct femininity in a uniquely appropriate way.

The girls-in-the-gang illustration reveals how social structures are constituted by social action and, in turn, provide resources for doing femininity. As resources for doing femininity, the particular types of youth crime are ultimately based on these social structures. In this way social structures both constrain and enable social action and, therefore, femininities and youth crime.

Gender patterns of crime are not static, but vary situationally. Outside parental and school surveillance, the gang provides greater space for the negotiation of gender. Consequently, females and males engage in 'gender-appropriate' crimes but sometimes commit similar types of crimes. By developing a sense of gender as structured action and situational accomplishment, we isolate not only the social actions that sustain but also those that undermine the construction of gender and crime as difference. The gang provides a milieu within which girls can experiment with, and possibly dismantle, the bounds of emphasized femininity. Girl gang members use the resources available to construct gender and, in so doing, challenge notions of gender as merely difference. Thus, rather than conceptualizing gendered crime simplistically in terms of, for example, 'males commit violence and females commit theft', new directions in feminist theory enable us to explore which males and which females commit which crimes, and in which social situations.

Acknowledgements

I am especially grateful to Piers Beirne, Bob Connell, Barbara Perry, Frances Heidensohn, Nicky Hahn Rafter, Dusan Bjelic, Bob Miller and Tony Jefferson for offering valuable comments on earlier drafts of this chapter.

Notes

1 The first wave of the US feminist movement is usually dated from the abolitionist movement of the 1830s to the successful passage of the Nineteenth Amendment (guaranteeing women the right to vote) in 1920.

2 Not all female gangs are connected to male gangs. Independent girl gangs do exist but seem to be rare. A recent notable example of such a gang is the Potrero Hill Posse in San Francisco (see Lauderback *et al.* 1992).

3 Other primary money-making activities by girl gangs are drug dealing and shoplifting (for an example, see Lauderback *et al.* 1992).

4 This is *not* to suggest, as is regularly portrayed in the mass media, the emergence of a 'new violent female criminal'. On the contrary, I agree with Meda Chesney-Lind (1993: 339), who documented that 'girls have long been members of gangs, that their roles in these gangs have been considerably more varied than early stereotypes would have it, and that girls' occasionally violent behavior has, during other decades, been largely ignored.'

5 This raises an important issue that has been ignored in the criminological and feminist literature: intra-gang cross-gender violence as a form of 'family violence'.

6 For example, in the 1850s, 'Lucy Ann Lobdell left her husband in upstate New York and passed as a man in order to support herself. 'I made up my mind to dress in men's attire to seek labor,' she explained, and to earn 'men's wages'. Later, she became the Reverend Joseph Lobdell and set up house with Maria Perry, living for ten years as man and wife' (D'Emilio and Freedman 1988: 124–5). Similarly, in another case in mid-1800s New York, 'A woman took the name Murray Hall and began to dress as a man. She opened an employment bureau, settled down with the first of her two wives, and later adopted a daughter. Hall became influential in the Tammany Hall Democratic political machine and earned a reputation for drinking, playing poker, and being "sweet on women"' (D'Emilio and Freedman 1988: 125).

References

Adler, F. (1975). *Sisters in Crime*. New York: McGraw-Hill.

Ashbury, H. (1927). *The Gangs of New York*. New York: Capricorn Books.

Campbell, A. (1984). *The Girls in the Gang*. Cambridge, MA: Basil Blackwell.

Campbell, A. (1987). Self definition by rejection: the case of gang girls. *Social Problems*, 35(5), 451–66.

Campbell, A. (1990). Female participation in gangs. In C.R. Huff (ed.) *Gangs in America*. Newbury Park, CA: Sage.

Campbell, A. (1991). *The Girls in the Gang*, 2nd edn. Cambridge, MA: Basil Blackwell.

Campbell, A. (1993). *Men, Women, and Aggression*. New York: Basic Books.

Carrington, K. (1993). *Offending Girls*. Sydney: Allen & Unwin.

Chesney-Lind, M. (1993). Girls, gangs and violence: anatomy of a backlash. *Humanity and Society*, 17(3), 321–44.

Chesney-Lind, M. and Shelden, R.G. (1992). *Girls, Delinquency and Juvenile Justice*. Belmont, CA: Wadsworth.

Connell, R.W. (1987). *Gender and Power*. Stanford, CA: Stanford University Press.

Connell, R.W. (1995). *Masculinities*. Stanford, CA: Stanford University Press.

Daly, K. and Chesney-Lind, M. (1988). Feminism and criminology. *Justice Quarterly*, 5(4), 497–538.

D'Emilio, J. and Freedman, E.B. (1988). *Intimate Matters: a History of Sexuality in America*. New York: Harper and Row.

Devor, H. (1987). Gender bending females: women and sometimes men. *American Behavioral Scientist*, 31(1), 12–40.

Faith, K. (1993). *Unruly Women*. Vancouver: Press Gang Publishers.

Fishman, L.T. (1988). The Vice Queens: an ethnographic study of black female gang behavior. Paper presented at the annual meeting of the American Society of Criminology, Chicago, 11 November.

Fishman, L.T. (1993). Slave women, resistance and criminality: a prelude to future accommodation. Paper presented at the annual meeting of the American Society of Criminology, Phoenix, AZ, 29 October.

Fox-Genovese, E. (1988). *Within the Plantation Household*. Chapel Hill: University of North Carolina Press.

Giddens, A. (1989). A reply to my critics. In D. Held and J.B. Thompson (eds) *Social Theory of Modern Societies: Anthony Giddens and His Critics*. New York: Cambridge University Press.

Hagedorn, J. (1988). *People and Folks: Gangs, Crime and the Underclass in a Rustbelt City*. Chicago: Lake View Press.

Harris, M.G. (1988). *Cholas: Latino Girls and Gangs*. New York: AMS Press.

Heidensohn, F. (1985). *Women and Crime*. New York: New York University Press.

hooks, b. (1984). *Feminist Theory: from Margin to Center*. Boston: South End Press.

Joe, K. and Chesney-Lind, M. (1993). 'Just every mother's angel': an analysis of gender and ethnic variations in youth gang membership. Paper presented at the annual meeting of the American Society of Criminology, Phoenix, AZ, 27 October.

Kessler, S. and McKenna, W. (1978). *Gender: an Ethnomethodological Approach*. New York: John Wiley.

Lauderback, D., Hansen, J. and Waldorf, D. (1992). 'Sisters are doin' it for themselves': a black female gang in San Francisco. *Gang Journal*, 1, 57–72.

Leonard, E.B. (1982). *Women, Crime and Society: a Critique of Criminology Theory*. New York: Longman.

Mann, C.R. (1993). Sister against sister: female intrasexual homicide. In C.C. Culliver (ed.) *Female Criminality: the State of the Art*. New York: Garland.

Messerschmidt, J.W. (1986). *Capitalism, Patriarchy and Crime: toward a Socialist Feminist Criminology*. Totowa, NJ: Rowman and Littlefield.

Messerschmidt, J.W. (1993). *Masculinities and Crime: Critique and Reconceptualization of Theory*. Lanham, MD: Rowman and Littlefield.

Millett, K. (1970). *Sexual Politics*. New York: Doubleday.

Moore, J. (1991). *Going down to the Barrio: Homeboys and Homegirls in Change*. Philadelphia: Temple University Press.

Naffine, N. (1987). *Female Crime: the Construction of Women in Criminology*. Boston: Allen & Unwin.

Quicker, J. (1983). *Homegirls: Characterizing Chicana Gangs*. San Pedro, CA: International Universities Press.

Schwendinger, H. and Schwendinger, J. (1985). *Adolescent Subcultures and Delinquency*. New York: Praeger.

Simpson, S.S. (1991). Caste, class, and violent crime: explaining difference in female offending. *Criminology*, 29(1), 115–35.

Sommers, I. and Baskin, D. (1992). Sex, race, age, and violent offending. *Violence and Victims*, 7(3), 191–201.

Steffensmeier, D. and Allan, E. (1991). Gender, age, and crime. In J.F. Sheley (ed.) *Criminology: a Contemporary Handbook*. Belmont, CA: Wadsworth.

Thorne, B. (1990). Children and gender: constructions of difference. In D.L. Rhode (ed.) *Theoretical Perspectives on Sexual Difference*. New Haven, CT: Yale University Press.

Thorne, B. (1993). *Gender Play: Girls and Boys in Schools*. New Brunswick, NJ: Rutgers University Press.

Thrasher, F.M. (1927). *The Gang*. Chicago: University of Chicago Press.

US Department of Health and Human Services (1993). *Health, United States, 1992*. Washington, DC: US Government Printing Office.

Vigil, J.D. (1988). *Barrio Gangs*. Austin: University of Texas Press.

West, C. and Fenstermaker, S. (1993). Power, inequality and the accomplishment of gender: an ethnomethodological view. In P. England (ed.) *Theory on Gender/Feminism in Theory*. New York: Aldine.

West, C. and Zimmerman, D.H. (1987). Doing gender. *Gender and Society*, 1(2), 125–51.

Williams, C.L. (1989). *Gender Differences at Work*. Berkeley: University of California Press.

Williams, T.M. and Kornblum, W. (1985). *Growing up Poor*. Lexington, MA: Lexington Books.

10

The 'dark figure' of criminology: towards a black and multi-ethnic feminist agenda for theory and research

KATHLEEN DALY AND
DEBORAH J. STEPHENS

In the United States, the public discussion of crime has become synonymous with race, and in particular, the face of young black men. But as Vernetta Young and Anne Sulton point out, 'African-American perspectives are virtually excluded from major treatises' on crime (Young and Sulton 1991: 114). A related, but different, race problem prevails in US literary theory. As articulated by Ann duCille (1994: 592), the issue is: why have 'we – black women – become the subjected subjects of so much contemporary scholarly investigation . . . in the 1990s?' These scholars share a concern with an over 'visibility' of black men and black women as subjects of inquiry in criminology and literature, respectively. However, the discipline-based contexts in which their concerns arise are distinctly different: black feminist thought has had an impact on literature (as well as history and law) in academic research and writing, but its presence in criminology is almost nil. This uneven impact of black feminist thought is encapsulated in duCille's concern with an 'explosion of interest in black women as literary and historical subjects' (p. 596), in contrast to Young and Sulton, who focus on an absence of African-American perspectives in criminology.

Our chapter aims to bring black feminist thought more fully into criminology.[1] It is organized in four parts. First, we discuss problems in naming one's self or enterprise 'black feminist' or 'multi-ethnic feminist', and we speak as a black woman and white woman about our aims. Second, we compare arguments on race and gender across several bodies of literature: black feminist theory in sociology and literature, feminist and critical race theory in law and black women's scholarship in criminology. Next, we review the criminological literature on black women, victimization, crime and justice. From these reviews we identify a theoretical and research agenda for black (or multi-ethnic) feminist perspectives in criminology.

Naming the enterprise: black feminist, multi-ethnic feminist and other identifications

Our focus is on black feminist theory and research in the United States,[2] but we realize that by not including Latina, Native-American, Asian-American or other groups, our analysis is limited. Racial and ethnic relations are compressed into a simplified black–white dualism, giving the impression of homogeneity within racial groups (when there is ethnic variation), rendering race relations oppositional (when there can be points of overlap) and reinforcing black as Other from a white referent. More-over, the black–white dualism thwarts an understanding of the relational histories of African-Americans, Latino(a)s, Native-Americans and Asian-Americans to each other in US history. We do not address international expressions of black feminism in this chapter; while potential affinities exist with black feminists in African and Caribbean nations and in the UK and Canada (among other countries), we give attention to black women in the USA.[3]

Naming conundrums

How do we come to identify ourselves? Naming one's scholarly or politi-cal identity is something we can choose and something about which his-tory or biology may give us little choice. Terms can be confusing. Does black feminist stand for the *racial identity* of a theorist or the *perspective* taken on a subject? Or does it refer to the *phenomenon* being analysed? Hazel Carby (1987: 7–19) addresses these questions for black feminist theory in literature; her analysis is helpful in outlining what a black femi-nist perspective could mean for criminology.

Carby contrasts Mary Helen Washington's (1975) anthology of black women's fiction, which gathered black women's texts but without a black feminist critical perspective, with Barbara Smith's (1977) call for a black feminist criticism, one by and on black women writers. Carby points out these problems. First, Smith asserts 'the existence of an essential black female experience and an exclusive black female language in which this experience is embodied' (p. 9). Second, her assumption of common experi-ences means that black feminist criticism is narrowed to 'black women critics of black women artists depicting black women' (p. 9). These ques-tions of how to define black feminist criticism continued in the 1980s. Deborah McDowell (1980) proposed 'any criticism written by a Black woman regardless of her subject or perspective' (cited in Carby 1987: 12), which collapsed the meaning of black feminist to anything written by a black woman. Another theorist, Barbara Christian (1985), used the term black feminist criticism in the title of her book, but she was uncertain how to define the enterprise: 'What is a literary critic, a black woman critic, a black feminist literary critic [?] ... How does one distinguish them?' (cited in Carby 1987: 14).

Carby proposes that 'black feminist criticism be regarded critically as a problem, not a solution, as a sign that should be interrogated, a locus of contradiction' (p. 15). The contradiction stems from the location of black feminist criticism in the academy, where black intellectuals may seek legitimation, but where racism and sexism flourish under the gloss of humanistic scholarship. Carby warns against essentialist and ahistorical assumptions of a common, shared experience between 'black women as critics and black women as writers who represent black women's reality' (p. 16). She calls for feminist work on the racial specificity of ideologies of 'womanhood' (which often means 'whiteness') and for analyses that 'use race as a central category' but are not necessarily about black women (p. 18).

Thus, when the term black feminist is used, some may be referencing: a theoretical and political identity as a black woman; the subjects of inquiry (that is black and/or women); and both an identity and the subjects of inquiry.[4] Let us consider how each might affect one's approach to criminology.

1 *A theoretical-political identity*. Self-identifying as black feminist can mean many things, but a common element is a self-conscious and reflexive analysis of the combined forces of race and gender (and also class and sexuality) on one's individual and group existence as a black woman.[5] A black feminist analysis in criminology would mean applying a (black) racialized gender consciousness to any feature of the crime and justice domain.

2 *Subjects of inquiry*. Some scholars may focus on black people, on racial-ethnic differences among women or on black women.[6] A recent example of this stance is articulated by Katheryn Russell (1992). She calls for a black criminology, which she defines as one concerned with 'developing and expanding *theoretical* research on crime committed by blacks' (p. 668, emphasis in original). Russell suggests that those engaged in black criminology may be conservative or radical, but that criminologists who are black must begin the process.

3 *A theoretical-political identity and subjects of inquiry*. Some scholars may apply a black feminist perspective on studies of black women, as victims, law-breakers or justice system workers. Those taking this approach include Beth Richey (1985), Amina Mama (1989) and Regina Arnold (1990). Working in a direction encouraged by Barbara Smith, they research and write 'out of their own identity' as black women (Smith, as cited in Carby 1987: 8).

Positions 2 and 3 can be limiting for criminology in the same ways that Carby has discussed for literature. While it is important that black scholars analyse the 'experiences'[7] of black victims and offenders, black feminists (or black criminologists) should not be limited to studying black women or men. Nor can we assume that black criminologists are best able to study black people.[8] Further, we may find that black and white scholars experience and explain crime or victimization in similar and different ways.[9] We turn then to the question of collaboration: can black and white women work together towards black feminist or multi-ethnic perspectives in criminology?[10]

Our 'voices' and collaborative questions

Over a decade ago Maria Lugones and Elizabeth Spelman (1983) wrote a paper about women's differences that took their collaboration as a Hispaña and a white woman as a substantive point of departure. We want to do the same.

Deborah's voice

I am speaking from the voice of a black woman who identifies as a black feminist. One of my research interests is the study of black women, but my analysis is not confined to this group. Writing this chapter and developing this argument brought about ambivalent feelings for two reasons. First, I want to connect two groups of people and their writings, which do not seem to overlap: one is work by black scholars in criminology, few of whom identify as black feminist, and the other is black feminist theory. Like other black scholars in criminology, I feel that a different way of theorizing and analysing multiple identities, inequalities and oppressions is needed and must be developed in the field. I think this can be successfully accomplished with a black feminist or multi-ethnic perspective of crime. The second reason for my ambivalence is that I am attempting to develop such an analysis with a white woman. This causes ambivalence because I, like many other black women, am suspicious of white feminists, their motivations, their use of their privileges, their role in oppression and their failure to acknowledge women's differences in the past; and because I am sensitive to what is being said about my people, 'our community' and 'our experiences'. In criminology, the black, low-income, inner-city experience is a primary focus of research. This experience is not different from my own. However, I have crossed the line from subject to researcher and must now recognize that I am somewhat different from many that I wish to research. I still have more in common with them than most white researchers, but to rely solely on common experience is limiting and essentialist. Although there are questions about whether it is desirable or even possible for black and white women to work together, it can be successful if there is genuine and reciprocal dialogue between the two women and the collaboration is out of genuine concern for and commitment to the subject of research, not out of self-interest or because it is the popular thing to do. Researchers need not take separatist positions in studying oppressed groups.

This will only lead to a slower transformation of a criminology in desperate need of change.

Kathy's voice

I may be speaking in a white voice, but all I can be sure about is my skin colour. I identify more as working than middle class, and thus Collins's (1986, 1990) ideas about being an 'outsider within' the academy have always resonated for me. I cannot be a black feminist, although *perhaps* I could be a multi-ethnic feminist, drawing from my (largely mythical) Irish roots. I am interested in how class, gender and race (and age and sexuality) construct the normal and deviant, in how these inequalities put some societal members at risk to be rendered deviant or to engage in law-breaking, and in how law and state institutions both challenge and reproduce these inequalities. While I do not think I belong in one of the three positions described above, I could identify with a fourth position, feminist and critical race theorist (see below on critical race theory). While naming is important, I worry that scholars can become more absorbed with essentialized and professionalized anxieties than with the substance of the social issues we confront. My greatest worry is that difference discourse will trivialize to individualistic concerns with 'my story' and 'my oppression'. I decided to write this chapter with Deborah because I wanted to figure out how I, as a white woman, could relate to and come to grips with black (and multi-ethnic) feminist thought. I have been wondering what white women's roles should be in doing research and producing theory on race and gender, and I have been dissatisfied with the way in which race and gender have been theorized in criminology, including my own work. I have been challenged by Regina Austin's call to 'work the line between street and straight, straddling it . . . pushing it' (Austin 1992b: 887). Austin's reference is not simply to a 'colour line', but to many other boundaries we need to understand and push.

Three trajectories of scholarship

The development of black feminist (or multi-ethnic) perspectives in criminology will be advanced by drawing from work outside of criminology. We review selected black feminist scholars in sociology and literature, and black feminist and critical race scholars in law, before turning to the arguments of selected black women scholars in criminology.

Black feminist theory in sociology and literature

DuCille's (1994) essay, together with Carby's (1987) review of black women writers, provide a good survey and introduction to black women and literature. We sketch ideas of Frances Beale, the Combahee River Collective,

Audre Lorde, June Jordan, bell hooks, Patricia Hill Collins and Deborah King.[11]

The concept of multiple oppressions is central to black feminist theory. Frances Beale (1970), an early critical voice in the black power movement, analysed the 'double jeopardy' of being black and female. The analysis of the connectedness and mutuality of class, race, gender and sexuality was stated forcefully by the Combahee River Collective (1979). For the Collective and other black feminist writers in the 1970s and early 1980s, two themes were central: class, race and gender relations were connected and interlocking, and unless all were considered, an understanding of inequality was incomplete (see review in Daly 1993). Audre Lorde and June Jordan developed themes of difference in the mid-1980s. Lorde focused on relations both among black people (addressing gender and sexuality) and between black and white (addressing race and class); she noted problems with the 'denial of difference', where those in positions of power over others denied that difference. She also raised questions about the facade of black community, where 'the need for unity is often misnamed as a need for homogeneity' (Lorde 1984: 119). Jordan raised questions about how 'factors of race and class and gender . . . collapse . . . when you try to use them as automatic concepts of connection.' She asserted that 'It is not who you are . . . but what we can do for each other that will determine the connection' (Jordan 1985: 46–7). Jordan posed unsettling questions about racial or gender solidarity: such alignments could not be readily adduced from one's class, racial or ethnic, or gender location. bell hooks (1981, 1984, 1989, 1990) acknowledged and reclaimed the term feminist as a theoretical-political identity for black women. That meant to challenge sexism within black communities and racism within 'feminist movement' (as hooks puts it), among other sites of struggle. Like Lorde and Jordan, she established a black feminist stance that did not constrain her from aligning with other groups.

Patricia Hill Collins and Deborah King, both sociologists, drew from black feminist works to chart a black feminist standpoint and to apply a class–race–gender analysis to women's paid employment, respectively. Collins (1986, 1989, 1990) developed an epistemological standpoint of 'outsider within' and one termed Afrocentric-feminist; both combined feminist and Afrocentric ideas, experiences and histories. Among the elements were concrete and experiential wisdom (rather than abstract knowledge), using dialogue (not just adversarial debate) to assess knowledge claims, an ethic of caring and an ethic of personal accountability. Like other black feminists, Collins called for analysis of a 'matrix of domination', along interlocking axes of race, class and gender oppression. King's (1988) analysis of paid employment data is unique in applying a class–race–gender analysis. She showed the importance of seeing these relations as multiplicative (or interactive), not simply additive.

Several themes are evident in this work. First, there are multiple sites of inequality, which are interwoven and interactive. Second, attributes of people (for example, their class, race and ethnicity, or gender) may not be an accurate guide to their political engagement or alignment. Third, multiple differences or a matrix of domination call for a 'both/and conceptual stance' (Collins 1990). This means that an individual or group can, depending on the context, 'be an oppressor, a member of an oppressed group, or both' (p. 225). Finally, some (e.g. Collins) call for new ways of producing and verifying knowledge because traditional forms objectify and suppress the knowledge of subordinated groups. Collins suggests a diversity of groups with different standpoints – for example, African-American women, African-American men, Latina lesbians – with each group[12] 'perceiv[ing] its own truth as partial, its knowledge . . . unfinished' (Collins 1990: 236).

Feminist and critical race theory in law

Legal scholars taking feminist and critical race perspectives argue that relations of inequality are structured and reproduced in law and legal process. They are critical of presumptive neutral legal principles, which mask a male, white and middle-class[13] point of view. Derrick Bell (1980, 1987, 1992), an early pioneer in critical race theory, argues that racism towards black people is so firmly structured in US culture and political economy that legal reforms cannot deliver racial justice. Kimberle Crenshaw (1989) shows how black women's employment discrimination claims cannot be registered because legal arguments must be framed within either race or gender anti-discrimination law but not both, and Richard Delgado (1989) demonstrates that apparently neutral legal standards, coupled with a top-down view of discrimination, deny the subjective experience of racial discrimination. Patricia Williams (1991) writes of the disjuncture between the ways in which she (and others) experience gender and racial discrimination in daily life and how those experiences are legally framed and interpreted.

A leitmotif of critical race theory is that racial injustice flourishes under a post-sixties regime of 'race-neutral' or 'colour-blind' law (Calmore 1992; Cook 1992; Greene 1993), as it did under the older regime of white superiority. Cook (1992: 1009) characterizes the dilemma this poses for race theory and politics:

> Blacks have had to vindicate standards of sameness (colorblind universalism) when different (race-conscious particularism) is used as an instrument of oppression. [Yet] Blacks have had to sing the praises of difference (race-conscious particularism) when sameness (colorblind universalism) is the instrument of oppression.

Feminists confront the same dilemma in the gender sameness–difference debates (see Daly 1990; Vogel 1993). Thus, we may extend on Cook's ideas by joining race with gender: both 'overtly racist' (and sexist) and 'ostensibly race-neutral' (and gender-neutral) law can be in the service of racial (and gender) domination (Cook 1992: 1010).

Comparatively fewer feminist and critical race analyses have been carried out in the crime area, and when they are, authors focus on police and trial procedures (e.g. Maclin 1991; Clay 1993; Johnson 1993; on this point generally, see Peller 1993). The works of Regina Austin, Dwight Greene and Dorothy Roberts are exceptions.

In a 1989 article Austin announced that 'the time has come for us to get truly hysterical, to take on the role of "professional Sapphires" in a forthright way . . . to combat the systematic denigration of minority women' (Austin 1989: 542). She then analysed how the idea of 'the black community' related to crime and black women's law-breaking (Austin 1992a,b). She argues that 'the black community' is an ideal, not a reality; and among the 'multiple threats to the ideal [is] black criminal behavior and the debates it engenders' (Austin 1992a: 1770). The 'black community' can respond to black law-breakers in two ways: by a politics of distinction or by a politics of identification. A politics of distinction relies on 'traditional values of hard work, respectable living, and conformity to law. [While] it furthers the interests of a middle class', it does so at the cost of intensifying community divisions (p. 1773). A politics of identification, which can take several forms, acknowledges community members' deviance, links it to a political agenda and relates it to race resistance (p. 1774). Drawing from Stuart Hall's (1988) ideas on a politics of identification, 'which works with and through difference', Austin argues for an integrated politics of identification. This would connect segments of the black middle class with black law-breakers; it would need bridge people who can straddle both worlds. Bridge people 'work the line between the legal and the illegal [and between] the merely different and the truly deviant' (Austin 1992a: 1817). Fissures in a black sisterhood are the subject of Austin's (1992b) analysis of a black woman who sued a television network for defamation, arguing she was wrongly portrayed as a prostitute. In this case the plaintiff was 'required to distinguish herself from and participate in the broader societal put down of other black women'. She had to walk 'a narrow strait in which bourgeois black women are supposed to channel their sexuality [as neither] matron or prostitute' (p. 885). Austin suggests the need to analyse the 'class cleavages that separate black women' (p. 887) and argues that one way to hasten the liberation of both 'deviant and non-deviant' black women would be to 'acknowledg[e] that sometimes it is . . . difficult to tell "us" from "them"' (p. 887).

Dwight Greene and Dorothy Roberts focus, in varying ways, on how 'race . . . is embedded in the very foundation of our criminal law' (Roberts 1993: 1945). Both analyse the abuses of prosecutorial discretion in criminalizing drug-using women who give birth to children (Greene 1991; Roberts 1991, 1993). Roberts's writings centre on constitutional questions and the ways in which gender, race and class hierarchies are sustained in these prosecutions. Greene's work calls for methods of creating a more democratic criminal law system. For example, he proposes that one way to challenge prosecutorial power and to incorporate feminist and multi-racial/cultural perspectives would be the development of boards to monitor what prosecutors do; for example, to record why decisions were made to go forward with or to drop particular cases. Greene wants to bring in 'outsider voices' – feminist and race-conscious – into the legal system. For example, in developing drug policy, Greene (1990) says that drug dealers, users, their family members and those in the community ought to be part of the 'choral fugue we call democracy' (p. 492) in establishing methods of controlling drugs. Theirs 'may be the only voices that hold the keys to a non-tyrannical solution to the drug problem' (p. 492).

A striking feature of feminist and critical race legal scholarship is that participants are familiar with and draw from both feminist and critical race analyses (see Calmore 1992: 2192–4 for a meditation on this issue). One practical and positive lesson we draw is that feminist and critical race perspectives can work together. Can scholars in criminology join forces with feminist and critical race scholars? Let us turn to a review of their ideas.

Black women scholars in criminology

We summarize writings by selected black women scholars who have raised questions about the substance of criminological theory; they are Loretta Caldwell, Helen Taylor Greene, Jacqueline Huey, Marcia Rice, Katheryn Russell, Anne Sulton and Vernetta Young. Some address the impediments to analysing black crime (Caldwell and Greene 1980; Young and Sulton 1991; Russell 1992); others focus on black women (Rice 1990; Huey 1992). Common themes are the low numbers of black scholars in criminology, the need for blacks to be engaged in theory construction and the exclusion of works by black scholars in the criminological literature. Although black scholars may be marginal to the field, these authors stress that their unique perspectives and experiences as black people ought to be central.

Caldwell and Greene (1980) note that blacks have been writing on crime, especially in the black community, since the turn of the century. They argue for the development of a black perspective that is based on recurring themes in black scholars' research. One theme is that black crime is linked to economic, political and social conditions; a second is that statistical information offers a distorted view of black crime. A black perspective, coupled with the recognition that blacks are under-represented as policy-makers and officials in the criminal justice system, is critical, the authors suggest, for an effective strategy towards crime.

Young and Sulton (1991) argue that African-Americans' contributions to criminology have been ignored: excluded from books edited by white authors or journals with white editorial boards, not on policy-making boards of criminology organizations, nor members of public policy groups, among other areas. In addition to the areas noted by Caldwell and Greene (1980), Young and Sulton argue that myths and misconceptions about African-Americans go unchallenged by white criminologists. Instead, such myths are incorporated into criminological theories and justify racist views of white superiority. The problems with white-centred criminology are errors of omission (denying qualities of cultural or racial difference) and commission (mischaracterizing qualities of cultural or racial difference); in addition, class may be ignored and conflated with race.

Russell's (1992) call for a black criminology was sketched above. Her position differs from Caldwell and Greene's and Young and Sulton's in that the 'black' in black criminology refers primarily to the subjects of research. Russell suggests, however, that the 'seeds for developing a black criminology need to be planted by black criminologists' (p. 680). Once they were established, all criminologists could contribute. Russell considers whether or not a black criminology should focus on racial differences; she concludes that a black criminology does not conflict with interests in examining racial or ethnic differences. Other black scholars, not reviewed in detail here (Bailey 1991; Mann 1993; Hawkins 1994), have conducted comparative racial-ethnic analyses; such an approach can shift a perceived social problem of black crime to a more theoretical and historical problem of racial-ethnic (and class) variation in crime and its control.

Huey (1992) and Rice (1990) want to develop a black feminist perspective in criminology. Huey argues that there needs to be more 'contextual development' in feminist work. Like Young (1986), she suggests that social constructions of black women in popular culture, such as mammy, whore, castrating matriarch or welfare mother, should be a focus for research on black women, crime and their treatment in the justice system. More generally, Huey argues for drawing from black feminist theoretical work that examines the relationships of class, race and gender.

Marcia Rice (1990), who is British, is critical of black criminology in Britain (e.g. Hall et al. 1978; Gilroy 1987) for its focus on black men. She devotes more sustained critical attention, however, to feminist criminology for its focus on gender without consideration of race, and she discusses the implications of such ethnocentrism for explaining victimization and lawbreaking. In the light of black women's experience under slavery and colonialism, Rice points out that their relations with black men 'produce a more complex mesh of struggles both within and outside the family' (p. 63). Moreover, Rice urges an understanding of black women, not simply as subject to greater disadvantage than white women, but as subject to 'oppression . . . of a qualitatively different kind' (p. 64). The approach she commends is precisely what black feminists in the USA endorse: an interactive (and historicized) coupling of class, race and gender relations. In reflecting on the relationship of gender and race, Rice suggests the need to understand how 'racism not only divides but draws together gender identities and how gender is experienced through racism' (p. 66). Although others have called for a way to theorize the experiences of black women and crime (Laub and McDermott 1985; Arnold 1990; Simpson 1991), Rice has been most explicit to date about what ought to be in a black feminist theory. She proposes these elements: not using ethnocentric or racist models of women; avoiding unspecified categories such as 'women' and 'blacks'; making race and racism integral to the analysis; comparing justice system responses to men and women that consider class and race; situating law-breaking within a wider political, economic and social sphere; and using a model of research that is concerned with the relationship of the researcher and subjects of research (p. 68).

To summarize this group of black women in criminology, some have self-defined as feminist and want to use black feminist theory, while others define themselves as black or African-American scholars and want to develop theories and research *on* black crime or to make visible and vocal black scholars' perspectives in criminology. Those in the latter group (Caldwell and Greene 1980; Young and Sulton 1991; Russell 1992) suggest that black criminologists have a unique perspective on the field; as such, they would agree with Collins's (1986) claim that the historical marginalization of black people confers to them a special status today as 'outsider within'.[14] A common assumption is that black researchers can better study and understand black people and crime. This is reasonable in that living in a racist society produces shared experiences and empathy; moreover, black researchers may establish relations of trust better and gather more accurate information from the black people studied. However, there is a downside to this assumption, as Carby (1987) has noted for black women who analyse black women's fiction: thinking there is an essential (commonly shared and known) 'black experience'. Austin's (1992a) call for an 'integrated politics of identification' between middle-class black intellectuals and law-breakers is an important corrective to arguments by black scholars that do not address class and educational differences between black criminologists and black subjects of crime studies.

Because naming what we call ourselves is important, it would be unfortunate if black criminology (Russell 1992) or a black perspective (Caldwell and Greene 1980) was misconstrued as a separatist enterprise, i.e. as something reserved only for black criminologists. While these authors emphasize the importance of black scholars in developing these perspectives, they encourage white scholars to become involved or to collaborate with them. In that regard, we may want to pay attention to how legal scholars name themselves: feminist and critical race. These terms are more aggregated, but they allow for flexibility in how scholars may want to state their perspective. In trying to build a more inclusive theoretical and research agenda, we should be aware that one name (such as 'black feminist' or 'multi-ethnic feminist') may not be capable of satisfying a large enterprise; at the same time, the identities of scholars and the histories of theoretical traditions (such as 'black feminist') are well established.

Research on black women's victimization, law-breaking and treatment in the criminal justice system

In our move from the conceptual questions raised in two previous sections to a review of the research literature in this section, readers will see a sharp break. That is because while we may have a grasp of what *ought* to be done, little research has met the challenge. A core element of black feminist, feminist and critical race theories – the need to address the multiple relations of class, gender and race – cannot be accomplished with national data on arrests or criminal court outcomes. As noted by many others, the Uniform Crime Reports (UCR) arrest data show rates by race and age, by gender and age, but not by gender and race. Published court data evince the same problems (Bureau of Justice Statistics 1990). The National Crime Victimization Survey (NCVS) is better in providing breakdowns by race and gender groups. If there is one bright spot, it is that recent publications from the Bureau of Justice Statistics (BJS) are providing more detailed information by race and gender on victimization (BJS 1994a), rates of imprisonment (BJS 1994b) and profiles of those in jail (BJS 1992).

We find that researchers' analytical strategies vary: many focus on only one or perhaps two relations simultaneously. We also find that different definitions are used for class and racial classifications, e.g. race may be dichotomized black–white, and the non-white category may include other non-black minority groups (see Simpson's 1991 review and Gelsthorpe 1993 on problems of racial classification in Britain). In sum, national data on crime have not been gathered or analysed with black feminist theory in mind. What, then, do we hope to learn from our review? With due regard for the limits of official crime data and the flat renderings of crime and justice from quantification, we want to see what patterns emerge for black women.

National statistical patterns

Victimization

Using NCVS data, Ronet Bachman (BJS 1994a: 2) finds that while women's victimization rate for violent crime (about 25 per 1000) is about 60 per cent of men's (41 per 1000), black women's rate of violent crime victimization (32 per 1000) is greater than white women's (24 per 1000). Black women's higher violent crime victimization is especially evident for robbery and to a lesser degree aggravated assault, but not for rape or simple assault. Gender ratios in violent crime victimization are identical for blacks and whites (60 per cent). The victim–offender relations for violent crime victimizations show that black and white women experience similar rates of violence committed by intimates and other relatives; however, black women are more likely than white women to be victimized by acquaintances and strangers. Class-related indicators of education and income show differences in women's victimization by intimates: college graduates are three times less likely to be victimized than high school graduates or those with some college education; women with less than $10 000 in family income are five times more likely to be victimized than women with family incomes of $30 000 or more. Overall, theft victimization rates are higher for men (72 per 1000) than women (64 per 1000); white women's theft victimization rate is somewhat higher than black women's, but black men experience theft victimization somewhat more than white men.

Offending

Studies by Vernatta Young (1980), Diane Lewis (1981), John Laub and Joan McDermott (1985), Roland Chilton and Susan Datesman (1987), Gary Hill and Elizabeth Crawford (1990) and Sally Simpson (1991) conclude that although women as a group are less likely than men to commit crime, black women's rates are higher than white women's. The race-gender hierarchy from most to least likely to be arrested for common crime (or to be perceived as an offender) is black men, white men, black women and white women.[15] This racial hierarchy within gender groups in rates of arrest (or perceived race of offender in NCVS data) is especially marked for violent crime.

Whether one draws from self-report data, NCVS data on perceived offenders or UCR arrest data, black women's involvement in crime appears to be higher than white women's. Simpson's review of the violent crime literature finds that black women have higher rates of homicide and aggravated assault; for both juveniles and adults, black women's rates of law-breaking are closer to those of white males than white females, and for some offences young black females' rates exceed those of young white males. Using UCR larceny arrest data from five cities, Chilton and Datesman (1987) find that non-white (almost all were black) women's rates of arrest are the same as white men's; thus the four-level gender-race hierarchy collapses into three levels. Hill and Crawford (1990: 611) find that, for a sample of women aged eighteen to twenty-three, white women's reported use of marijuana and other drugs[16] is significantly higher than black women's, but black women's reported involvement in serious property and assaultive acts is significantly higher than white women's. In analysing the spousal 'sex ratio of killing' (SROK), Margo Wilson and Martin Daly (1992) find that US women are far more likely to kill male spouses ('spouses' includes those married and cohabiting) than are women in other countries. Further, they note that the spousal homicide rates (like total homicide rates) are higher for blacks than whites in the USA. In explaining these racial differences, Wilson and Daly suggest that they are specific to the USA and cannot be accounted for by underclass theory or by supposed gender convergence in black violent crime, as Laub and McDermott (1985) speculate. Rather, they argue for a better understanding of 'the special characteristics of the marital relationship' and the particular contexts in which spousal conflict arises for black women in the USA (e.g. defending children from stepfathers).

Smaller-scale and interview studies

Victimization

While many emphasize the lack of information on black women law-breakers, there is even less on black women's experiences with violent crime victimization, especially domestic violence and rape. This is all the more important since, as we saw from Wilson and Daly's (1992) study, a portion of black women's homicides (and perhaps also serious assaults) is related to their victimization by violent intimates (see also Mann 1988). On domestic violence, Mama's (1989) study of London-area women is the only book-length treatment we are aware of. There are other reviews or analyses (Rasche 1988; Richey 1985), and some indirect knowledge from studies of police responses to domestic violence (e.g. Ferraro 1989; Chaudhuri and Daly 1992). From this research, we learn that black women can be caught between their concerns for safety and being tagged as disloyal to 'the race'; they may be pressured to endure the pain and keep silent. For rape, one exemplary study examined white, black and Mexican-American women's experiences after having been raped (Williams and Holmes 1981). The authors found that community supports and perceptions of the women were essential to the women's own recovery: on a continuum, black women were least negatively affected and Mexican-American women most negatively affected. Organizational responses to rape must therefore be responsive to such differences (Matthews 1989).

Victimization and offending

Interview studies of incarcerated women by Meda Chesney-Lind and Noelie Rodriguez (1983), Eleanor Miller (1986), Kim Romenesko and Eleanor Miller (1989), Regina Arnold (1990) and Mary Gilfus (1992) posit a model of black and white women's crime that links victimization and criminalization. Gilfus (1992: 86) puts the 'blurred boundaries' thesis well: 'criminalization is connected to women's subordinate position in society where victimization by violence coupled with economic marginality related to race, class, and gender all too often blur the boundaries between victims and offenders.' Arnold's (1990) interpretation of black women's offending combines victimization, structural dislocation and resistance to victimization. Such resistance is another way of describing women's survival strategies on the street (Chesney-Lind 1989).

Are there racial differences in women's routes to the street or in patterns of law-breaking? There is insufficient research to know. Miller (1986) argues that domestic networks – households linked by kinship, pseudo-kinship and reciprocal personal and economic relationships – which commonly feature for poor urban black households, allow for greater exposure to other deviant individuals. She takes the position that the intersection of domestic and deviant street networks more frequently provides a path to the street for black than white women; however, drug use and running away from abusive families were common to both white and black women's routes to the street.

Cathy Widom (1989) studied the link between victimization when growing up and arrest as an adult. She found that for both black and white women who were adjudicated abused or neglected as children, their rates of arrest as adults were greater (28 and 17 per cent, respectively) than those of control groups of black and white women (19 and 11 per cent, respectively). It is evident that whether or not they were adjudicated to be abused or neglected, being black puts women at 'increased risk' of arrest. Using court documents on women convicted in felony court, Daly (1992) found no racial differences in women's pathways to court. However, it is argued that the 'blurred boundaries' theme of victimization and criminalization, while an important feminist contribution to criminology, evades core questions about how to represent women who abuse, harm and hurt others.

Questions about explaining crime

In explanation of crime, three areas of debate or development have emerged. One is the 'convergence thesis': arrest rates for black men and women are converging more rapidly than those for white men and women (Adler 1975). Most studies find no support for this thesis (Young 1980; Laub and McDermott 1985; Chilton and Datesman 1987), although one did (Smith and Visher 1980). The second is whether structural sources of inequality may play an even greater role in black than white women's crime. Underclass theory, when linked to race, has been used by Chilton and Datesman (1987) and Miller (1986) to explain black women's greater involvement in crime as illicit work. Moreover, Hill and Crawford (1990) find that a cluster of variables they term structural (e.g. unemployment rate, gap between educational aspiration and achievement) more directly affected black women's law-breaking, whereas for white women, variables reflecting social-psychological processes (e.g. self-esteem, gender role traditionalism) were more influential. Third is whether the blurred boundaries theme of victimization-criminalization takes a racially specific form. Research on black and white women (Daly 1992; Gilfus 1992) and multi-ethnic women (Chesney-Lind and Shelden 1992: 166–82) highlights problems of abuse in families and problems in school; racial variation was either not found or it was not a focus of these studies. Rather, as Gilfus (1992: 86) puts it, 'when extreme victimization is accompanied by poverty and racial discrimination, women may have very few options for survival by legal avenues.' Arnold (1990), who interviewed black women only, identified structural dislocation from families and the educational system.

One problem in conceptualizing racial differences for women is that we may conveniently, but perhaps wrongly, overlay racial and gender dichotomies. That is, women's deviance may be split as 'mad' (white) and 'bad' (black) or as psychological (white) and structural (black). While we would caution against such simple schemes, state officials may be using them in responding to women's law-breaking, as Nicole Rafter's (1990) historical study of women's prisons and reformatories reveals.

Justice system responses

The limited research on justice system responses suggests that black women are more likely to be subject to arrest than white women (Visher 1983; Smith *et al.* 1984) but that race-based differences in criminal court outcomes are less evident (Daly 1989a). Racial disproportionalities in prison populations are clear: for women imprisoned in 1991, 46 per cent were black, 36 per cent white, 14 per cent Latina and 4 per cent other (largely Native-American and Asian) (Maguire *et al.* 1993: 622, Table 6.69). The extraordinary increases in women incarcerated in state and federal correctional facilities, from about 6000 in 1970 and 11 500 in 1980 to over 40 000 in 1990 (Maguire *et al.* 1993: 606, Table 6.2), are a consequence of more punitive sentencing policies, including mandatory terms for some drug offences (Chesney-Lind 1991). In the USA, we lack contemporary studies of women's experiences in prison and of their post-prison release experiences.

For court research, some suggest a focus on how racial stereotypes of black women – as dominant, nagging or sexually promiscuous – differ from those of white women – as gentle or dependent (Young 1986; Huey 1992). While Huey (1992) considers general issues concerning images of black women in popular culture, Young (1986) suggests more explicitly that these images affect court officials' responses towards black women in a more punitive manner. Conducting research on how these images are played out and with what consequences would be challenging. Some groundwork has been laid by legal scholars on courtroom racial imagery (Clay 1993; Johnson 1993), though it is on black men.

One problem in the legal and sociological literature on race in justice system practices is a preoccupation with differential treatment. As discussed elsewhere (Daly 1994), it is useful to conceptualize the impact of race (and gender) with a three-part scheme: criminal law and justice system practices as racist (and sexist), white (and male) and racialized (and gendered). This scheme, which borrows from Carol Smart's (1992) analyses of feminist developments in law, allows for different theoretical and research strategies. Practices-as-racist (and sexist) focuses on ways of exposing different treatment and on eradicating it. Practices-as-white (and male) assumes that the point of view of criminal law and justice system practices is white, middle class and male. Neutral and objective standards and policies are shown to be systematically skewed against the poor, minority group members and women. Practices-as-racialized (and gendered) assumes that race and gender relations structure criminal law and justice system practices so profoundly that legal subjects can be expected to be saturated with racializing (and gendered) qualities. Majority group members do not always benefit; nor are minority group members (and women) always subordinated. Most criminological research focuses on officials' responses from a practices-as-racist (and sexist) framework. By contrast, feminist and critical race theorists operate from a practices-as-white (and male) framework; and black feminists in literature and sociology operate from a practices-as-white (and male) *and* practices-as-racialized (and gendered) framework.

Black and multi-ethnic feminist perspectives in criminology: an agenda for theory and research

Fifteen years ago, Deborah McDowell said with respect to black feminist criticism: 'theories have been marred by slogans, rhetoric, and idealism' (McDowell 1980: 188). We should learn from that history in forging black and multi-ethnic feminist perspectives in criminology. Three bodies of ideas – black feminist theory, feminist and critical race theory in law and work by black scholars in criminology – should be joined in developing a broader consciousness about crime and justice.

We have used several terms – black feminist, multi-ethnic feminist, feminist and critical race theories – to describe a range of scholars' identities and perspectives. We are not interested in policing the boundaries of what should count as 'black feminist', who can be a 'multi-ethnic feminist' or who can take a 'critical race perspective'. But, by building on the elements identified by Rice (1990), we are interested in clarifying for ourselves and others what a fully racialized analysis of gender would mean and what it would look like. We find that there are several meanings of the term 'black feminist' that are keyed to a scholar's identity, subjects of research or a combination of the two. There are also scholars, such as Carby, who argue for using race as a central category but not necessarily focusing on black women. Legal scholars have devised the term 'critical race theory' to analyse how legal structures and social processes are racialized or have a 'white' point of view. We have argued for the need to draw from these several literatures in creating new theories of crime and justice. But as our literature review reveals, we should expect that participants in this enterprise may move in different directions and with different assumptions. For example, some may focus their research on black women, while others may use race as a central category of analysis in analysing white women (as Frankenberg 1994 has done). Some may study particular groups of women (or men), with the aim of theorizing and generalizing from that group alone; this could produce distinctive theories of white women's and black women's law-breaking. Others may start with a general framework about women's experience with violence and then explore how race and ethnicity structure variation in experiences with violence and responses to it. Still others may begin with a theory of masculinity and explore its meaning in racialized terms. Theoretical terms used may vary: from familiar criminological terms (such as 'offender') to those less familiar (such as 'criminalized women' or 'racialized subject position'). It is crucial that we become aware of the different assumptions, terms and priorities we have in building knowledge.

As calls for a 'multicultural literacy' in criminology are made in the USA (Barak 1991), they must not repeat the problems noted by Rice (1990) in Britain: a lack of attention to how gender constructs men's crime and victimization, and a focus only upon men's experiences with racism. We propose two strategies that should be pursued simultaneously: a call for community and a call for collaboration. A 'community'[17] of black and multi-ethnic scholars must be mobilized; we need to unify ourselves and the scholarship we present. We must work collectively on the problem of exclusion of minority group voices from the field. A call for collaboration begins with Carby's admonition against essentialist understandings of the 'black' or 'Latino' or 'Asian' or 'Native-American' experience in conducting research. Yet shared experiences of racism, of sexism, of victimization etc. can matter in the relationships formed between researchers and the subjects of their research. We need to incorporate such experiences and make them count without naturalizing them. Separatist notions (that is, white criminologists should only study white people, or men should only study other men) must be avoided for practical and theoretical reasons. Collaborations across gender and racial-ethnic groups may be an optimal way to work together 'as equals in joint enquiry' (Lugones and Spelman 1983: 579).

We return, then, to our separate 'voices' in reflecting on what we learned from our collaboration.

Kathy's voice. The process of doing this chapter helped me to see several things. It may be easier for white feminists to be glib in theorizing about race; that is, to be facile and clever with terms. Such apparent ease may reflect another version of racist expression. When I am thinking and writing by myself, I view race and gender as a theoretical puzzle, but when Debbie and I are struggling with passages and ideas, this is not possible. Collaborating with a black woman makes the words more real, more like life is lived.

Deborah's voice. The collaborative effort of this chapter was a worthwhile project. However, it was not easy for many reasons. For instance, I had to confront some issues within myself as well as the assumptions and preconceptions I have about whites researching and generating theory about black people. These issues were always present in my mind during the entire process of writing this chapter, including our discussions and disagreements, and my reluctance to make revisions to my original ideas. It was illuminating to see through the lens of another whose experiences and theoretical approach are different from my own.

What is our enterprise? The theoretical starting point is that there are multiple and cross-cutting relations of class, race-ethnicity, gender, sexuality and age. This produces a matrix of domination taking a 'both/and' form; that is, shifting and contingent relations of power. Although many claim that black women are at the intersection of class, race and gender, that statement is misleading. Black women are *marked* at the intersection as being on the subordinate side of these three relations, but all social groups (including middle-class white men) are at the intersection. Moreover, as we know from UCR, NCVS, court and prison statistics, it is black men not black women who are most likely to be subject to official criminal justice control. Thus, a 'both/and' stance, not a simple additive model of structural subordinate relations, is required.

What, more precisely, does it mean to take a class-race-gender analysis of crime, victimization and justice? In tracing the history of class-race-gender, we find its emergence in black women's struggles within the Civil Rights Movement to name a set of simultaneously experienced oppressions (Daly 1993).[18] Its development has flowered in literature and cultural studies, but far less so in the social sciences and especially in criminology. In these fields, a class-race-gender analysis has translated to mean a comparison of different groups (e.g. employment and wage differences for white and black women by type of job) or an analysis of interaction effects, in a statistical sense, of class-, race- or gender-related variables. While such quantitative work can be useful in depicting patterns or making comparisons, it is not capable of revealing the relational and socially constructed ways in which crime and justice are experienced and enacted.

Many criminologists have suggested that black women are 'uniquely situated' as subjects of research on crime and justice. Their reasoning is that femaleness is associated with decreased criminal activity and blackness is associated with increased criminal activity. The image they generate is of an alien being – half woman, half black – one side racing towards conformity, the other towards deviance. Criminological theory has constructed this alien being, and we worry that she will become 'infinitely deconstructable "othered" matter', just as duCille (1994: 591) describes for black women writers. Can we work against this tendency?

Our review of the research literature suggests that beyond statistical profiles, our lack of historical and contemporary information is profound. Ethnographic and neighbourhood studies are rare (exceptions are Stack 1974; Valentine 1978; Dunlap 1992; Maher and Curtis 1992; Maher 1995). Neighbourhood-level analyses offer a good way to understand how the processes of conformity and deviance are gendered and racialized, the conditions of street life and illicit work for women, and how once they are immersed in the street life and subject to criminalization, women's options are narrowed. Mercer Sullivan's (1989) three-neighbourhood comparison of black, white and Latino young men showed how different opportunities – for both crime and work – and different family connections to law enforcement and the courts affected the young men's crime patterns and abilities to avoid arrest and incarceration. Such studies have not been done for women. As important to note is that studies of men (such as Sullivan's or gang studies by Hagedorn (1988) and Sanchez-Jankowski (1991)) do not address how gender structures these men's lives and their relations to women.

Racism in criminological theories occurs when racial or cultural differences are overemphasized or mischaracterized *and* when such differences are denied. Feminist and critical race theorists see similar problems in law: in the creation of racial and gender difference (which generates notions of black and female deficiency) and in the creation of colour-blind and gender-neutral law (which operates on a white and male standard). Black (or multi-ethnic) feminist perspectives need to move into a third stage of theoretical and research inquiry: to focus on sources of racial and gender specificity without reinforcing or engaging in racist and sexist imagery. That will mean: the development of a language to talk about 'blackness', 'Latinoness', 'whiteness' etc.; elucidation of the content of cultural differences; and identification of the linguistic and cultural mechanisms by which domination and subordination are enacted and negotiated.

Although we have noted differences across several bodies of literature reviewed, we see a 'choral fugue' singing these themes: sociological, legal and criminological theories and policies are informed from a top-down (white, male, middle class) standpoint of the social order; legal and social reforms of the past several decades have just barely loosened structured inequalities; and there is a need for a more fully democratic and bottom-up presence in academic theories, the creation of law and policy, and its interpretation. The bridge people identified by Austin (1992b), who can walk the line between street and straight in re-creating communities of colour, are also needed to forge multi-ethnic and feminist bridges across disciplinary and personal boundaries. We take a measure of hope from Dwight Greene's (1993: 798) observation that 'feminist perspectives on male domination, when joined with critical race perspectives reflecting the slave and other experiences of people of color, offer transformative coalition possibilities.' The need to build such coalitions could not be more urgent.

Acknowledgements

In addition to the editors, we thank Katheryn Russell, Vernetta Young, Michele Berger and Teri Rosales for their careful reading of and comments on an earlier draft. Thanks are also due to Stephanie Phillips for citations to crime and critical race theory. We commend the editors for their energy and commitment in continuing the spirit of Mont Gabriel.

Notes

1 Our title is taken from Marcia Rice's (1990: 58) observation that black women are the 'dark figure' of criminological literature, having been 'overshadowed by both black men and white women'.

2 We focus on black feminism not because we think it is special or better than other multi-ethnic approaches, but because the original idea of this chapter stemmed from an interest in how a black feminist analysis could better analyse black female offenders (Stephens 1993). We hope our ideas can help to make sense of multiple oppressions of other groups, although we recognize that groups differ and that existing feminist theories may do little to articulate the experiences of women of colour. We see black feminism as one strand of multi-ethnic feminism, and it can also be viewed as one articulation of feminist and critical race theories.

3 Black women in the USA glosses over many black ethnicities, such as Dominican, Jamaican or Haitian, or racial-ethnic mixes such as black Puerto Rican.

4 We discuss black feminism within academic work, but there are, of course, many other sites where black feminist thought and activism flourish.

5 We are aware that for some black women the term 'feminist' carries such white racialized overtones that the preferred self-identify may be 'womanist' (see Walker 1983: xi–xii). A white woman could reverse the usual qualifiers and disrupt the racial hierarchies by calling herself a white womanist.

6 We take it as axiomatic throughout this chapter that criminalized populations are composed disproportionately of economically and politically marginalized members of society. Thus, questions of class emerge most visibly in criminology when we examine the class location of criminologists (middle class, conventional) and the subjects of most criminologists' theories of crime (working class, poor).

7 As Carby (1987) noted and Scott (1992) has developed more fully, the concept of 'experience' should not be viewed as an ahistorical 'bedrock of evidence upon which explanation is built' (Scott 1992: 25). Rather, as Scott proposes 'one must historicize the terms by which experience is represented' (1992: 36). Like many other categories of analysis used in this paper (e.g. black, women, race, crime) the term 'experience' is socially and historically constructed.

8 Black scholars' studies of whites may be as, if not more, important (our thanks to Vernetta Young for reminding us). Judith Rollins's (1985) study of black women domestic workers and their white women employers provides an important discussion of the dilemmas she faced analysing white women as a black woman passing as a domestic worker.

9 Evidence of racially based differences in women's understandings of crime and victimization comes from several sources. One is the reception to Coramae Richey Mann's (1988) analysis of domestic homicide when it was presented at a professional meeting (where members of the audience challenged her for not saying more about previous abuse in the relationship). Others come from our experiences in teaching certain texts in the classroom. For example, black students often challenge how Eleanor Miller (1986) describes and interprets the experiences of black street women, and minority group women challenge the characterizations that Rasche (1988) makes of the experiences of domestic violence for women of colour.

10 It is useful to reiterate the distinction between *identifying* as a black feminist and *taking* a black feminist perspective. The former is concerned with how one's social location (as black and female) is politicized and theorized as a point of view or standpoint; the latter is a theoretical point of view that is not necessarily anchored to a black and female body. While all those identifying as 'black feminist' are likely to take a black feminist perspective, we do not assume that all those who take a black feminist perspective are black and female.

11 Our review omits important new work in cultural studies, such as that by Michele Wallace (1990), the contributors in Gina Dent's edited collection (1992)

and Tricia Rose (1994). Nor do we review the contributions of black women writers prior to the 1950s Civil Rights Movement or the historical meanings of race in the USA. See Giddings (1984), Higginbotham (1992), Brewer (1993) and James (1993) for analyses of the historical contexts of black feminist thought.

12 Collins's concept of standpoint reflects difficulties in feminist theory more generally about what constitutes the basis for the standpoint. In the passage summarized here, Collins assumes that the gender, race and sexual identities of the scholars produce the 'standpoint'. Standpoint could be conceptualized another way: by identification with a set of theoretical and political assumptions that orient a person's outlook. Thus, a white man may take a socialist-feminist analysis on crime.

13 In using terms such as 'white' or 'male' or other designated voices, we assume decoupling from a biological referent. That is, here and in the section describing justice system practices, we assume that whiteness and masculinity need not be anchored to white or male bodies.

14 We would like to acknowledge that with this status comes hardships; for example, 'outsiders within' may have a unique perspective but are not allowed to express it, or outsiders may be ignored or penalized when expressing ideas.

15 For varieties of white-collar crime, however, we know less. Daly's (1989b) study of defendants convicted in federal court for petty to more serious forms of white-collar crime found that antitrust and securities fraud violations were almost entirely committed by white men; however, for other offences (such as bank embezzlement) women made up 45 per cent of convictions; the non-white share of embezzlement convictions was far higher for women (41 per cent) than men (14 per cent). These race/gender differences can be explained, but only in part, by occupational position. Maher and Waring (1990: 48–9) found that of clerical workers convicted of embezzlement, the non-white shares for women and men were 38 and 22 per cent, respectively. See analyses by Harris (1991) and Russell (1994) on the class–race relationship in common and white-collar crime.

16 Detail on which drugs were in the 'other drug' category was not given by the authors.

17 We use the term 'community' here like Austin (1992a,b) does in referring to 'the black community': it is an ideal and a partial reality; it suggests commonalities and differences.

18 The history of class-race-gender could be linked to nineteenth-century black women's writings in the USA; however, its use as an analytical term first appears in academic feminist scholarship during the 1970s.

References

Adler, F. (1975). *Sisters in Crime: the Rise of the New Female Criminal*. New York: McGraw-Hill.

Arnold, R. (1990). Processes of victimization and criminalization of black women. *Social Justice*, 17, 153–65.

Austin, R. (1989). Sapphire Bound! *Wisconsin Law Review*, 1989, 539–78.

Austin, R. (1992a). 'The black community', its lawbreakers, and a politics of identification. *Southern California Law Review*, 65, 1769–817.

Austin, R. (1992b). Black women, sisterhood, and the difference/deviance divide. *New England Law Review*, 26, 877–87.

Bailey, F.Y. (1991). Law, justice, and 'Americans': an historical overview. In M.J.

Lynch and E.B. Patterson (eds) *Race and Criminal Justice*. New York: Harrow and Heston.

Barak, G. (1991). Cultural literacy and a multicultural inquiry into the study of crime and justice. *Journal of Criminal Justice Education*, 2, 173–92.

Beale, F. (1970). Double jeopardy: to be black and female. In T. Cade (ed.) *The Black Woman*. New York: New American Library.

Bell, D. (1980). *Race, Racism, and American Law*, 2nd edn. Boston: Little, Brown.

Bell, D. (1987). *And We Are Not Saved*. New York: Basic Books.

Bell, D. (1992). *Faces at the Bottom of the Well*. New York: Basic Books.

Brewer, R.M. (1993). Theorizing race, class and gender: the new scholarship of Black feminist intellectuals and Black women's labor. In S.M. James and A.P.A. Busia (eds) *Theorizing Black Feminisms*. New York: Routledge.

Bureau of Justice Statistics (1990). *Profile of Felons Convicted in State Courts 1986* (by P.A. Langan and J.M. Dawson). Washington, DC: US Department of Justice, Office of Justice Programs.

Bureau of Justice Statistics (1992). *Women in Jail, 1989* (by T.L. Snell). Washington, DC: US Department of Justice, Office of Justice Programs.

Bureau of Justice Statistics (1994a). *Violence against Women* (by R. Bachman). Washington, DC: US Department of Justice, Office of Justice Programs.

Bureau of Justice Statistics (1994b). *Prisoners in 1993* (by D.K. Gilliard and A.J. Beck). Washington, DC: US Department of Justice, Office of Justice Programs.

Caldwell, L. and Greene, H.E.T. (1980). Implementing a black perspective in criminal justice. In A.W. Cohn and B. Wards (eds) *Improving Management in Criminal Justice*. Beverly Hills, CA: Sage.

Calmore, J.O. (1992). Critical race theory, Archie Shepp, and fire music: securing an authentic intellectual life in a multicultural world. *Southern California Law Review*, 65, 2129–230.

Carby, H.V. (1987). *Reconstructing Womanhood: the Emergence of the Afro-American Woman Novelist*. New York: Oxford University Press.

Chaudhuri, M. and Daly, K. (1992). Do restraining orders help? Battered women's experience with male violence and legal process. In E.S. Buzawa and C.G. Buzawa (eds) *Domestic Violence: the Changing Criminal Justice Response*. Westport, CT: Auburn House.

Chesney-Lind, M. (1989). Girls' crime and woman's place: toward a feminist model of female delinquency. *Crime and Delinquency*, 35, 5–29.

Chesney-Lind, M. (1991). Patriarchy, prisons, and jails: a critical look at trends in women's incarceration. *The Prison Journal*, 71, 51–67.

Chesney-Lind, M. and Rodriguez, N. (1983). Women under lock and key: a view from the inside. *The Prison Journal*, 63, 47–65.

Chesney-Lind, M. and Shelden, R.G. (1992). *Girls, Delinquency, and Juvenile Justice*. Pacific Grove, CA: Brooks/Cole Publishing Company.

Chilton, R. and Datesman, S.K. (1987). Gender, race, and crime: an analysis of urban arrest trends, 1960–1980. *Gender and Society*, 1, 152–71.

Clay, D.A. (1993). Race and perceptions in the courtroom: nonverbal behaviors and attribution in the criminal justice system. *Tulane Law Review*, 67, 2335–55.

Christian, B. (1985). *Black Feminist Criticism: Perspectives on Black Women Writers*. New York: Pergamon Press.

Collins, P.H. (1986). Learning from the outsider within: the sociological significance of black feminist thought. *Social Problems*, 33, 14–32.

Collins, P.H. (1989). The social construction of black feminist thought. *Signs: Journal of Women in Culture and Society*, 14, 745–73.

Collins, P.H. (1990). *Black Feminist Thought: Knowledge, Consciousness, and the Politics of Empowerment*. London: Harper Collins Academic.

Combahee River Collective (1979). The Combahee River Collective Statement. In Z. Eisenstein (ed.) *Capitalist Patriarchy and the Case for Socialist Feminism.* New York: Monthly Review Press.

Cook, A.E. (1992). The spiritual movement towards justice. *University of Illinois Law Review,* 1992, 1007–20.

Crenshaw, K. (1989). Demarginalizing the intersection of race and sex: a black feminist critique of antidiscrimination doctrine, feminist theory, and antiracist politics. *University of Chicago Legal Forum,* 1989, 139–67.

Daly, K. (1989a). Neither conflict nor labeling nor paternalism will suffice: intersections of race, ethnicity, gender, and family in criminal court decisions. *Crime and Delinquency,* 35, 136–68.

Daly, K. (1989b). Gender and varieties of white-collar crime. *Criminology,* 27, 769–93.

Daly, K. (1990). Reflections on feminist legal thought. *Social Justice,* 17, 7–24.

Daly, K. (1992). Women's pathways to felony court: feminist theories of lawbreaking and problems of representation. *Review of Law and Women's Studies,* 2, 11–52.

Daly, K. (1993). Class-race-gender: sloganeering in search of meaning. *Social Justice,* 20, 56–71.

Daly, K. (1994). Criminal law and justice system practices as racist, white, and racialized. *Washington and Lee Law Review,* 51, 431–64.

Delgado, R. (1989). Storytelling for oppositionists and others: a plea for narrative. *Michigan Law Review,* 87, 2411–41.

Dent, G. (ed.) (1992). *Black Popular Culture.* Seattle: Bay Press.

duCille, A. (1994). The occult of true black womanhood: critical demeanor and black feminist studies. *Signs: Journal of Women in Culture and Society,* 19, 591–629.

Dunlap, E. (1992). The impact of drugs on family life and kin networks in the inner-city African-American single-parent household. In A.V. Harrell and G.E. Peterson (eds) *Drugs, Crime, and Social Isolation.* Washington, DC: Urban Institute Press.

Ferraro, K.J. (1989). Policing woman battering. *Social Problems,* 36, 61–74.

Frankenberg, R. (1994). *White Woman, Race Matters.* Minneapolis: University of Minnesota Press.

Gelsthorpe, L. (1993). Approaching the topic of racism: transferable research strategies? In D. Cook and B. Hudson (eds) *Racism and Criminology.* London: Sage.

Giddings, P. (1984). *When and Where I Enter: the Impact of Black Women on Race and Sex in America.* New York: William Morrow.

Gilfus, M.E. (1992). From victims to survivors to offenders: women's routes of entry and immersion into street crime. *Women and Criminal Justice,* 4, 63–89.

Gilroy, P. (1987). *There Ain't No Black in the Union Jack: the Cultural Politics of Race and Nation.* London: Hutchinson.

Greene, D.L. (1990). Drug decriminalization: a chorus in need of Masterrap's voice. *Hofstra Law Review,* 18, 457–500.

Greene, D.L. (1991). Abusive prosecutors: gender, race and class discretion and the prosecution of drug-addicted mothers. *Buffalo Law Review,* 39, 737–802.

Greene, D.L. (1993). Justice Scalia and Tonto, judicial pluralistic ignorance, and the myth of colorless individualism in Bostick v. Florida. *Tulane Law Review,* 67, 1979–2062.

Hagedorn, J. (1988). *People and Folks.* Chicago: Lakeview Press.

Hall, S. (1988). New ethnicities. In L. Appignanesi (ed.) *Black Film, British Cinema.* London: Institute of Contemporary Arts.

Hall, S., Critcher, C., Jefferson, T., Clarke, J. and Roberts, B. (1978). *Policing the Crisis: Mugging, the State, and Order.* New York: Holmes & Meier Publishers.

Harris, A.R. (1991). Race, class, and crime. In J.F. Sheley (ed.) *Criminology.* Belmont, CA: Wadsworth.

Hawkins, D.F. (1994). Ethnicity: the forgotten dimension of American social control. In G.S. Bridges and M.A. Myers (eds) *Inequality, Crime, and Social Control.* Boulder, CO: Westview Press.

Higginbotham, E.B. (1992). African-American women's history and the metalanguage of race. *Signs: Journal of Women in Culture and Society,* 17, 251–74.

Hill, G.D. and Crawford, E.M. (1990). Women, race and crime. *Criminology,* 28, 601–26.

hooks, b. (1981). *Ain't I a Woman? Black Women and Feminism.* Boston: South End Press.

hooks, b. (1984). *Black Feminist Theory: from Margin to Center.* Boston: South End Press.

hooks, b. (1989). *Talking Back: Thinking Feminist, Thinking Black.* Boston: South End Press.

hooks, b. (1990). *Yearning: Race, Gender, and Cultural Politics.* Boston: South End Press.

Huey, J.F. (1992). A contextual analysis of a feminist-oriented criminology: race and popular culture. Paper presented at the annual meeting of the American Society of Criminology, New Orleans, November.

James, S.M. (1993). Introduction. In S.M. James and A.P.A. Busia (eds) *Theorizing Black Feminisms.* New York: Routledge.

Johnson, S.L. (1993). Racial imagery in criminal cases. *Tulane Law Review,* 67, 1739–805.

Jordan, J. (1985). *On Call: Political Essays.* Boston: South End Press.

King, D.K. (1988). Multiple jeopardy, multiple consciousness: the context of a black feminist ideology. *Signs: Journal of Women in Culture and Society,* 14, 42–72.

Laub, J.H. and McDermott, M.J. (1985). An analysis of serious crime by young black women. *Criminology,* 23, 81–98.

Lewis, D. (1981). Black women offenders and criminal justice: some theoretical considerations. In M. Warren (ed.) *Comparing Female and Male Offenders.* Beverly Hills, CA: Sage.

Lorde, A. (1984). *Sister Outsider.* Trumansburg, NY: Crossing Press.

Lugones, M.C. and Spelman, E.V. (1983). Have we got a theory for you! Feminist theory, cultural imperialism and the demand for the 'woman's voice'. *Women's Studies International Forum,* 6, 573–81.

McDowell, D. (1980). New directions for black feminist criticism. *Black American Literature Forum,* 14, 153–9.

Maclin, T. (1991). 'Black and blue encounters' – some preliminary thoughts about Fourth Amendment seizures: should race matter? *Valparaiso University Law Review,* 26, 243–79.

Maguire, K., Pastore, A.L. and Flanagan, T.J. (eds) (1993). *Sourcebook of Criminal Justice Statistics 1992.* Washington, DC: US Department of Justice, Bureau of Justice Statistics.

Maher, L. (1995). Dope girls: gender, race and class in the drug economy. Unpublished PhD thesis, Rutgers University School of Criminal Justice.

Maher, L. and Curtis, R. (1992). Women on the edge of crime: crack cocaine and the changing contexts of street-level sex work in New York City. *Crime, Law, and Social Change,* 18, 221–58.

Maher, L. and Waring, E.J. (1990). Beyond simple differences: white collar crime, gender and workforce position. *phoebe,* 2, 44–54.

Mama, A. (1989). *The Hidden Struggle: Statutory and Voluntary Sector Responses to Violence against Black Women in the Home*. London: London Race and Housing Research Unit.

Mann, C.R. (1984). *Female Crime and Delinquency*. Montgomery: University of Alabama Press.

Mann, C.R. (1988). Getting even? Women who kill in domestic encounters. *Justice Quarterly*, 5, 33–51.

Mann, C.R. (1993). *Unequal Justice: a Question of Color*. Bloomington: Indiana University Press.

Matthews, N.A. (1989). Surmounting a legacy: the expansion of racial diversity in a local anti-rape movement. *Gender and Society*, 3, 518–32.

Miller, E.M. (1986). *Street Woman*. Philadelphia: Temple University Press.

Peller, G. (1993). Criminal law, race, and the ideology of bias: transcending the critical tools of the sixties. *Tulane Law Review*, 67, 2231–52.

Rafter, N.H. (1990). *Partial Justice: Women, Prisons, and Social Control*, 2nd edn. New Brunswick, NJ: Transaction.

Rasche, C. (1988). Minority women and domestic violence: the unique dilemmas of battered women of color. *Journal of Contemporary Criminal Justice*, 4, 150–71.

Rice, M. (1990). Challenging orthodoxies in feminist theory: a black feminist critique. In L. Gelsthorpe and A. Morris (eds) *Feminist Perspectives in Criminology*. Milton Keynes: Open University Press.

Richey, B. (1985). Battered black women: a challenge for the black community. *The Black Scholar*, 16, 40–4.

Roberts, D.E. (1991). Punishing drug addicts who have babies: women of color, equality, and the right of privacy. *Harvard Law Review*, 104, 1419–82.

Roberts, D.E. (1993). Crime, race, and reproduction. *Tulane Law Review*, 67, 1945–77.

Rollins, J. (1985). *Between Women: Domestics and Their Employers*. Philadelphia: Temple University Press.

Romenesko, K. and Miller, E.M. (1989). The second step in double jeopardy: appropriating the labor of female street hustlers. *Crime and Delinquency*, 35, 109–35.

Rose, T. (1994). *Black Noise*. Middleton, CT: Wesleyan University Press.

Russell, K.K. (1992). Development of a black criminology and role of the black criminologist. *Justice Quarterly*, 9, 667–83.

Russell, K.K. (1994). White crime. Unpublished manuscript, Institute of Criminology and Criminal Justice, University of Maryland.

Sanchez-Jankowski, M. (1991). *Islands in the Street: Gangs and American Urban Society*. Berkeley: University of California Press.

Scott, J.W. (1992). Experience. In J. Butler and J.W. Scott (eds) *Feminists Theorize the Political*. New York: Routledge.

Simpson, S. (1991). Caste, class, and violent crime: explaining difference in female offending. *Criminology*, 29, 115–35.

Smart, C. (1992). The woman of legal discourse. *Social and Legal Studies*, 1, 29–44.

Smith, B. (1977). Toward a black feminist criticism. *Conditions*, 2, 25–44.

Smith, D.A. and Visher, C. (1980). Sex and involvement in deviance/crime: a quantitative review of the empirical literature. *American Sociological Review*, 45, 691–701.

Smith, D.A., Visher, C. and Davidson, L. (1984). Equity and discretionary justice: the influence of race on police arrest decisions. *Journal of Criminal Law and Criminology*, 75, 234–49.

Stack, C.B. (1974). *All Our Kin: Strategies for Survival in a Black Community.* New York: Harper Colophon Books.

Stephens, D.J. (1993). Crime, victimization and the black women. Paper presented at the annual meeting of the American Society of Criminology, Phoenix, AZ, October.

Sullivan, M.L. (1989). *'Getting Paid': Youth Crime and Work in the Inner City.* Ithaca, NY: Cornell University Press.

Valentine, B. (1978). *Hustling and Other Hard Work.* Glencoe, IL: Free Press.

Visher, C. (1983). Gender, police arrest decisions, and notions of chivalry. *Criminology*, 21, 5–28.

Vogel, L. (1993). *Mothers at Work: Maternity Policy in the US Workplace.* New Brunswick, NJ: Rutgers University Press.

Walker, A. (1983). *In Search of Our Mothers' Gardens.* New York: Harcourt Brace Jovanovich.

Wallace, M. (1990). *Invisibility Blues: from Pop to Theory.* New York: Verso.

Washington, M.H. (ed.) (1975). *Black-eyed Susans.* New York: Anchor Press.

Widom, C. (1989) Child abuse, neglect, and violent criminal behavior. *Criminology*, 27, 251–71.

Williams, J.E. and Holmes, K.A. (1981). *The Second Assault: Rape and Public Attitudes.* Westport, CT: Greenwood Press.

Williams, P.J. (1991). *The Alchemy of Race and Rights: Diary of a Law Professor.* Cambridge, MA: Harvard University Press.

Wilson, M.I. and Daly, M. (1992). Who kills whom in spouse killings? On the exceptional sex ratio of spousal homicides in the United States. *Criminology*, 30, 189–215.

Young, V.D. (1980). Women, race and crime. *Criminology*, 18, 26–34.

Young, V.D. (1986). Gender expectations and their impact on black female offenders and victims. *Justice Quarterly*, 3, 305–27.

Young, V.D. and Sulton, A.T. (1991). Excluded: the current status of African-American scholars in the field of criminology and criminal justice. *Journal of Research in Crime and Delinquency*, 28, 101–16.

11

Crime through gender's prism: feminist criminology in the United States

DORIE KLEIN

Introduction

The present and future of feminist criminology in the United States can be illustrated with a story. As I write, a political battle has ended over recently enacted crime legislation in Congress. By current standards nearly everything in the Bill was routine, and most of it completely antithetical to anything that would be advocated by a feminist criminology: new prisons, new capital crimes, more mandatory incarcerations and more police. However, this time the Congressional Black Caucus initially refused to support the legislation unless it contained a so-called 'Racial Justice Act'. Optimistic title nothwithstanding, the provision would merely have allowed convicted defendants facing the death penalty – who are disproportionately black – to appeal their sentences based on statistical research evidence of racial bias. The provision would have overturned a Supreme Court decision invalidating such a defence, wherein one justice had written that, after all, the entire US criminal justice system could be challenged on the basis of racial bias statistics. The Clinton administration, pushing to enact the crime Bill, opposed the controversial clause and persuaded most Caucus members to acquiesce. The new Attorney General, admired as a feminist, toured the country to promote the legislation, the content of which she reportedly had no role in; at a function in Oakland which I attended, she was stressing the Bill's funding for community youth projects and battered women's shelters. Ironically, the Bill, shorn of the Racial Justice Act, still nearly did not pass the Congress: conservatives complained about the youth projects, shelters and other crime prevention programmes. In the end, funding for these programmes was cut dramatically.

Here advocates of feminist or progressive crime policies typically find themselves today: ricocheting between the optimism of potentially staggering public revelations about the nature of justice (from institutional racism to tolerance of violence against women) and the pessimism of a systemic political slide deeper into repression. In particular, women's advocates, having been admitted as legitimate spokespersons on certain issues, such as violence against women, are asked to accept the constraints imposed by business as usual. Like the Congressional Black Caucus, they can occasionally refuse to play by these rules, over which they have no say, even if it cedes the field to the reactionaries, but if they wish to remain in the game . . . And so it is with their academic sisters in criminology.

Feminist criminologists, like all criminologists, have even fewer gains to celebrate than do their policy-minded colleagues. One important footnote to the Racial Justice Act is this: if racism in the US justice system is now a topic of debate, it is, with a few exceptions (e.g. on the death penalty: Radelet 1981; Baldus *et al.* 1983), no thanks to criminologists and their largely technical work on procedural bias. Rather, in addition to the astonishing numbers of drug arrests in recent years, of which well over half are of black or Latino people, the major intellectual catalyst was a short and horrifying report issued by a handful of activists dependent on voluntary donations. This group, the Sentencing Project, calculated that one out of four young African-American men is in the correctional system (Mauer 1992). My account is symptomatic in that for almost every important question raised about crime and justice in the USA in recent decades, criminologists have been among the last to know.

For questions of gender and crime, despite the wealth of academic material today, most of the important first steps in the USA were taken outside universities. The first influential feminist book on women and prison was by a journalist (Burkhart 1973); the first analysis of rape was in a magazine article by a freelance political writer (Griffin 1971); and the first publications on wife battering were paperbacks and pamphlets by community-based activists (Martin 1976; Warrior 1976). The relative absence of criminologists could also be noted among the authors of early important feminist work on pornography, serial killing of women, killing by women, sex work and political prisoners, and books on 'the life' or 'the streets'.

This chapter will not trace the development of feminist criminology in the USA over its lifetime of a quarter century. Such a historical account, even though potentially voluminous, could illuminate the points I want to make only if it were exhaustively to critique criminological works for what has been *left out* of them. A shorter route for me to take is to 'transgress' criminology, to use Maureen Cain's term (Cain 1989).

My objective is to stimulate a re-envisioning of the kind of feminist thinking on crime and justice in the USA that could make an intellectual and socio-political difference. My metaphor for the re-envisioning will be the prism, which, under the right conditions, breaks up a beam of white light into colours visible to our eyes. This spectrum of the rainbow is used for creating science, art and sheer pleasure.

Gender through the prism of criminology

A feminist criminology has struggled to be born in the USA since the rise of the women's movement amidst the social ferment of the late 1960s, most strikingly through the mobilizations to redefine rape and wife battering. Over two decades later there now exists a scholarly literature comprising pro-feminist views on women and crime, or consisting of work on women-related criminological subjects (these are not necessarily the same thing, of course, or necessarily feminist criminology).[1]

In a few areas, feminist perspectives have gained prominence, most notably in theories and empirical studies of sexual and domestic violence. Fought-for policy victories, such as the growth of battered women's shelters and the reform of rape laws, have been accompanied by hard-won intellectual triumphs. In a number of areas, work on women is accepted, such as in studies of women working in the justice system and surveys of justice system discretion and bias. Mainstream criminological theories on crime causation and victimology have been tested for their applicability to women's behaviours, and for their ability to explain rates of offending by and victimization of women. The federal government has initiated funding for research on women victims and on women's alcohol and drug use, and now encourages the inclusion of women and ethnic minority members as research subjects. Studies with exclusively male samples have begun to include the modifying adjective in the titles of their publications.[2] The Division on Women and Crime exists alongside other special-interest divisions in the American Society of Criminology.

Much of this progress has been characterized by feminists as an 'add women and stir' adjustment rather than as a conceptual paradigm shift. In fact, the main currents of criminological theory in the USA have been relatively impervious to feminist and other critical challenges. While there are many reasons for this, one powerful factor has been the explosion of crime and victimization as political media issues in the 1970s and 1980s. The narrow high beam focused on deterring and punishing street crime (a discussion of which is beyond the scope of this chapter) has engulfed criminology and eclipsed most radical approaches to social problems, including feminism.

In this climate, the pro-feminist position that has succeeded best has been the advocacy of criminalizing individual violations (e.g. battering, sexual assault) and arresting and punishing the identified offenders (Klein 1988). Law and criminology have accepted with relative willingness, albeit ill grace, those pro-woman perspectives centred on violent crimes, especially those involving relatively powerless offenders and respectable or 'legitimate' victims. Also relatively accepted have been studies and projects concerning internal system decision-making bias against individual offenders, victims and workers on the basis of gender. These perspectives can be incorporated into the traditional paradigms. Less successful has been the advocacy of alternatives to punishment and incarceration for female and other offenders. Feminist attacks on organized sexual exploitation (e.g. pornography and mass media objectification) have been mostly frustrated, and even less visible have been attempts to highlight other systemic victimizations of women (Klein 1981), such as medical maltreatment and government abuses. In short, the deeper forms of feminist critique and advocacy, with their cutting implications for mainstream theories of crime and justice, have been stymied.

This leaves us in a contemporary dilemma well expressed by Sandra Harding's protest that 'feminists are not arguing that anti-sexist theory, research and politics have an equal *right* to be recognized as legitimate or desirable *alongside* sexist theory, research and politics' (Harding 1986: 108, emphasis in original). In both science (i.e. research and teaching) and law (i.e. the criminal justice system and crime policy), the inching of feminist thought from margin towards centre has so far tamed feminism more than it has transformed the centre. From the prism of criminology, women are only another interest group to be acknowledged, and gender is just another variable to be included.

A small group continues to dream of a profound critique of the discipline, and for a growing proportion of this group feminist thought has the capability of provoking such a critique. A few areas for such a feminist critique that I will touch on here are the criminologist's subject, method and commitment. Since space is limited, my remarks will of necessity be suggestive and schematic.

Criminology through the prism of gender

The field of criminology has always defined crime through the prism of gender, one way or another. There has been a sparse criminological literature contrasting men and women. The male usually is the unproblematic norm, and it is the female who needs to be explained. Close attention has been paid to this 'gender-biased' schema since the early feminist critiques of traditional theories of female law-breaking and the feminist studies uncovering biased criminal justice treatment. A related issue has been explorations of female versus male rates of offending, which try to sort out the effects of gender-biased interventions.

More commonly, criminology has gazed without regard to gender at the caught criminal, who (like the criminologist) empirically often happens to be male. The 'gender-blind' assumption has been one of universal applicability of the research, with the unproblematic, practically ungendered, male as norm. Such approaches have been examined in recent years by feminist-influenced criminologists for their relevance to women, but rarely have the implicit assumptions of these approaches been analysed. That is, pro-feminist research has mostly asked whether the 'gender-blind' approaches and assumptions empirically 'work' for women offenders, but has rarely asked how, by whom and for what purpose these approaches and assumptions were developed.

An everyday analogy to the consequences of 'gender blindness' is presented in the processes used by commercial laundries to iron women's and men's shirts in California. Women are charged considerably more than men for this service; hence an Equal Pricing Act was proposed. The fact emerged that the alleged reason for charging women more is that women's shirts must be hand-ironed, because the ironing 'forms' were designed for men's shirts (i.e. bigger sizes, buttons on the right side). Despite the pro-liferation of women's shirts, apparently no one has thought to alter the 'forms', which are seen as the ungendered norm.

In criminology, while we are now 'adding women in', the conceptual forms remain unaltered. But *should* we alter the forms, 'engender' crim-inology, as the term goes? Perhaps it is time, to use another current phrase, to 'reinvent' criminology completely, using our 'engendered' sight.

A gendered sight

The ongoing feminist strategic work to uncover gender bias and gender blindness in Western thought has been enormously illuminative. This is because a narrow and intense beam of light switched on from a particular personal social location (an 'identity') has the power to shed considerable new light on a subject, and can transform the viewer as well. Wanda Coleman comments on her vision as a self-conscious African-American in a way that may strike a responsive chord in many:

> I have grown yet another eye, a primal orb density which provides me constant double vision. Thus I may observe with such intense focus I become emotionally cock-eyed; so skewed I can't know of any racial incident without relating it to my personal circumstances. It's impos-sible to read a book or newspaper, watch television or a movie, or listen to music without perceiving the racist ramifications. I even see racism under my bed.
>
> (Coleman 1993: 209–10)

When activated on behalf of a group, the gendered sight of personal iden-tity grows even stronger, as that of a 'standpoint'. The striving for an independent definition of one's self and a space of one's own is widened to constitute a politics of group affirmation and positive empowerment. Thus a stigma imposed from above is transformed into a choice from below.

That an oppressive social site or marginalized identity can confer a sub-jugated knowledge has long been recognized. In *The Souls of Black Folk* (1903), W.E.B. DuBois referred to the 'second sight' of African-Americans.

For women, the female-dominated worlds of caregiving, mothering, sexuality, female physicality, female labour and work can give rise to a 'different voice' (Gilligan 1982). But 'different' is not 'separate but equal' to (i.e. no better than) the dominant voice: women know intimately both their own worlds *and* the worlds of men, as expressed in the phrase that women 'sleep with the enemy' ('give birth to the enemy' would be just as apt). The same can be said for black Americans, who must negotiate their way in white America, or for slaves in a slave society, or for gays and lesbians in the straight world.

For feminist criminologists, a second sight, double vision or different voice would have to incorporate the experiences and perceptions of those who are overlooked or avoided by the privileged. These people include the 'social garbage' lining our streets and the 'social dynamite' filling our institutions (Spitzer 1975), as well as the silent servants (paid and unpaid) in the big houses and service stations. The situations of these people are dissected as constituting one social problem after another in the USA (e.g. crime, violence, gangs, illegal drug use, homelessness, teenage pregnancy, welfare dependence, AIDS), but rarely are the problematized allowed to speak for themselves or have their contributions acknowledged.

Consciously assuming the gendered sight carries with it the obligation to reflect critically on one's own site, one's self. Electrifying as the prism of identity or standpoint may be, it has its distortions and its limitations. For middle-class white feminists, there has sometimes been an obsessive attention paid to gender, until one does see sexism under the bed. In an ironic mirroring of the sexists' '*la difference*', there is sometimes such a differentiation of the genders by this group that one might suspect, in the words of John Gray's currently popular book title, that 'men are from Mars, women are from Venus'.[3]

Double vision is inadequate as a metaphor in any event, for we all possess at any given moment multiple identities of gender, ethnicity, age, generation, socio-economic class, religion (or the absence of one), nationality, sexual orientation and physical abilities. There is also the need to acknowledge one's changing identity, or the potential for changing one's identity, through the shifts wrought over time (i.e. age) and space (i.e. nationality), or orientation (i.e. sexuality). One individual may see through a prism of many shifting colours. An argument for us to be wary of blinkered gender vision, and to expand beyond it, has been made by Laura Fishman (cited in Bertrand *et al.* 1992) in her observation, which I will paraphrase, that, if we look for the witches of sexism everywhere, we will find them – and miss, perhaps, the warlocks of racism lurking elsewhere.

Furthermore, there is the potential for assuming others' viewpoints. One would be extraordinarily constrained if one's concerns were limited to one's personal identity or group standpoint, provocative as they may be. The ability to see from other locations is particularly vital for feminist criminologists, since we rarely belong to the most discarded or dangerous or vulnerable classes. To conduct feminist research will inevitably require us to step outside ourselves and assume others' perspectives. Furthermore, our policy advocacy should not be based on narrow interest group perceptions. The dilemma for feminists who have done so is exemplified in the trap of centrist legitimacy I alluded to with respect to advocates of crime victims. Thus personal 'standpointism' is insufficient for the feminist criminologist.

Finally, we must keep our eyes open and our visions receptive to new sights, not let our identities and standpoints harden and freeze. Identities and standpoints are based on experiences and interpretations, or empathetic observations, of relationships. In exchanges among women and men, black and white, young and old, worker and employer, and so forth, all persons – the privileged as well as the subjugated, the distant witnesses as well as the immediate parties to the conflict – are affected. A key theme in many feminist and Afrocentric perspectives is connectedness: the connection between individual and community, between oppressed and oppressor, and between one political issue and another (Haraway 1991; Baca Zinn and Dill 1994).

A natural woman

I have suggested that gender and other identities are usually relational and experiential, rather than essential or natural. Criminology, on the other hand, whether gender-blind, gender-biased, or feminist-influenced, nearly always posits the gendered subject as natural or essential, and the gender division as an unproblematic dualism based on biological sex. The discipline has as yet been barely touched by the postmodern feminist theoretical project of deconstruction, which has been to challenge the category of the natural, and to trace the scientific construction of biological sex or gender itself, much as feminist social scientists have already examined socio-cultural gender.

Simone de Beauvoir in The Second Sex (1949) made the famous observation that women are not born but made; going beyond this, one might say that 'women and men are not just made, but made up' (Klein 1994). Woman herself is a constructed Other, in de Beauvoir's classic phrase. This does not require an idealist assumption, but a constructionist one:

> The fact that every object is constituted as an object of discourse has nothing to do with whether there is a world external to thought, or with the realism/idealism opposition. An earthquake or the falling of a brick is an event that certainly exists ... What is denied is not that such objects exist externally to thought, but the rather different assertion that they would constitute themselves as objects outside any discursive condition of emergence.
>
> (Laclau and Mouffe, quoted in Gordon 1990: 489)

What feminist deconstruction has argued about gender being a construction can be said even more forcefully about race and about crime. These phenomena are not discovered when they are named, they are invented; one might recall *Time* magazine's old practice of capitalizing weighty terms, such as Crime in the Streets or Modern Woman.

It is important to emphasize that because something is constructed that does not mean that it is not real, as symbolic interactionists have long noted. There certainly is subjugation and identity based on gender and ethnic relations, and there certainly are experiences of inflicted harm. Scientific deconstruction does not wish any of this away, but brings to our attention how the boundaries of these experiences and relationships are constituted.

Traditional science and social science has viewed the female, like the non-European, as the Other, to be discovered and conquered, like nature itself. Implicitly, these Others may be contrasted to the 'civilized' white man, who, while arguably 'unnatural', ironically becomes the constructed norm. As Lombroso might say, borrowing from Orwell, all genders and races are natural, but some (the devalued ones) are more natural than others. The overlapping discourses of gender, sex, race, normalcy and nature take on new and largely hidden twists all the time. This goes on at a near-invisible level, a below the surface marginalization of biological thought, in most mainstream US criminology.[4]

Contemporary social science and popular culture each seek for innate characteristics to explain violence among caught street criminals or to explain pathology among such labelled deviants as illegal drug users or welfare mothers. These innate characteristics, sought in the individual or in her home culture, are posed as natural, as essences awaiting discovery, rather than as socially constructed concepts. They are also defined as abnormal, in implicit relation to the presumed civilized norm. In the USA these undersirable characteristics are sought in poor and minority individuals and communities. The recent report of a major national commission on violence, chaired by a criminologist, notes:

> researchers have identified many correlates and antecedents of aggressive childhood behavior that are presumed to reflect psychosocial influences:
>
> - in infancy: pregnancy and birth complications, low birthweight, and an uninhibited, fearless temperament;
> - in the preschool years: fearless behavior, hyperactivity-impulsivity-attention deficit, restless behavior, and poor concentration;
> - in the early school years: daring and risk-taking behavior, poor ability to defer gratification, low IQ, low empathy, and abnormally frequent viewing of violence on television.
>
> (Reiss and Roth 1993: 105)

That traditional criminologists continue to worship what may be termed the 'natural abnormal' is suggested by the fact that, although nearly every 'objective risk factor' associated with 'violence' identified in this report is correlated with low income (i.e. low birthweights, low 'IQ scores', high rates of television viewing), which in turn is concentrated among blacks and Latinos, the report confines itself to individual-level variables and discusses neither income distribution nor societal racism in the USA.[5] Surely a logical conclusion is that if low birthweight, low 'IQ scores' and so forth are the problems, alleviating poverty is the solution.[6]

The 'natural abnormal' image of the female deviant at this time in the USA is increasingly pathetic, repugnant, frightening, one-dimensional, unquestionably poor and statistically likely to be African-American. The 'drug-dependent woman' is described by leading ethnographers as someone:

- who has never paid a taxi driver with money, but with sex;
- who has left her child as collateral at the dope house;
- whose probation or parole officer represents the most predictable relationship in her life;
- whose grandmother was an alcoholic and mother a prostitute, and who started using drugs at twelve and began prostituting with her mother at fourteen;
- who was raised in foster care;
- who watches TV and sees a life she knows she will never participate in;
- who feeds her child out of dumpsters (Inciardi *et al.* 1993: 138).[7]

The deviant mother plays an increasingly large role in discussions of public policy. A recent editorial by a Republican former White House official argues that a condition for mothers receiving welfare, of whom nearly all are unmarried and two-thirds are black or Latina, should be 'universal, regular drug tests' (DuPont 1991), and an even more recent review by a Democratic former US Cabinet member claims that nearly one-third of mothers receiving welfare 'abuse or are addicted to drugs and alcohol' (Center on Addiction and Substance Abuse 1994). Thus treatment of their physical addiction should, in the authors' view, precede educational and vocational assistance.

It is not really a long road from Lombroso's prototypical primitive, dark-skinned, female offender (Klein 1973) to the contemporary American stereotype of the pathological female. As Collins notes in her critique of the white male image of the 'aggressive matriarchal' African-American woman, a stereotype functions as an instructive warning:

> a powerful symbol for both Black and white women of what can go wrong if white patriarchal power is challenged. Aggressive, assertive women are penalized – they are abandoned by their men, end up impoverished, and are stigmatized as being unfeminine.
>
> (Collins 1991: 74–5)

This particular image of the Other is built on the constructed imaginary norm of the compliant, 'civilized', feminine, white woman in the affluent nuclear family.

I want to argue here that it is no longer sufficient, and indeed it should be unnecessary, to challenge exhaustively every pseudo-scientific gender and ethnic stereotype. To risk a biological metaphor, these stereotypes persist through continuous mutation: mental defective, nymphomaniac, kleptomaniac, matriarch, addict, teenage mother, welfare dependent, low IQ scorer, heavy TV watcher. We must refuse to play this game, whose rules are not on our terms. We must instead question the construction of the fundamental dichotomies: feminine versus masculine, black versus white, stupid versus smart, criminal versus law-abiding, abnormal versus normal (see essays in Benhabib and Cornell 1987; Nicholson 1990; Sunstein 1990).[8]

For feminist criminologists, the acknowledgement of the construction of the devalued Other is crucial, because binary poles permeate the field. Not only do mainstream theoreticians, including those sympathetic to feminism, still unreflexively utilize gender and ethnic categories as natural variables. Most centrally, criminologists rely on a deviant Other: the offender and victim are defined as the opposites of each other, and are both set apart from the normal, law-abiding, unharmed citizen. This sleight of hand is what permits traditional criminologists to search endlessly for distinguishing characteristics of the abnormals. Yet this demonization of the Other actually represents quite poorly people's experience of harm.

The double-blind scientist

The traditional paradigms of crime are defended by those who cling to the ideal of blind science: value-neutrality, objectivity, positivism. This ideal persists even as feminist and philosophical critiques, not to mention the ongoing scientific revolution, demonstrate both the impossibility and the undesirability of such an ideal. It is increasingly clear, in this era of relativity, quantum mechanics and chaos theory, that our ability to do science is bounded by our human scale and sensory perceptions. For humans, a hurricane is a scientific problem worthy of study, but to a flea a sudden gust of wind would present a formidable and interesting phenomenon. Scientific findings are also affected by our actions as observers, by the partiality and indeterminacy of our observations and by the vast array of still-unknown interactions of 'things' or subjects 'out there', as in Lorenz's proverbial butterfly whose flap of its wings in China ultimately sets off a tornado in Texas. Given the limits on our ability to conceptualize object, cause and effect, Niels Bohr understandably remarked: 'It is wrong to think that the task of physics is to find out how nature *is*. Physics concerns what we can say about nature' (emphasis in original; quoted in Polkinghorne 1985: 79). Of course, we would want to add, 'what we can say about what we *call* nature'.

Furthermore, human science is neither universal nor timeless, but has culturally and historically transitory priorities; nowhere can this be truer than in social science, specifically in criminology. To take a pedestrian example, nowadays in most of the world an accidental bump between passers-by constitutes no breach of conduct, no crime and no problem for study. In another culture, however, it might be perceived as a grave breach of conduct, or perhaps a public health problem. However, the collision of two car drivers, even unintended, can be a serious offence and hence involve research on environmental and behavioural contexts. More generally, how science frames the basic questions and methods is variable; witness our current mania for reducing events or units to their lowest common denominator and then summing the parts. For all these reasons, the questions and methods of all the sciences inevitably reflect gender, ethnic and other social relations. In short, accusations of inherent bias or unacceptable subjectivity in *feminist* social science should be greeted with grave suspicion, if not scornful laughter.

More seriously, mainstream criminology in the USA has been content to occupy a very narrow niche in terms of 'what we can say about crime'. Criminology has looked for crime in only the most obvious and accessible of places; it resembles the proverbial drunk outside her front door who looks for her lost house keys under the street lamp because that is the only place she can see. The convenient lamp is the cherished Uniform Crime Reports, with an occasional flicker of light from the National Crime Victimization Survey. Thus the discipline is more than merely a product of its time; it is stuck in time. Criminology looks for the whole as only the sum of its parts, and, given its increasing specialization, it is less and less likely to see the whole.

I noted earlier that criminology on its own, despite its scientific resources, failed to problematize or even notice violence against women, until forced to by feminist activists. Despite all its studies on the minutae of racial bias, criminology was also unable to perceive that among young African-American men, one in four is in the correctional apparatus. And despite its command of the details of crime statistics, criminology has been unable to focus on the devastating level of killings in the inner cities, leaving it to public health researchers to identify, recently, an 'epidemic' of violence among young African-American men.

If criminology has been chronically unable to perceive glaring social crises, narrowly focused on minor technicalities and stubbornly blind to its own shortcomings, the feminist critique would have it that this is no accident. For criminology, the following observation of science rings true with an absolute clarity:

> the objects of inquiry are the very same objects that are manipulated through social policy. It is not that the results of scientific research are misused or misapplied by politicians, as the ideology of pure vs. applied science holds. Rather, social policy agendas and the conceptualization of what is significant among scientific problems are so intertwined from the start that the values and agendas important to social policy pass – unobstructed by any merely methodological controls – right

through the scientific process to emerge intact in the results as implicit and explicit policy recommendations.

(Harding 1986: 77)

This intertwining of scientific and policy priorities is particularly acute for all social science, of course, and not only for criminology:

Much of the phenomenal universe of sociology has its ground in . . . institutional processes, which together organize, coordinate, regulate, guide, and control contemporary societies. They perform a work of ruling. Phenomena providing much of the familiar stuff of sociology, such as mental illness, violence, juvenile delinquency, intelligence, unemployment, poverty, motivation, and the like, come into being as integral constituents and products of the bureaucratic, legal, and professional operations of this apparatus.

(Smith 1987: 152)

The applied and policy-minded character of much of social science is not necessarily a vice; one need not and should not argue for detached or 'pure' research unconnected to a 'social problems' agenda. The question is, in considering these social problems and institutions: what and whose standpoint does our science adopt? From their earliest years, critical, Marxist and feminist criminologies have attacked the discipline as one bent in the service of power, as one which embraces the privileged. In the USA, ties between academic researchers and government funding agencies are very dense and close. This embrace affects research in everything from the selection of fundable topics to the framing of plausible hypotheses to the scientific definitions of crime.[9]

It is not merely that US criminology is enmeshed in the state apparatus of control and beholden to state funding mechanisms, or that it protests the 'crimespeak' of officialese only feebly and intermittently: its very definition is suspect. It is the science of seeking out the causes of crime, operationalized as the bio/psycho/social characteristics of criminal actors. Ironically, neither crime nor criminality can be even remotely defined or defended purely on scientific grounds, despite long agonizing by criminologists over this, but are constituted through law, administration and, above all, politics, as noted above. Yet it is rare for a criminologist to explore or question the state-bestowed definition of a crime such as juvenile delinquency or cocaine use. It is even rarer to call attention to the absence of criminal sanctions for a harm such as corporate malfeasance (e.g. the tobacco industry for selling a deadly product). Rather, criticisms of the penal code and justice system revolve largely around evaluations of their 'effectiveness' on their own terms.

As feminists, we are at only the beginning of understanding precisely how women and devalued Others are made the objects of this dominant scientific power, of the white male identification of the omniscient gaze of experts (see essays in Benhabib and Cornell 1987; Diamond and Quinby

1988). Feminist researchers, for example, have analysed the obsessive problematization of female sexuality and motherhood, which was focused on young immigrant women at the turn of the century and, both then and now, has focused on young black women and other poor women of colour (Chesney-Lind 1973; Rafter 1990; Nathanson 1991). While the obsessive study may partly reflect cultural voyeurism (e.g. a white male gaze on black women's sex lives), it is also linked to the institutional regulation of sexuality and parenting along gender and racial lines (e.g. the controlling sexual stereotypes, limited reproductive rights, punitive welfare and child custody laws).

From a feminist perspective, our science should begin in a very different place from the blind service of power: from the standpoints of women and men affected by the social problems and institutions of control that constitute crime and justice. For those attempting to reorient their gaze from that of the controller to the standpoints of the dominated, the initial research questions will slowly change. They are transformed from the realm of 'What should the discipline and the state do with these people?' to something resembling 'How can groups of people use the discipline to address their harms and problems?'

That the creation of an alternative allegiance is not an easy task is pointed out by recent feminist and postmodern critiques that suggest that the very constitution of a discipline is itself an act of domination. The insights of Foucault have enlightened us to the lack of innocence in any social science, and this must especially be true for criminology (see Foucault 1977). If, as Foucault has argued, knowledge and power are intertwined, then in our field knowledge is 'discipline' in two senses of the word: the discipline of criminology and the discipline of crime control and punishment. Feminist criminology can acknowledge the power–knowledge connection by subjecting its own work to the same scrutiny to which it has subjected gender-biased and gender-blind work. A beginning has been made in recent critiques of and reflections on the racial assumptions in white feminist theory (e.g. descriptions of wife battering as 'caused' by 'patriarchal society' based solely on European-identified society).

Before I leave the topic of mainstream criminology, I should respond to an anticipated question: given everything I have said, why should we reinvent criminology at all? Why not discard the discipline? I would like to say, briefly, that for all the discipline's lack of appeal as a fruitful intellectual terrain for us to inhabit, the fact is that it addresses key problems in the USA today: crime and justice. Criminal justice is not the 'centre' of social injustice or social control (Klein 1990), but it is vital to the nightmarish possible future described succinctly by Donna Haraway:

> formation of a strongly bimodal social structure, with the masses of women and men of all ethnic groups, but especially people of colour, confined to a homework economy, illiteracy of several varieties, and general redundancy and impotence, controlled by high-tech

repressive apparatuses ranging from entertainment to surveillance and disappearance.

(Haraway 1991: 169)

Crime through the prism of gender

My proposed project for feminist criminology is not the rescuing of a discipline, but the reinvigorating of the study of crime and justice. It the remaining pages, I would like to discuss what and how we might reinvent in the name of feminist criminology: examples of new assumptions, new questions and new methods.

To refract crime through gender's prism is to do several quite different and contrary things at once. I am reminded of F. Scott Fitzgerald's wry dubbing of intelligence as the ability to hold two opposed ideas at the same time and still function, as well as of Lewis Carroll advocating that we believe six impossible things before breakfast. For us, these things are engaging in several stages in Harding's (1986) project to build a 'successor science': simultaneously create a 'feminist empiricism', and 'equity studies', produce 'woman worthies' (these are well under way in US criminology), critique the 'uses and abuses' of criminology, create a female 'standpoint' and keep in mind that crime, gender, science and justice are all ambiguous and troubled social constructions, even as we reconstruct them.

Glimpses of a paradigm other than the traditional discourse of victim and offender are provided by feminist research and activism concerning the different forms of violence against women and the experiences of female offenders. While details of this alternative must be left to another time and place, the outlines can be briefly suggested. Harms are constituted through both everyday human interactions and overarching structural conditions. Inflicting and suffering harm are connected to one another (e.g. the past victimizations of many offenders). There is a thin line between the abnormal and the normal (e.g. between prostitution and marriage, between rape and sex). Just as offenders do not necessarily see themselves as the demonized criminals (e.g. 'rapists'), so victims do not necessarily view themselves in such one-dimensional terms (e.g. 'battered wives') (Klein 1992). As suggested by Christine Alder (1992), we might begin to move away from the paradigm of individual pathology towards the notion of damaging circumstances. Finally, which harms are criminalized, and to what extent, change historically and culturally, depending on shifts in power relations and in the criminalized activities themselves (e.g. the recent criminalization of violence against women; the new harsher penalties for crack cocaine, mostly used by blacks, compared with powder cocaine, common among whites). As suggested by Tamar Pitch (1992), we might consider turning away from justice rooted in individual culpability towards justice based on relational responsibilities.

There are potential inclusions of new study topics in feminist criminology that explore experiences of damage, stigma or social control that affect women, but may not have been defined as crime. These may include impoverished single motherhood, people's lives on the street and the welfare and public health systems' shaping of motherhood among the poor. In other words, to capture the full reality of the lives of those with whom we are concerned, those who struggle to survive and interact daily with the system, we researchers will move beyond the usual questions posed in the confines of our discipline. For example, criminology has long neglected institutions and strategies of social control that affect impoverished women but take place outside the criminal justice system, such as child protection services and public mental institutions. Even many privileged women have long been trapped or, in a sense, imprisoned by what may be called 'the soft disciplines', which we have omitted from our gaze. These webs include: their bodies, over which they lack control and with which they feel little comfort; their families, the constituting of which may rest on abuse or, more commonly, on petty tyranny; and their homes, whose very security against the threatening outside may encourage a kind of 'house arrest' (Griffin 1971).

We also need to look at different cultures of resistance to social control, the ways women challenge the dominant order and cope with adversity. As criminologists, accustomed to seeking and seeing pathology and deficiency everywhere, we have sometimes failed to appreciate the strength and creativity of women's diverse viewpoints and cultures.

What the new topics share is a starting point of commitment to women's lived experiences and concerns. Dorothy Smith, for example, calls for feminist sociologists to abandon the dreams of grand theory or testing of generalizable propositions, and instead to take the everyday as the problematic and as the point of entry into the world, rather than as a case study (Smith 1987: 151–79). Each relationship, life, situation is intrinsically linked to structural issues; thus the connection between private troubles and public issues, to use C. Wright Mills's description of the sociological imagination (1959). As William Blake observed (and as chaos theory suggests) sometimes one can 'see the world in a grain of sand' (and perhaps even in deviant and outlier cases). This does *not* mean that feminists should abandon 'macro' studies of social structure, history and policy. It means that our studies, whether 'micro' or 'macro', should not have as their sole *raison d'être* the development or testing of academic criminological theory.

If it is far easier to identify what feminist criminology is not than to describe what it is or should be, this is not merely because of the newness of the project or the scarcity of exemplary studies. It is also because, perhaps, inherent in feminist thinking and in the deconstructive critique is the caution that we should not be creating universal feminist questions. Rather, they will arise out of interactions and observations, and we will need to be constantly self-reflexive concerning our own assumptions. Perhaps only after the fact will we see what our problematics and theories have in common.

With respect to a feminist methodology in criminology, as in other disciplines it is important to try to involve our constituent-subjects in the research design wherever possible as participants rather than as objects. Findings can be described in non-technical language, distributed to respondents and activists, and made accessible in lay publications. More difficult is the development of methods of analysis which do not rely on multivariate labels that carve people up into one-dimensional identities as prisoners, victims, drug users and so forth. Our hypotheses and our conclusions may have to break with the either/or, the universal, the timeless and the absolute, and incorporate ambiguity, fluidity, complexity and specificity. For example, how can we describe individuals as simultaneously involved in victimization and harm infliction?

Concerning my own particular current research, on perinatal substance use issues, I have had to grapple with how difficult it is to develop feminist questions and methods in a specific context, in this case funded applied research.[10] This includes, in an assessment of women's needs, adequately representing marginalized persons' voices, avoiding the language of pathology and attempting to 'de-centre' illegal activity and emphasize what the women themselves express as their day-to-day concerns (Klein *et al.* 1994). For instance, in data analysis we have tried, not always successfully, to transcend the standard scientific comparisons based on individual variables: 'pregnant' versus 'non-pregnant', 'drug-using' versus 'non-using' etc. Similarly, we have tried to use the terminology of experiences rather than identities, difficult as this is (e.g. 'heavy cocaine use' rather than 'heavy cocaine user'). We have sought patterns of connection among the women in their experiences as well as differences among them, and we have explored how their individual experiences might be common in their communities. Fortunately, the project also includes a policy study involving data collection on and analysis of the official construction of the problem of 'perinatal substance use', and specific institutional responses (e.g. hospitals' and child welfare agencies' procedures).[11] All this has been carried out in a complex political context, where there is the opportunity for additional benefits and services for the group known as 'substance-involved pregnant and parenting women', and at the same time there is always the possibility of increased scrutiny and punishment of these women. And, throughout, I have tried to be conscious of the boundaries that shape the investigation, try as one might to escape them: the state's agendas, to be sure, but also my own training and biases.

We may be most inspired to invent feminist criminology by models totally outside the field. A particular vision recently presented itself to me in my seeing an exhibit of the work of Dorothea Lange and reading about her life (Ture 1994). Lange photographed impoverished 'Okie' and other migrants streaming into California during the Great Depression (whose experiences were also portrayed in John Steinbeck's fiction), and later Japanese-Americans interned during the Second World War. Lange, while neither impoverished nor interned, explained that her ability to identify with her subjects was influenced by her having had polio as a child and the experience of always walking with a limp. In partnership with Berkeley social scientist Paul Taylor, she travelled to mills and coops and camps in the 1930s on behalf of government relief administrations.

> Lange had a natural ability, Taylor recalled, to put people at ease and let them know she cared. She would never intrude with her camera. If nothing was said but she felt unwelcome, she would fool around with her equipment or sit down in a corner and let people look her over. She would talk with them about who she was and what her family was like, where she came from, and what she represented. Then if she asked questions, it seemed a fair exchange.
>
> (Ture 1994: 10)

Regarding the subjects of her photos, Lange said:

> The only background they had was a background of utter poverty. It's very hard to photograph a proud man against a background like that, because it doesn't show what he's proud about. I had to get my camera to register the things about those people that were more important than how poor they were – their pride, their strength, their spirit.
>
> (Ture 1994: 10)

Lange's most celebrated photo, 'Migrant Mother' (1936), was taken during a last-minute impulse drive out to a pea-pickers' camp:

> I did not ask her name or her history. She told me her age, that she was 32. She said that they had been living on frozen vegetables from the surrounding fields, and birds that the children killed. She had just sold the tires from her car to buy food. There she sat in the lean-to tent with her children huddled around her, and seemed to know that my pictures might help her, and so she helped me.
>
> (Ture 1994: 11)

Lange's photos, which were exhibited among other places on the Berkeley campus at the very site of the University of California School of Criminology, were widely seen, had a sizeable impact on social policy of their day and are admired today.

I was struck by the lessons for us in Lange's work and life: the choice of topics to highlight social upheaval and injustice, the use of one's personal experience to empathize with others, a method of respectfully working with individuals and a concern for conveying the dignity of one's subjects. As a footnote, one might mention that Lange also took in her stride the professional slights she received: she initially received no credit for 'Migrant Mother' and was listed and paid as 'clerk-stenographer' for the research team.

Towards a feminist vision of justice

A changing methodology will be accompanied by changing commitments to justice. A wide-reaching critique of justice has been initiated by feminist legal scholars and moral philosophers in the USA, although participation by feminist criminologists to date has been by and large lamentably rare (for exceptions, see Harris 1987; Daly 1989). While this chapter can only touch on some of the important themes, the question of feminist justice should be prioritized in the years ahead. Whatever a feminist vision of justice might incorporate, I predict that it would bear little resemblance to the present system of cyclical processing and confining of people at the economic bottom of our society.

The conventional ideal of justice as objective, impartial or 'blind' is a sort of legal twin of the ideal of value-free, neutral, blind science. It also incorporates in its universal categories fundamental adversarial dualisms (i.e. legal and illegal, victim and offender, good and bad) (Young 1987: 62). The central actor in law has traditionally been the autonomous citizen, implicitly a white male. In theory, the normal, reasonable, law-abiding citizen stands in opposition to the criminal whose mess spills over from his unregulated private life to make a blot on the orderly public square.

Feminists have extensively used and challenged the distinction of public versus private law and justice in exploring 'woman's place'. In the most profound and most mundane ways, the assumptions of where public law starts and stops create a no-woman's-land for those caught up in the justice system. These difficulties range from prison-bound single mothers caring for small children to wives forced to testify against battering men with whom they live. But the assumptions of 'public versus private' are themselves contingent upon one's identity and standpoint, and vary in time and place. The personal lives of African-Americans have historically never been private or publicly unregulated. In contrast, many seemingly public disputes are privatized through civil law, such as those involving corporate and other elite wrongs. Furthermore, the penal law has always reached beyond the ranks of participating citizens and now threatens to put to death individuals who are not even yet voting adults. Today there is growing surveillance over more and more people's private lives, although there is a large difference between the invited protection of suburban home security and the intrusive street patrolling of city police. The public square and private space are not easily defined in a USA increasingly composed of shopping malls, gated suburbs, mean streets and virtual cyberspace (Davis 1992). Still, the public–private dichotomy may yet be a useful metaphor despite, or perhaps because of, its very imprecision, with which to critique both the rhetoric of crime control for the 'public good' and the reality of differential access to safety depending on one's 'private' resources.

The point must be to re-envision justice, not to assure equal access to our justice system as it is currently construed. Feminist discussions of justice so far have debated modifying what is categorized as impersonal justice or rule-laden 'just desserts' with a more context-specific 'ethic of care' sensitive to the individual need (Gilligan 1982; see essays in Larrabee 1993). 'Care' might also serve as a prompt for consideration of prevention or protection, the assurance of safety and security before the fact, in contrast to compensation or retribution after damage is done. Feminists have also debated the early political ideal of the homogeneous community of 'sisters' with shared values versus the more contemporary model of continuously fissioning affinity groups of different individuals (Young 1990), but how one reconciles social diversity with an ethic of care remains unclear. Some theorists working in a feminist or anti-colonialist/anti-racist inspired framework point to ways out of the vice of competing group interests, focusing on interdependence among oppressed groups (Baca Zinn and Dill 1994) or the fluidity of individual affinity and vision (Young 1990; Haraway 1991: 149–201).

Discussions of feminist justice should now move from the abstract to the concrete, and here is where a valuable contribution could be made by feminist criminologists and criminal justice advocates. Compared with philosophers, we are perhaps relatively knowledgeable about social power and poverty, justice system discretion and discrimination. For example, the criminological and socio-legal literatures on informal or community justice give us some appreciation of the difficulties of organizing 'caring' or any kind of restitution, and controlling its potential abuses, in a society with vast power differentials and social polarizations.

Continuing in the vein of the concrete, our work as feminist criminologists is deeply affected by the gains and losses experienced by the subjugated in the USA, such as the simultaneous growing formal legal ethnic and gender equality and rising marginalization and criminalization of many African and Latino Americans. The equality trend has been couched by both detractors and supporters in terms of special interest benefits, as the vocabulary of splintered and hardened group identity increasingly dominates political and intellectual life. The criminalization trend has been officially described as 'blind justice', allegedly a racially neutral response to conditions 'out there'. The discussions of how to address both the formal inequality of groups and the far more substantive socio-economic inequities are dominated by debates on whether to celebrate and codify, or denigrate and nullify, group differences, including gender.[12] We obviously need to pay close attention: to what kind of differences are we referring?

Having begun this chapter with a double-edged legislative tale, I will conclude with two more tales from the justice system. The Supreme Court has ruled that a juror cannot be excused from serving in a trial on the basis of her race or gender. Exclusions based on other experiences, such as occupation, which are believed to influence a juror's viewpoint, are permitted. The decision is the only acceptable one, and a gain in that it attacks gender- and race-based, or 'partial', justice (Rafter 1990). But the decision also reminds us, perversely, that in one sense the race for justice requires us to close our eyes to people's different experiences. Ethnic and gender experiences affect the jury, as criminology and jury selection surveys corroborate. To claim that there is a 'universal juror' may be the same logic that led the same court to rule against racial bias evidence in death penalty cases; after all, the death penalty is 'universal'.[13]

Perhaps a good response to this dilemma for us as feminist criminologists is suggested by what may be a 'giant step for (hu)mankind' recently taken by law enforcement in Minnesota. Like all states, Minnesota routinely releases crime statistics. But after protests by urban leaders regarding the unreflexive publishing of racial data on offenders, the new state report now reads:

> Racial or ethnic data [on crime] must be treated with caution . . . The use of racial or ethnic descriptions may reflect social custom rather than genetic or hereditary origins. Moreover, existing research on crime has generally shown that racial or ethnic identity is not predictive of crime behavior within data which has been controlled for social or economic factors.
>
> (*Law Enforcement News* 1994)

It used to be said about the US criminal justice system that it sends to prison or death a greater proportion of its citizens than any other country save the Soviet Union and apartheid South Africa. Now the US justice system stands alone, even as Americans' fears of insecurity and violence increase.[14] The challenge for us is: can we create a criminology inspired by feminist questions – a homegrown feminist criminology that does not quite yet exist – that can make an intellectual and political difference?

Acknowledgements

The author thanks Lynn Cooper for her suggestions, and acknowledges a special debt to Nicole Hahn Rafter. This is not only for her years of encouragement, but for her tough and absolutely on-target criticisms of an earlier draft of this chapter, which caused the author to tear her hair out and ultimately write a better version. Of course, all shortcomings are the author's own.

Notes

1 See generally the journal *Women and Criminal Justice*; for a theoretical overview see Daly and Chesney-Lind (1988); for a review of theories see Leonard (1982); for edited collections see Rafter and Stanko (1982) and Price and Sokoloff (1982, 1994); for a new direction see Harris (1987). There are studies on female offenders: for early collections see Crites (1976), Adler and Simon (1979) and Datesman and Scarpitti (1980); for comprehensive views see Chapman (1980) and Chesney-Lind (1986); for ethnographies see Rosenbaum (1981) and Miller (1986). There are materials on women and girls as victims

of violent crime: for early work see Russell (1975), Holmstrom and Burgess (1978) and Walker (1979); for an edited collection see Yllo and Bogard (1988); for different perspectives see Gordon (1988), Schechter (1982), Stanko (1985), Russell (1982) and Caputi (1989); for work on men, see Scully (1990). There is work on women's experiences with the justice system: generally see Feinman (1980); on prisoners see Rafter (1985, 1990) and Freedman (1981); on offenders see Daly (1994); on courts see Hepperle and Crites (1978) and Crites and Hepperle (1987); on women police officers see Martin (1980, 1990). These broad criminological categories include specific topics, such as sex work and its control, rape, battering, women white-collar criminals, women political prisoners, women and the judiciary, justice system discretion and bias, girls and juvenile justice, women witnesses, policing and women, rape trials, gender and ethnic bias interaction, women's drug use and women's safety concerns. Outside of criminology, US feminist social scientists and legal scholars have written on related topics, such as sexual harassment, pornography, reproductive rights, corporate victimization of women, witches and deviant women, the control of female mental illness, women's drinking practices and controls, marginalization and scapegoating of women of colour, feminist legal theory and the social construction of female sexuality and motherhood.

2 For example, compare the titles of two articles on biological causes of crime, published ten years apart in the journal of the American Society of Criminology: 'Urban environment, genetics and crime' (Gabrielli and Mednick 1984) and 'Neuropsychological tests predicting persistent male delinquency' (Moffitt et al. 1994). Both articles describe, and limit their findings to, male-only samples. But only in 1994 was the fact thought newsworthy.

3 From a very different perspective, it has been argued that the vision of the subjugated inevitably mirrors the hegemonic values and beliefs of the dominant group (Fanon 1967). From this framework of 'internalized oppression', whatever women want today cannot be a basis for an alternative future, because, in Mackinnon's play on Marxist phrase-making, 'all women live in sexual objectification like fish live in water' (Mackinnon 1990: 233).

4 The marginal status of biological thought in current US criminology must be qualified, in that increasingly biological research is reappearing, especially around 'violence', 'the underclass', 'disorderly families' and 'illegitimacy'.

5 In contrast, another recent report on violence by a national professional commission, this one comprised ironically of psychologists, flatly states that, psycho-social factors notwithstanding, 'violence is most prevalent among the poor' owing to 'socioeconomic inequality', and that anti-violence interventions may have limited success if there are no structural societal changes (American Psychological Association 1993).

6 The only argument might be from those highly visible conservative US social scientists who are arguing that mental and moral defects ('low IQ scores' and/ or 'irresponsibility') cause poverty.

7 These authors offer a solution for the 'drug-dependent woman' they have described: 'Rather than entertaining such solutions as restructuring society, redistributing capital resources, and legalizing drugs, more realistic endeavors can be addressed, in such areas as HIV/AIDS prevention/intervention, drug abuse treatment, and health care' (Inciardi et al. 1993: 139).

8 Ironically, even as philosophical theorists challenge conventional Western dualist thinking, the digital logic of the electronic computer may reinforce binary categorization.

9 These effects are by no means negated by the fact that academics are usually more liberal than government officials regarding crime policy; in recent years

academic liberalism has had little influence on policy, whereas the government has had a great deal of influence on academics.

10 This work is being undertaken with my primary collaborator, Elaine Zahnd, and several other colleagues, and owes a great deal to the work conducted by another member of the team, Amanda Noble.

11 The opportunity to do this work is one in which I am fortunate, since it is difficult to receive support in the USA for policy analysis, i.e. studying the powerful rather than the powerless.

12 I want to thank Kathleen Daly for continuously bringing this issue to my attention over the years, and for ignoring my objections that it was unimportant.

13 This dilemma is far from new; recall Anatole France's famous saying that the law in its majestic equality forbids the rich as well as the poor from sleeping under bridges and begging in the streets. A sobering footnote is that when I first found that saying on a poster years ago and hung it on my wall, unlike today hardly any Americans were homeless or panhandling.

14 Specifically, a study by the Center on Juvenile and Criminal Justice finds the US rate of incarceration per 100 000 to be 517, versus 355 in the Republic of South Africa and 335 in the Russian Federation (*San Francisco Chronicle* 1994).

References

Adler, F. and Simon, R.J. (eds) (1979). *The Criminality of Deviant Women*. Boston: Houghton Mifflin.

Alder, C. (1992). Economic conditions, gender and family. In M-A. Bertrand et al. (eds) *Proceedings of the International Feminist Conference on Women, Law and Social Control, 1991*. Vancouver: International Centre for the Reform of Criminal Law and Criminal Justice Policy.

American Psychological Association (1993). *Violence and Youth: Psychology's Response. Volume I: Summary Report of the APA Commission on Violence and Youth*. Washington, DC: Author.

Baca Zinn, M. and Dill B.T. (1994). Difference and domination. In M. Baca Zinn and B.T. Dill (eds) *Women of Color in US Society*. Philadelphia: Temple University Press.

Baldus, D.C., Pulaski, C. and Woodworth, G. (1983). Policy review of death sentences: An empirical study of the Georgia experience. *Journal of Criminal Law and Criminology*, 74, 661–753.

Benhabib, S. and Cornell, D. (eds) (1987). *Feminism as Critique*. Minneapolis: University of Minnesota Press.

Bertrand, M-A., Daly, K. and Klein, D. (eds) (1992). *Proceedings of the International Feminist Conference on Women, Law and Social Control, 1991*. Vancouver: International Centre for the Reform of Criminal Law and Criminal Justice Policy.

Burkhart, K.W. (1973). *Women in Prison*. New York: Doubleday and Co.

Cain, M. (1989). Introduction: feminists transgress criminology. In M. Cain (ed.) *Growing Up Good: Policing the Behaviour of Girls in Europe*. Newbury Park, CA: Sage.

Caputi, J. (1989). The sexual politics of murder. *Gender and Society*, 3, 4.

Center on Addiction and Substance Abuse (1994). *Substance Abuse and Women on Welfare*. New York: Columbia University, CASA (J.A. Califano, Chairman).

Chapman, J.R. (1980). *Economic Realities and the Female Offender*. Lexington, MA: Lexington Books.

Chesney-Lind, M. (1973). Judicial enforcement of the female sex role: The Family court and the female delinquent. *Issues in Criminology*, 8, 2.

Chesney-Lind, M. (1986). Women and crime: the female offender. *Signs: Journal of Women in Culture and Society*, 12, 1.

Coleman, W. (1993). Primal orb density. In G. Early (ed.) *Lure and Loathing: Essays on Race, Identity and the Ambivalence of Assimilation*. New York: Penguin.

Collins, P.H. (1991). *Black Feminist Thought*. Routledge: New York.

Crites, L.L. (ed.) (1976). *The Female Offender*. Lexington, MA: Lexington Books.

Crites, L.L. and Hepperle, W.L. (eds) (1987). *Women, the Courts, and Equality*. Newbury Park, CA: Sage.

Daly, K. (1989). Criminal justice ideologies and practices in different voices: some feminist questions about justice. *International Journal of the Sociology of Law*, 17, 1.

Daly, K. (1994). *Gender, Crime and Punishment*. New Haven, CT: Yale University Press.

Daly, K. and Chesney-Lind, M. (1988). Feminism and criminology. *Justice Quarterly*, 5, 4.

Datesman, S.K. and Scarpitti, F.R. (eds) (1980). *Women, Crime and Justice*. New York: Oxford University Press.

Davis, M. (1992). *City of Quartz: Excavating the Future in Los Angeles*. New York: Vintage.

de Beauvoir, S. (1949). The Second Sex. London: Picador.

Diamond, I. and Quinby, L. (eds) (1988). *Feminism and Foucault: Reflections on Resistance*. Boston: Northeastern University Press.

Dubois, W.B. (1903). *The Souls of Black Folk*. Chicago, IL: A.C. McClung & Co.

DuPont, R.L. (1991). Random drug tests, mandatory treatment should be conditions of receiving welfare. *Wall Street Journal*, 4 March.

Fanon, F. (1976). *Black Skin, White Masks*. New York: Grove Press.

Feinman, C. (1980). *Women in the Criminal Justice System*. New York: Praeger.

Foucault, M. (1977). *Discipline and Punish*. New York: Random House.

Freedman, E.B. (1981). *Their Sisters' Keepers: Women's Prison Reform in America 1830–1930*. Ann Arbor: University of Michigan Press.

Gabrielli, W.F. and Mednick, S.A. (1984). Urban environment, genetics and crime. *Criminology*, 22, 4.

Gilligan, C. (1982). *In a Different Voice: Psychological Theory and Women's Development*. Cambridge, MA: Harvard University Press.

Gordon, A. (1990). Feminism, writing and ghosts. *Social Problems*, 37, 4.

Gordon, L. (1988). *Heroes of Their Own Lives: the Politics and History of Family Violence*. New York: Viking.

Griffin, S. (1971). Rape: the all-American crime. Ramparts, 10, 3.

Haraway, D.J. (1991). *Simians, Cyborgs, and Women: the Reinvention of Nature*. New York: Routledge.

Harding, S. (1986). *The Science Question in Feminism*. Ithaca, NY: Cornell University Press.

Harris, M.K. (1987). Moving into the new millenium: toward a feminist vision of justice. *Prison Journal*, 67, 2.

Hepperle, W.L. and Crites, L.L. (eds) (1978). *Women in the Courts*. Williamsburg, VA: National Center for State Courts.

Holmstrom, L.L. and Burgess, A. (1978). *The Victim of Rape: Institutional Reactions*. New York: John Wiley.

Inciardi, J.A., Lockwood, D. and Pottieger, A.E. (1993). *Women and Crack-Cocaine*. New York: Macmillan.

Klein, D. (1973). The etiology of female crime: a review of the literature. *Issues in Criminology*, 8, 2.

Klein, D. (1981). Violence against women: some considerations on its causes and on its elimination. *Crime and Delinquency*, 27, 1.

Klein, D. (1988). Women and criminal justice in the Reagan era. Presented at the Academy of Criminal Justice Sciences.

Klein, D. (1991). Losing the (war on the) war on crime. *Critical Criminologist*, 2, 4.

Klein, D. (1992). Women offenders, victims and false labels. In U. Kruger (ed.) *Kriminologie: eine feministische Perspektive*. Pfaffenweiler: Centaurus-Verlagsgesellschaft.

Klein, D. (1994). Twenty years ago . . . today: afterword to 'The Etiology of Female Crime'. In B.R. Price and N. Sokoloff (eds) *The Criminal Justice System and Women*, 2nd edn. New York: McGraw-Hill.

Klein, D., Zahnd, E. and Holtby, S. (1995). Designing an agency-based drug problem needs assessment. *Contemporary Drug Problems*.

Larrabee, M.J. (ed.) (1993). *An Ethic of Care: Feminist and Interdisciplinary Perspectives*. New York: Routledge.

Law Enforcement News (1994). 15 April. New York: John Jay College.

Leonard, E. (1982). *Women, Crime and Society: a Critique of Criminology Theory*. New York: Longman.

Mackinnon, C.A. (1990) Sexuality, pornography and method: 'pleasure under patriarchy'. In C.R. Sunstein (ed.) *Feminism and Political Theory*. Chicago: University of Chicago Press.

Martin, D. (1976). *Battered Wives*. San Francisco: Glide Publications.

Martin, S.E. (1980). *Breaking and Entering: Policewomen on Patrol*. Berkeley: University of California Press.

Martin, S.E. (1990). *On the Move: the Status of Women in Policing*. Washington, DC: Police Foundation.

Mauer, M. (1992). *Young Black Men and the Criminal Justice System: a Growing Problem*. Washington, DC: Sentencing Project.

Miller, E. (1986). *Street Woman*. Philadelphia: Temple University Press.

Mills, C.W. (1959). *The Sociological Imagination*. New York: Oxford University Press.

Moffitt, T.E., Lynam, D.R. and Silva, P.A. (1994) Neuropsychological tests predicting persistent male delinquency. *Criminology*, 32, 2.

Nicholson, L. (ed.) (1990). *Feminism/Postmodernism*. New York: Routledge.

Nathanson, C.A. (1991). *Dangerous Passage: the Social Control of Sexuality in Women's Adolescence*. Philadelphia: Temple University Press.

Pitch, T. (1992). Gendered justice, gendered law: the Italian debate. In M-A. Bertrand *el al*. (eds) *Proceedings of the International Feminist Conference on Women, Law and Social Control, 1991*. Vancouver: International Centre for the Reform of Criminal Law and Criminal Justice Policy.

Polkinghorne, J.C. (1985). *The Quantum World*. Princeton, NJ: Princeton University Press.

Price, B.R. and Sokoloff, N. (eds) (1982). *The Criminal Justice System and Women* New York: Clark Boardman.

Price, B.R. and Sokoloff, N. (eds) (1994). *The Criminal Justice System and Women*, 2nd edn. New York: McGraw-Hill.

Radelet, M.L. (1981). Racial characteristics and the imposition of the death penalty. *American Sociological Review*, 46, 918–27.

Rafter, N.H. (1985). *Partial Justice: Women in State Prisons, 1800–1935*. Boston: Northeastern University Press.

Rafter, N.H. (1990). *Partial Justice: Women, Prisons and Social Control*, 2nd edn. New Brunswick, NJ: Transaction Books.

Rafter, N.H. and Stanko, E. (eds) (1982). *Judge, Lawyer, Victim, Thief: Women, Gender Roles, and Criminal Justice*. Boston: Northeastern University Press.

Reiss, A. and Roth, J. (eds) (1993). *Understanding and Preventing Violence*. Washington, DC: National Academy Press.

Rosenbaum, M. (1981). *Women on Heroin*. New Brunswick, NJ: Rutgers University Press.

Russell, D.E.H. (1975). *The Politics of Rape: the Victim's Perspective*. New York: Stein and Day.

Russell, D.E.H. (1982). *Rape in Marriage*. New York: Macmillan.

San Francisco Chronicle (1994). State tops nation in imprisonment rate. 15 July.

Schechter, S. (1982). *Women and Male Violence*. Boston: South End Press.

Scully, D. (1990). *Understanding Sexual Violence: a Study of Convicted Rapists*. Boston: Unwin Hyman.

Smith, D. (1988). *The Everyday World as Problematic*. Milton Keynes: Open Unversity Press.

Spitzer, S. (1975). Toward a Marxian theory of deviance. *Social Problems*, 22, 638–51.

Stanko, E. (1985). *Intimate Intrusions: Women's Experiences of Male Violence*. Boston: Routledge.

Sunstein, C.R. (ed.) (1990). *Feminism and Political Theory*. Chicago: University of Chicago Press.

Ture, M. (1994). The contemplation of things as they are: the photographic journey of Dorothea Lange. *East Bay Express*, 13 May.

Walker, L. (1979). *The Battered Woman*. New York: Harper and Row.

Warrior, B. (1976). *Wifebeating*. Somerville, MA: New England Free Press.

Yllo, K. and Bogard, M. (eds) (1988). *Feminist Perspectives on Wife Abuse*. Newbury Park, CA: Sage.

Young, I.M. (1987). Impartiality and the civic public: some implications of feminist critiques of moral and political theory. In S. Benhabib and D. Cornell (eds) *Feminism as Critique*. Minneapolis: University of Minnesota Press.

Young, I.M. (1990). *Justice and the Politics of Difference*. Princeton, NJ: Princeton University Press.

Index

FEMICIDE
THE POLITICS OF WOMAN KILLING
Jill Radford and Diana E.H. Russell (eds)

The first of its kind – and a classic. This book should be required reading for everyone: college students and their professors, policy makers, and business-people, lawyers and judges, police officers and members of the clergy. It raises our consciousness and inspires resistance to femicide.

Phyllis Chesler

While the issues of date rape and sexual harassment have finally entered into mainstream discourse, femicide, the most brutal form of sexist behaviour, has yet to be widely acknowledged and understood. In this wide-ranging study, more than 40 contributors document and describe the phenomenon of femicide as it occurs across continents and cultures, analyse the roles that our social values and institutions play in perpetuating it, and articulate the actions that can be taken to combat it. *Femicide: The Politics of Woman Killing* is at once a disturbing testimony to the many women who have been victims of femicide and an act of resistance.

Contents
Part 1: Femicide is as old as patriarchy – Part 2: The patriarchal home – Part 3: Femicide and racism – Part 4: The mass media, pornography, and gorenography – Part 5: Femicide and travesties of justice – Part 6: Women fighting back against femicide – Summary and conclusion – Sources – Index.

400pp   0 335 15178 7 (Paperback)

MAKING VIOLENCE SEXY
FEMINIST VIEWS ON PORNOGRAPHY

Diana E.H. Russell (ed.)

A crucially important collection of feminist voices challenging the pornocrats. Even if you read nothing else on the subject, read this.

Robin Morgan

Making Violence Sexy is a courageous book that chronicles women's resistance to pornography over the last twenty years. It does this in a collection of feminist articles, including testimonies by victims/survivors of pornography that together make a convincing case for the view that pornography (as distinct from erotica) causes harm to women, including acts of violence.

This book will appeal to students and lecturers of women's studies and sociology, political activists, public officials, social scientists, legal and medical professionals – those who consider it a form of discrimination against women. Women's studies teachers will find it a welcome addition to their required reading lists, and those working against sexual violence will appreciate it as a primary, up-to-date, and comprehensive source and inspiration.

Contents
Introduction – Part I: Survivors of pornography – Part II: Overview – Part III: Feminist research on pornography – Part IV: Feminist strategies and actions against pornography – Notes – References – Index.

320pp   0 335 19200 9 (Paperback)

POWER IN STRUGGLE
FEMINISM, SEXUALITY AND THE STATE

Davina Cooper

What is power? And how are social change strategies shaped by the ways in which we conceptualize it? Drawing on feminist, poststructuralist, and Marxist theory, Davina Cooper develops an innovative framework for understanding power relations within fields as diverse as queer activism, municipal politics, and the regulation of lesbian reproduction. *Power in Struggle* explores the relationship between power, sexuality, and the state and, in the process, provides a radical rethinking of these concepts and their interactions. The book concludes with an important and original discussion of how an ethics of empowerment can inform political strategy.

Special features:

- brings together central aspects of current radical, political theory in an innovative way
- offers a new way of conceptualizing the state, power and sexuality

Contents
Introduction – Beyond domination?: productive and relational power – The politics of sex: metaphorical strategies and the (re)construction of desire – Multiple identities: sexuality and the state in struggle – Penetration on the defensive: regulating lesbian reproduction – Access without power: gay activism and the boundaries of governance – Beyond resistance: political strategy and counter-hegemony – Afterword – Bibliography – Index.

192pp   0 335 19211 4 (paperback)   0 335 19212 2 (hardback)